ACHI 2021

The Fourteenth International Conference on Advances in Computer-Human Interactions

July 18 – 22, 2021

Nice, France

ACHI 2021 Editors

Marie Sjölinder, PhD, Senior Researcher, RISE Research Institutes of Sweden, Sweden
Prima Oky Dicky Ardiansyah, Iwate Prefectural University, Japan

Printed from e-media with permission by:

Curran Associates, Inc.
57 Morehouse Lane
Red Hook, NY 12571

Some format issues inherent in the e-media version may also appear in this print version.

Printed with permission by Curran Associates, Inc. (2023)

International Academy, Research, and Industry Association (IARIA)
412 Derby Way
Wilmington, DE 19810

Phone: (408) 893-6407
Fax: (408) 527-6351

petre@iaria.org

Additional copies of this publication are available from:

Curran Associates, Inc.
57 Morehouse Lane
Red Hook, NY 12571 USA
Phone: 845-758-0400
Fax: 845-758-2633
Email: curran@proceedings.com
Web: www.proceedings.com

Table of Contents

ACHI 2021

Forward

The Fourteenth edition of The International Conference on Advances in Computer-Human Interactions (ACHI 2021) conference was held in Nice, France, July 18 - 22, 2021.

The conference on Advances in Computer-Human Interaction, ACHI 2021, was a result of a paradigm shift in the most recent achievements and future trends in human interactions with increasingly complex systems. Adaptive and knowledge-based user interfaces, universal accessibility, human-robot interaction, agent-driven human computer interaction, and sharable mobile devices are a few of these trends. ACHI 2021 brought also a suite of specific domain applications, such as gaming, social, medicine, education and engineering.

The event was very competitive in its selection process and very well perceived by the international scientific and industrial communities. As such, it is attracting excellent contributions and active participation from all over the world. We were very pleased to receive a large amount of top quality contributions.

The accepted papers covered a wide range of human-computer interaction related topics such as graphical user interfaces, input methods, training, recognition, and applications.
We believe that the ACHI 2021 contributions offered a large panel of solutions to key problems in all areas of human-computer interaction.

We take here the opportunity to warmly thank all the members of the ACHI 2021 technical program committee as well as the numerous reviewers. The creation of such a broad and high quality conference program would not have been possible without their involvement. We also kindly thank all the authors that dedicated much of their time and efforts to contribute to the ACHI 2021. We truly believe that thanks to all these efforts, the final conference program consists of top quality contributions.

This event could also not have been a reality without the support of many individuals, organizations and sponsors. In addition, we also gratefully thank the members of the ACHI 2021 organizing committee for their help in handling the logistics and for their work that is making this professional meeting a success.

We hope the ACHI 2021 was a successful international forum for the exchange of ideas and results between academia and industry and to promote further progress in the human-computer interaction field.

ACHI 2021 Chairs

ACHI Steering Committee
Flaminia Luccio, University Ca' Foscari of Venice, Italy
Marie Sjölinder, RISE, Sweden
Lasse Berntzen, University of South-Eastern Norway, Norway

ACHI 2021 Advisory Committee
Leslie Miller, Iowa State University - Ames, USA
Uttam Kokil, Kennesaw State University Marietta, USA

ACHI 2021 Publicity Chair
Alvaro Liebana, Universitat Politecnica de Valencia, Spain
Mar Parra, Universitat Politecnica de Valencia, Spain

ACHI 2021

COMMITTEE

ACHI Steering Committee

Flaminia Luccio, University Ca' Foscari of Venice, Italy
Marie Sjölinder, RISE, Sweden
Lasse Berntzen, University of South-Eastern Norway, Norway

ACHI 2021 Advisory Committee

Leslie Miller, Iowa State University - Ames, USA
Uttam Kokil, Kennesaw State University Marietta, USA

ACHI 2021 Publicity Chair

Alvaro Liebana, Universitat Politecnica de Valencia, Spain
Mar Parra, Universitat Politecnica de Valencia, Spain

ACHI 2021 Technical Program Committee

Mostafa Alani, Tuskegee University, USA
Marran Aldossari, University of North Carolina at Charlotte, USA
Obead Alhadreti, Umm Al-Qura University, Al-Qunfudah, Saudi Arabia
Mehdi Ammi, Univ. Paris 8, France
Prima Oky Dicky Ardiansyah, Iwate Prefectural University, Japan
Ahmad Azadvar, Ubisoft Entertainment Sweden A.B. - Ubisoft Massive / Malmo University, Sweden
Catalin-Mihai Barbu, University of Duisburg-Essen, Germany
Lasse Berntzen, University of South-Eastern Norway, Norway
Ganesh D. Bhutkar, Vishwakarma Institute of Technology (VIT), Pune, India
Cezary Biele, National Information Processing Institute, Poland
Christos J. Bouras, University of Patras, Greece
Christian Bourret, UPEM - Université Paris-Est Marne-la-Vallée, France
James Braman, The Community College of Baltimore County, USA
Pradeep Buddharaju, University of Houston - Clear Lake, USA
Idoko John Bush, Near East University, Cyprus
Minghao Cai, University of Alberta, Canada
Klaudia Carcani, Østfold University College, Norway
Meghan Chandarana, NASA Ames Research Center, USA
Lara Jessica da Silva Pontes, University of Debrecen, Hungary
Andre Constantino da Silva, Federal Institute of São Paulo - IFSP, Brazil
Lea Daling, Cybernetics Lab IMA & IfU - RWTH Aachen University, Germany
Antonio Diaz Tula, University of São Paulo, Brazil
Verena Distler, University of Luxembourg, Luxembourg
Krzysztof Dobosz, Silesian University of Technology - Institute of Informatics, Poland
Margaret Drouhard, University of Washington, USA
Robert Ek, Luleå University of Technology, Sweden

Galina Madjaroff, University of Maryland Baltimore County, USA
Sebastian Maneth, University of Bremen, Germany
Laura Maye, School of Computer Science and Information Technology - University College Cork, Ireland
Weizhi Meng, Technical University of Denmark, Denmark
Xiaojun Meng, Noah's Ark Lab | Huawei Technologies, Shenzhen, China
Daniel R. Mestre, CNRS Institute of Movement Sciences - Mediterranean Virtual Reality Center, Marseilles, France
Mariofanna Milanova, University of Arkansas at Little Rock, USA
Harald Milchrahm, Institute for Software technology - Technical University Graz, Austria
Leslie Miller, Iowa State University - Ames, USA
Alexander Mirnig, Center for Human-Computer Interaction | University of Salzburg, Austria
Arturo Moquillaza, Pontificia Universidad Católica del Perú, Peru
Nicholas H. Müller, University of Applied Sciences Würzburg-Schweinfurt, Germany
Sachith Muthukumarana, Auckland Bioengineering Institute | The University of Auckland, New Zealand
Roger Ng, The Hong Kong Polytechnic University, Hong Kong
Yoko Nishihara, College of Information Science and Engineering - Ritsumeikan University, Japan
Rikke Toft Nørgård, Aarhus University, Denmark
Yoshimasa Ohmoto, Shizuoka University, Japan
Tom Ongwere, University of Dayton, Ohio, USA
Aditeya Pandey, Northeastern University, Boston, USA
Athina Papadopoulou, Massachusetts Institute of Technology (MIT), USA
Evangelos Papadopoulos, National Technical University of Athens, Greece
Vida Pashaei, University of Arizona, USA
Freddy Alberto Paz Espinoza, Pontificia Universidad Católica del Perú, Peru
Jorge Henrique Piazentin Ono, New York University - Tandon School of Engineering, USA
Jorge Luis Pérez Medina, Universidad de Las Américas, Ecuador
Brian Pickering, IT Innovation Centre - University of Southampton, UK
Thomas M. Prinz, Friedrich Schiller University Jena, Germany
Annu Sible Prabhakar, University of Cincinnati, USA
Marina Puyuelo Cazorla, Universitat Politècnica de València, Spain
Yuanyuan (Heather) Qian, Carleton University in Ottawa, Canada
Rafael Radkowski, Iowa State University, USA
Mariusz Rawski, Warsaw University of Technology, Poland
Radiah Rivu, Bundeswehr University Munich, Germany
Carsten Röcker, Fraunhofer IOSB-INA, Germany
Joni Salminen, Qatar Computing Research Institute, Qatar
Sandra Sanchez-Gordon, Escuela Politécnica Nacional, Ecuador
Antonio-José Sánchez-Salmerón, Instituto de Automática e Informática Industrial - Universidad Politécnica de Valencia, Spain
Paulus Insap Santosa, Universitas Gadjah Mada - Yogyakarta, Indonezia
Diana Saplacan, University of Oslo, Norway
Hélène Sauzéon, Centre Inria Bordeaux, France
Trenton Schulz, Norwegian Computing Center, Norway
Kamran Sedig, Western University, Ontario, Canada
Sylvain Senecal, HEC Montreal, Canada
Fereshteh Shahmiri, Georgia Tech, USA
Yuhki Shiraishi, Tsukuba University of Technology, Japan
Marie Sjölinder, RISE, Sweden

Jesse Smith, University of California, Davis, USA
Zdzisław Sroczyński, Silesian University of Technology, Gliwice, Poland
Ben Steichen, California State Polytechnic University, Pomona, USA
Han Su, RA - MIT, USA
Federico Tajariol, University Bourgogne Franche-Comté, France
Sheng Tan, Trinity University, Texas, USA
Jiro Tanaka, Waseda University, Japan
Cagri Tanriover, Intel Corporation (Intel Labs), USA
Ranjeet Tayi, User Experience - Informatica, San Francisco, USA
Masashi Toda, Kumamoto University, Japan
Carlos Toxtli Hernandez, West Virginia University, USA
Milka Trajkova, Indiana University, Indianapolis, USA
David Unbehaun, University of Siegen, Germany
Simona Vasilache, University of Tsukuba, Japan
KatiaVega, University of California, Davis, USA
Nishant Vishwamitra, University at Buffalo - SUNY, USA
Konstantinos Votis, Information Technologies Institute | Centre for Research and Technology Hellas, Greece
Zhanwei Wu, Shanghai Jiao Tong University, China
Shuping Xiong, KAIST, South Korea
Panpan Xu, Bosch Research, Sunnyvale, USA
Sunny Xun Liu, Stanford University, USA
Ye Zhu, Cleveland State Unviersity, USA

Copyright Information

Toward the Development of a VR Simulator for Speed Sprayers

Yu Tanaka, Oky Dicky Ardiansyah Prima, Kanayo Ogura, and Koichi Matsuda
Graduate School of Soft. and Info. Science, Iwate Prefectural University
152-52 Sugo, Takizawa, Iwate, Japan
email: g231t024@s.iwate-pu.ac.jp, {prima, ogura_k, matsuda}@iwate-pu.ac.jp

Shoichi Yuki
YAMABIKO Corporation
10-2 Sugo, Takizawa, Iwate, Japan
email: s_yukixx@yamabiko-corp.co.jp

***Abstract*—The speed sprayer, an agricultural chemical spraying vehicle, has been used to efficiently control pests and diseases in orchards such as grapes and apples. The use of speed sprayers is also problematic from the perspective of environmental protection, such as the measures to prevent pesticides from drifting outside the field. It also requires a skilled operator to operate the vehicle, as adjustments to travel speed, pressure, and nozzle selection must be considered. To make the speed sprayer easier and safer to operate, improvements to the control panel are required. In this study, we report our effort on the development of a simulator based on Virtual Reality (VR) that can analyze the operator's body movements while driving and operating a speed sprayer. As reference data, we videotaped the operator at the actual site and extracted the characteristics of the body movements during operation using computer vision techniques. The characteristics of the body movements observed while operating the various panels provide useful information for improving the operation panels.**

Keywords-vr-simulator; speed sprayer; virtual reality; head pose; hand gesture.

I. INTRODUCTION

Most of the chemicals sprayed in orchards are liquids. There are several types of sprayers, including pipe sprayers, portable power sprayers, and speed sprayers. The introduction of speed sprayers has a great effect on the efficiency and labor saving of pesticide spraying in orchards. Many studies have been conducted on the prevention of pesticide drift and exposure to pesticides, and the application of small amounts of concentrated pesticides [1].

In Japan, speed sprayers were introduced in 1957. The Japanese Ministry of Health, Labor and Welfare (MHLW) introduced the positive list system for agricultural chemical residues, such as pesticides, feed additives, and veterinary drugs in foods [2]. The use of speed sprayers poses several challenges in terms of occupational safety and environmental protection. In the case of speed sprayers used in orchards, the amount of pesticides sprayed increases due to the large spray area. Therefore, there is an urgent need for measures to prevent drift of pesticides outside the field. A variety of unmanned pest control machines have been developed for more accurate spraying [3],, but they have not been widely used.

Speed sprayers require a skilled operator to operate due to the need to consider the relationship between travel speed, pressure, and nozzle selection. Furthermore, the complexity of the operation panel, in addition to the difficulty in seeing the surrounding environment from inside the vehicle, makes the work on this vehicle hard. Driving skills are required, especially in vineyards, where cars need to pass through the path between the branches.

Figure 1. The electric speed sprayer (SSV1091FSC) manufactured by the YAMABIKO Corporation used in this study.

As the number of agricultural workers in Japan has decreased and the population has aged in recent years, there has been a growing demand for the development of more efficient speed sprayers. Especially, simplifying the operations that require technical skills becomes critical. In the automobile industry, car simulators have been developed as a measure of vehicle performance. However, there are few examples of studies that simulate the operation and driving of tractors in agriculture [4][5].

In this study, we build a simulator using Virtual Reality (VR) to analyze the driving and operation of a speed sprayer. The simulator collects information on the driver's Six-Degree-of-Freedom (6-DoF) head pose, three-dimensional (3D) hand gestures, gas pedal and brake operations, and visualizes the characteristics of driving behavior based on the features of head and hand movements. In the physical environment, we set up two cameras to capture the cockpit and the driver at the same time. Computer vision techniques were used to track the body movements and the rotation of the steering wheel.

This paper is organized as follows. In Section II, we describe the VR simulator of a speed sprayer built for this study. Section III describes experiments using our VR simulator and their results. In Section IV, we present our computer vision techniques used to observe the operator behavior in the physical environment. Finally, Section V summarizes the results of this study and discusses future perspectives.

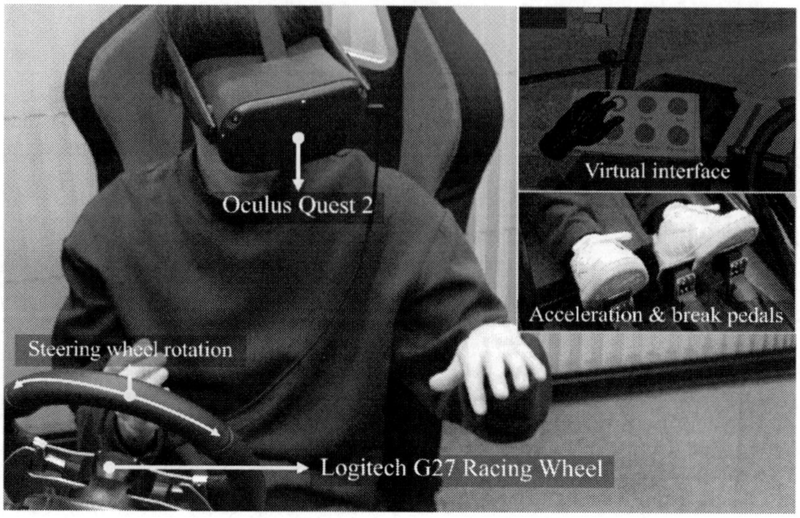

Figure 2. The VR simulator of a speed sprayer developed in this study.

II. VR Simulator of a Speed Sprayer

Figure 1 shows the speed sprayer (SSV1091FSC) that can carry 1000L of pesticide which was used in this study. The simulator of the speed sprayer developed in this study has the following conditions. First, the simulator must be able to track the driver's head pose and finger movements in 6-DoF. Next, the driver must be able to operate the vehicle using physical car controls. Finally, the driver should be able to perceive the car control in the virtual space and that in the physical space equally. Considering these constraints, we adopted a set of Logitech G27 Force Feedback Wheel and Pedal as the car control, and the Oculus Quest 2 as the VR device [6].

A. Logitech G27 Force Feedback Wheel and Pedal

The Logitech G27 is a gaming racing wheel compatible with PlayStation 2 and 3. It runs on Windows and Mac using the Logitech G27 driver and gaming SDK. The SDK for Windows is also available on the Unity Asset Store. Figure 2 shows the steering wheel and pedals of Logitech's G27 attached to the seat of a racing car fixed with a metal frame.

B. Oculus Quest 2

The Oculus Quest 2 is consumer-oriented Head-Mounted Display (HMD) based VR device developed by Facebook, Inc. featuring a 6-DoF angular and linear tracking system that can measure head pose and hand gestures. This system uses Inertial Measurement Units (IMUs) that assess linear acceleration and rotational velocity with low latency and cameras in the HMD that creates a 3D map of the room space and hand landmarks of the user. Figure 2 shows a user wearing the Oculus Quest operating a panel in a virtual space.

The simulator outputs information on car controls such as steering, gas pedal, and brake, as well as position and rotation information on the user's head pose and finger joints of both hands observed by the Oculus Quest 2. The initial position of the Oculus Quest 2 was calibrated against the position of the car control beforehand, since no auxiliary devices, such as base stations were used to obtain the absolute position of the user. For data recording, the Oculus Quest 2 was registered to the SteamVR Desktop application. By default, the Oculus Quest 2 runs at a frame rate of 72 Hz, however, to accommodate the frame rate drop caused by the program for the experiment, all data was recorded at a sampling rate of 60

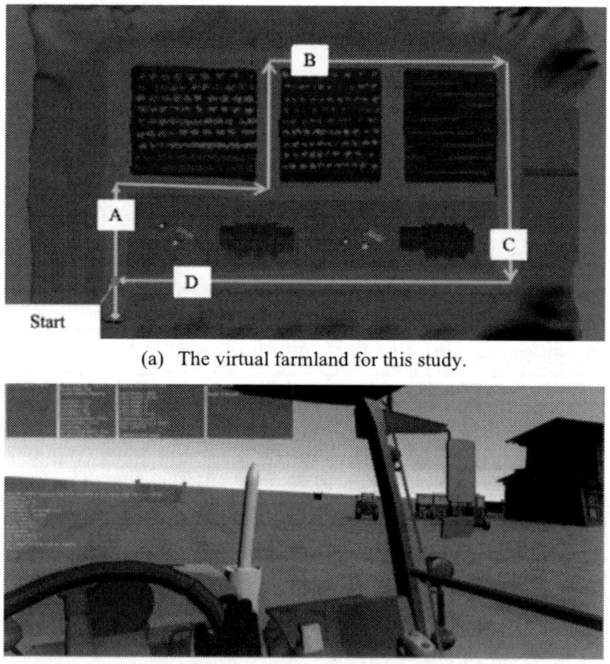

(a) The virtual farmland for this study.

(b) A view from the cockpit in a virtual environment

Figure 3. Virtual farmland used in the experiments of this study.

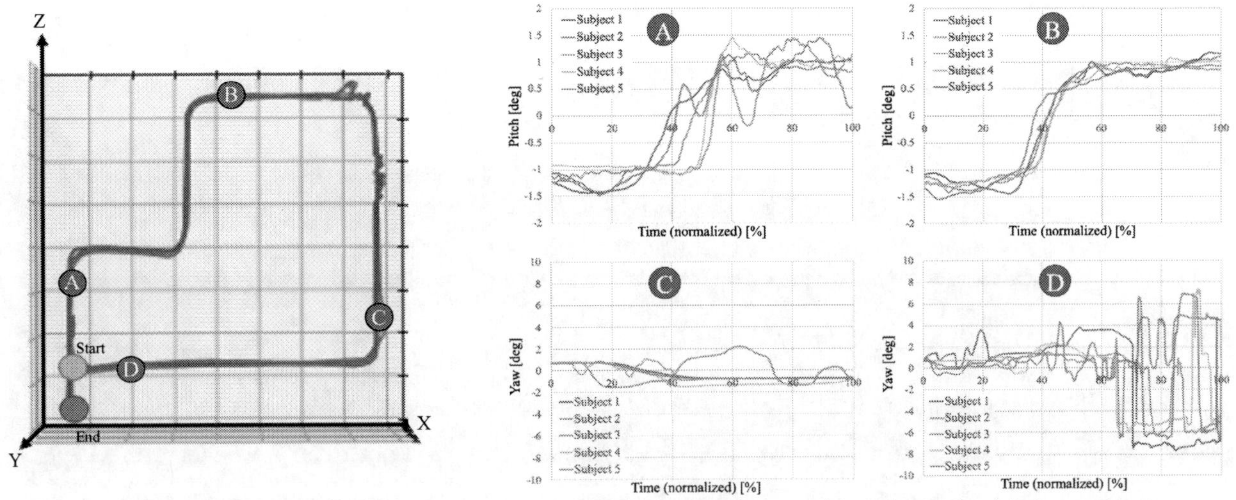

(a) Superimposed travel routes of all subjects

(b) Subjects' head poses as they perform each task in the experiment.

Figure 4. Routes traveled by the subjects and their head poses when performing each task of the experiment.

Hz. Sound feedback was implemented to make it easier to operate buttons and other interfaces in the virtual environment.

III. Experiments and Results

Using the developed simulator, the participants are asked to perform several tasks in a virtual farmland in different locations. The behavior during the tasks and the time required are measured. Figure 3 shows the virtual farmland we set up for the experiment. The field was set up with four points to perform the tasks, and audio instructions were played as the subject passed each point. The tasks are as follows. Following the voice instructions, the subject pressed a virtual button to spray to the left at point A, then another virtual button to spray to the right at point B, then turned off the ventilation fan at point C, and finally parked the car at point D.

In this experiment, we obtain the subject's driving path, head pose, and the time required for each task. The car's position (*x*, *y*, *z*) and the subject's head pose (*pitch*, *yaw*, *roll*) were all measured in the Unity coordinate system. For the head pose, clockwise is positive and counterclockwise is negative. The signal when the brake is pressed is recorded as a binary signal, a digital signal with two distinguishable levels.

For this experiment, five adult males between the ages of 20 and 23 were recruited as subjects. All of the subjects had obtained a car driving license, but had little experience using a driving simulator. Figure 4(a) show the routes traveled by the subjects when performing each task of the experiment. The subjects' routes are almost identical. This means that the subjects can navigate the vehicle along a predetermined route regardless of the virtual environment. Figure 4(b) shows subjects' head poses when performing each task of the experiment. At points A and B, we observed that, in order to press the virtual button, the subjects' heads turned down once to confirm the button's position (negative pitch angle), and then they raised their heads to confirm the direction of travel (positive pitch angle). At point C, the subjects were expected to check the condition of the fan in order to stop the rear ventilation fan, but as they used the rearview mirror to check, the yaw angle did not change significantly. On the contrary, at point D, when the subjects parked the car, they checked the left and right sides of the car, resulting in a significant variation of the yaw angle.

TABLE I. TIME TAKEN TO ACCOMPLISH EACH TASK FOR EACH SUBJECT.

Subject	Task 1 (s)	Task 2 (s)	Task 3 (s)	Task 4 (s)
1	1.9	2.9	2.1	57.1
2	3.1	2.4	8.4	106.3
3	9.0	4.2	18.0	111.1
4	3.3	2.9	3.4	79.9
5	2.8	2.8	2.5	59.0
Mean	4.02	3.04	6.88	82.68
Std. Dev.	2.835	0.680	6.710	25.438

This outcome can be attributed to the fact that the virtual environment can reproduce the relief of the terrain and scenery, so it is likely that subjects who see these scenes will behave in a similar manner. The time taken to accomplish the task for each subject is shown in Table I. The reason that task 4 took longer than the others is that it requires forward, backward, and stop actions to park the vehicle at point D.

These experimental results show that the developed simulator can reproduce the actual task work of pesticides spraying and quantify the operator's behavior in each task, which can be used to improve the interface design in the cockpit for efficient work.

IV. Observation of Operator Behavior in the Physical Environment

We installed two 4K 60fps cameras (GoPro Hero8) in the cockpit of the speed sprayer (SSV1091FSC), one on the dashboard near the door and the other next to the driver's seat. Each camera was used to observe the operator's head and hand movements, steering wheel and button operations.

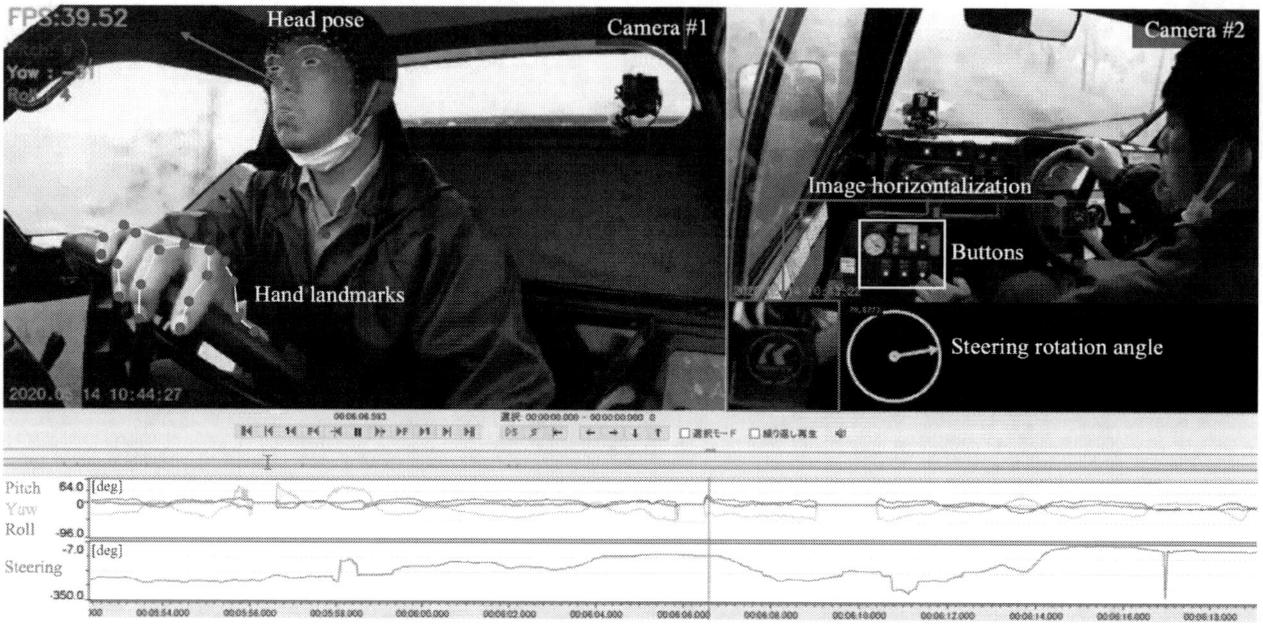

Figure 5. Data of operator behavior integrated into the ELAN.

A. Measuring head and hand movements

MediaPipe [7][8], a framework for building perception pipelines, was used to detect landmarks of faces and hands in real time from images captured by the camera on the dashboard. The head and hand movements can be quantified by obtaining the coordinate values for each landmark. We applied the Perspective-n-Point (PnP) solution to estimate the head pose in 6-DoF from the landmarks that consist of the face [9].

B. Detecting Pressed-Button

In this study, we detected that a button was pressed based on the inclusion of the fingertip coordinates with the range of pre-determined coordinates on the image of the button. This process is done on a frame-by-frame basis, but if a sequence of detected results occurs, these results are counted as a single pressing.

C. Measuring Steering Wheel Rotation

A relatively simple deep feed-forward neural network was constructed to estimate the steering wheel rotation angle. The network takes as input a 64x64 image of the steering wheel and performs convolution, batch normalization, and Rectified Linear Unit (RELU) four times to optimize the results. The network successfully estimated the steering rotation angle from low resolution steering images, where the SIFT features [10] are difficult to extract.

All the data, including video, head and hand movement measurements, steering wheel rotation, and pushed-button detection, is integrated into the ELAN (EUDICO Linguistic Annotator) [11]. ELAN provides a powerful tool for annotating and labeling data with time series characteristics. By statistically analyzing the statistical characteristics of these labels, further analysis can be performed to find out the operations that cause fatigue and how to overcome them. Figure 5 shows the data integrated into ELAN. In this way, ELAN enables us to analyze the data of head pose (*pitch*, *yaw*, *roll*), hand landmarks, and steering wheel rotation angles in a time series. We intend to verify the differences between the two environments by implementing similar tasks in the simulator using labeled tasks that correspond to the behavior of the operator obtained in the physical environment.

V. CONCLUSION

In this study, we have developed a simulator that allows the user to experience driving and operating a speed sprayer in a virtual environment using an HMD-type VR device and a car controller used in games. The simulator enables us to collect a time series of information on the driver's head pose, hand gestures, and gas pedal and brake controls measured by the simulator, and to visualize the characteristics of the driver's behavior during driving.

To achieve a more realistic simulator, data on the behavior of operators in the field was collected so that similar behavioral data could be reproduced in a virtual environment. The MediaPipe framework made it possible to extract data of operator behavior even in a light-sensitive environment such as that inside a cockpit. Next, we will conduct experiments with many tasks using the developed simulator and find valuable data for improving the operation interface of the speed sprayer.

ACKNOWLEDGEMENTS

This work was done in collaboration with YAMABIKO Corporation and the Faculty of Software and Information Science, Iwate Prefectural University.

REFERENCES

[1] H. L. Wong, D. G. Garthwaite, C. T. Ramwell, and C. D. Brown, "How Does Exposure to Pesticides Vary in Space and Time for Residents Living Near to Treated Orchards?," Environmental Science and Pollution Research, 24 (34), pp. 26444–26461, 2017.

[2] The Japanese Ministry of Health, Labor and Welfare (MHLW), "Introduction of the Positive List System for Agricultural Chemical Residues in Foods," https://www.mhlw.go.jp/english/topics/foodsafety/positivelist060228/introduction.html [retrieved: June, 2021]

[3] J. H. Han, C. H. Park, Y. J. Park, and J. H. Kwon, "Preliminary Results of the Development of a Single-Frequency GNSS RTK-Based Autonomous Driving System for a Speed Sprayer," Journal of Sensors, pp. 1-9, 2019.

[4] M. Watanabe and K. Sakai, "Development of a Nonlinear Tractor Model Using in Constructing a Tractor Driving Simulator," 2017 ASABE Annual International Meeting, pp. 1–6, 2017.

[5] D. O. Gonzalez et al., "Development and Assessment of a Tractor Driving Simulator with Immersive Virtual Reality for Training to Avoid Occupational Hazards," Computer and Electronics in Agriculture, 143, pp. 111–118, 2017.

[6] R. Venkatakrishnan et al., "Towards an Immersive Driving Simulator to Study Factors Related to Cybersickness," 26th IEEE Conference Virtual Reality and 3D User Interfaces, VR 2019, pp. 1201–1202, 2019.

[7] C. Lugaresi et al., "Mediapipe: A Framework for Building Perception Pipelines," arXiv preprint arXiv:1906.08172, pp. 1-9, 2019.

[8] F. Zhang et al., "MediaPipe Hands: On-device Real-time Hand Tracking," http://arxiv.org/abs/2006.10214, 2020.

[9] F.Rocca, M. Mancas, and B. Gosselin, "Head Pose Estimation by Perspective-n-Point Solution Based on 2D Markerless Face Tracking," Lecture Notes of the Institute for Computer Sciences, Social-Informatics and Telecommunications Engineering, LNICST, 136 LNICST, pp. 67–76. 2014.

[10] D. G. Lowe, "Object Recognition from Local Scale-Invariant Features," Proceeding of the International Conference on Computer Vision, pp. 1150–1157, 2004.

[11] ELAN (Version 6.0), "The Language Archive," https://archive.mpi.nl/tla/elan [retrieved: June, 2021]

Assessment of Drug Picking Activity using RGB-D Camera

Yuta Ono, Oky Dicky Ardiansyah Prima
Graduate School of Software and Information Science, Iwate Prefectural University
152-52 Sugo, Takizawa, Iwate, Japan
e-mail: g236s001@s.iwate-pu.ac.jp, prima@iwate-pu.ac.jp

Abstract—**Non-pharmacists have been allowed to pick drugs under the responsibility of pharmacists in order to reduce the burden on them in Japan. However, the activity tends to occur human errors since the name or shape of drugs are similar. While Bar-Code Medication Administration (BCMA) system and Automated Dispensing System (ADS) have been proposed to prevent such errors, these systems are cumbersome and costly. With the progress on human pose estimation technique using machine vision-based approach, it has become possible to measure the displacement and the posture of human body in real space. This approach makes us easy to measure the location of humans and other objects simultaneously. This study attempts to construct a drug picking activity judgement framework using RGB-D camera to detect the error easily at low-cost. This framework uses RGB-D camera to measure the location of hand landmarks and judges the activity by proposed judgement algorithm based on the position of those landmarks. In order to measure both hands accurately, we used Azure Kinect Body Tracking SDK and MediaPipe. Our experiments show that proposed framework is capable of the activity judgement on drug picking.**

Keywords-Medication administration error; 3D human pose estimation; MediaPipe; RGB-D camera; Azure Kinect.

I. INTRODUCTION

In Japan, non-pharmacists have become possible to perform the picking of drugs, such as Press Through Package (PTP) sheets, under the responsibility of pharmacists [1]. This is expected pharmacists to concentrate on more specialized tasks, such as checking prescriptions and providing medication guidance for patients. However, drug picking activities tend to occur human errors due to the similarity of drug names, shapes and so on [2]. The error during the activity may cause serious harm to patients and make the operator place a heavy burden. In addition, pharmacists need to check the drugs collected by operator. Therefore, there is a need for a method to prevent human errors during the activity.

Previous works have been proposed various method to prevent human errors during the activity. Bar-Code Medication Administration (BCMA) is a system that use bar-codes to identify such drugs, prescriptions, operators and verify that work is being performed correctly. This system is effective to prevent medication administration errors and it has been shown that introducing of the BCMA system can significantly reduce the error rate [3][4]. However, those methods are cumbersome because operator need to scan bar-code each time to check picking operation. Similar to the bar-code, Radio Frequency Identification (RFID) technology has been used for object identification. This technology uses a RFID reader to identify object with RFID tag. The reader can scan multiple tags simultaneously. However, as with BCMA system, we need to scan them in order to find human error during the activity. Automated Dispensing System (ADS) is a computer-controlled dispensing cabinet that provides safety medication management and has attracted attention as system that can reduce errors. This system has been shown to prevent errors, such as medication mix-ups [5][6]. However, ADS requires a high cost.

Operators need to spend a lot of concentration to carefully check prescriptions and drugs on the dispensing cabinet. In order to visualize where the correct drug is stored, some methods have been proposed by using LED or projector. Han et al. proposed a method that teaches the location of drugs to operators by controlling LEDs on the cabinet with a microcontroller for notification [2]. In addition, monitoring system is developed [7]. This system visualizes shelves with projector and LEDs and measures Augmented Reality (AR) markers installed shelves for monitoring the activity to help operators find out the shelf should be operated next. However, this system needs to install LEDs or projector or AR markers on each shelf.

With recent development of computer vision and deep learning, it is possible to easily measure 3D position of human body parts from vision cameras. Martinez et al. proposed a simple Deep Neural Network (DNN) that estimated root-relative 3D joint positions based on 2D joint positions estimated from single RGB image [8]. In contrast, Moon et al. proposed a method to measure 3D joint position in real space directly from an RGB image [9]. However, the accuracy achieved by this method is not enough for judgment of drug picking activities. On the other hand, hand tracking methods have been proposed using single RGB camera. Zhang et al. proposed a real-time lightweight hand tracking model from an RGB image [10]. Their model consists of the palm detector that detects 2D bounding box of hands and the hand landmark model that detects detailed skeleton.

Azure Kinect can measure the location of human body using depth sensor [11]. The Kinect captures the range of 0.25~5.46m in 30 Frame Per Second (FPS) and the provided Body Tracking Software Development Kit (SDK) can measure the 3D joint positions. Azure Kinect Sensor SDK also enables developers to measure the location of objects measured by RGB camera installed the Kinect.

This study attempts to construct a framework for judging drug picking activities using RGB-D camera in order to detect the errors easily at low-cost. The framework judges the activity based on relative positions of operator's hand and each shelf on dispensing cabinet. 3D hand tracking is performed from depth sensor. In addition, 2D hand landmarks

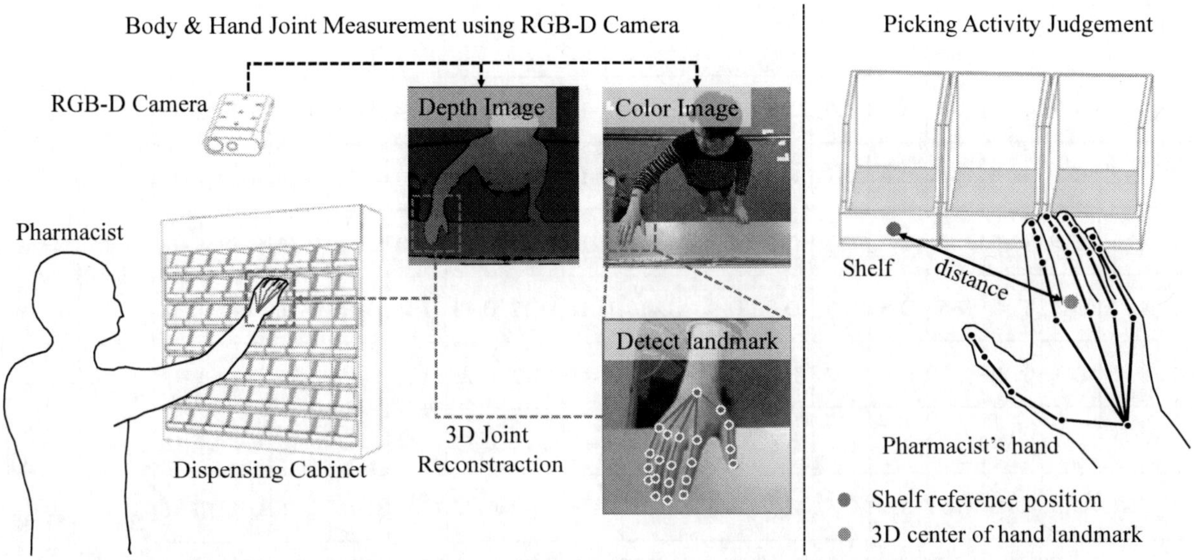

Figure 1. The illustration of drug picking activity measurement and judgement in our study.

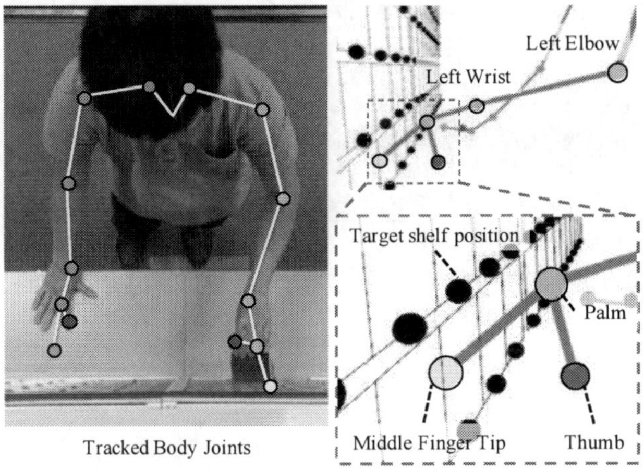

Figure 2. An example of body tracking failure on Azure Kinect.

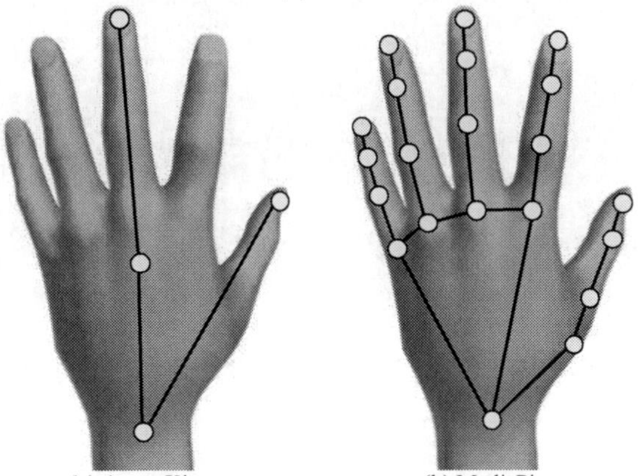

(a) Azure Kinect (b) MediaPipe

Figure 3. Hand landmarks detection in our study. Yellow landmarks are used to calculate hand center position in our study.

are tracked from RGB image using MediaPipe [10] in order to obtain stable hand measurements. 3D landmarks are inferred from the associated 2D landmarks detected by the RGB-D camera. In this study, we measure the activity of drug picking and clarify the judgement accuracy on proposed framework.

This paper is organized as follows. Section II describes the related work on human joint detection methods. Section III describes proposed methods to judge drug picking activities. Section IV describes how to assess our framework and shows result of our experiments. Section V considers about our framework's performance improvement. Finally, Section VI concludes our study.

II. Related Work

Various methods have been proposed to capture the motion of human body. The Leap Motion Controller and the Stereo IR 170 have been developed to capture hand movement [12][13]. These systems can track hands accurately, but multiple devices will be needed to measure movement during a wide range of drag picking activities. Some methods have been proposed to estimate 3D human pose from a single RGB image using DNN trained by large 3D human pose datasets [8][14][15]. Although these methods can estimate root-relative 3D location of human joints, it is difficult to directly capture their positional relationship with other object in real space. Moon et al. proposed a method to estimate the global position and posture of human based on the correlation between the size of the 2D human pose and 3D one [9].

Cabinet 1									Cabinet 2									
A-1	A-2	A-3	A-4	A-5	A-6	A-7	A-8	A-9	A-10	A-11	A-12	A-13	A-14	A-15	A-16	A-17	A-18	Top Shelf
B-1	B-2	B-3	B-4	B-5	B-6	B-7	B-8	B-9	B-10	B-11	B-12	B-13	B-14	B-15	B-16	B-17	B-18	
C-1	C-2	C-3	C-4	C-5	C-6	C-7	C-8	C-9	C-10	C-11	C-12	C-13	C-14	C-15	C-16	C-17	C-18	
D-1	D-2	D-3	D-4	D-5	D-6	D-7	D-8	D-9	D-10	D-11	D-12	D-13	D-14	D-15	D-16	D-17	D-18	
E-1	E-2	E-3	E-4	E-5	E-6	E-7	E-8	E-9	E-10	E-11	E-12	E-13	E-14	E-15	E-16	E-17	E-18	
F-1	F-2	F-3	F-4	F-5	F-6	F-7	F-8	F-9	F-10	F-11	F-12	F-13	F-14	F-15	F-16	F-17	F-18	
G-1	G-2	G-3	G-4	G-5	G-6	G-7	G-8	G-9	G-10	G-11	G-12	G-13	G-14	G-15	G-16	G-17	G-18	Bottom Shelf

Figure 4. The arrangement of the dispensing cabinets with shelves and their corresponding index viewed from subject.

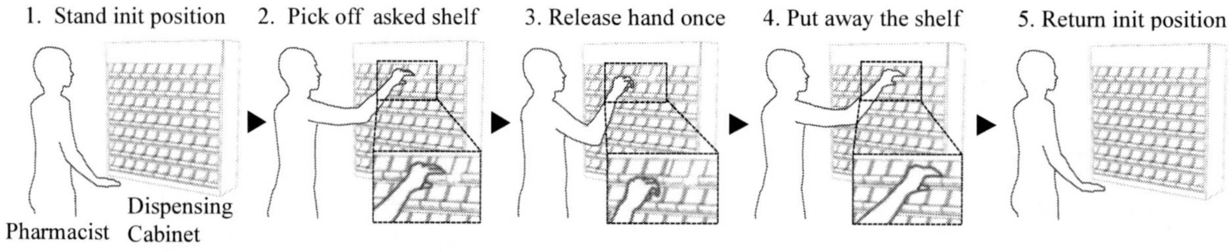

Figure 5. Drug picking activity defined in our study.

However, the measurement accuracy of this method depends on the human posture.

Azure Kinect is a device equipped with both a visible camera and depth sensor. The Kinect can directly capture human body and other objects using the depth sensor and the Body Tracking SDK. With the device-specific calibration data, the 3D position of the object can be measured from visible camera.

III. Proposed Framework

In this study, we attempt to construct a framework using RGB-D camera for judging drug picking activities to detect human errors easily at low-cost. Figure 1 shows a schematic diagram representing how to measure and judge the activity in our proposed framework. The framework uses Azure Kinect Body Tracking SDK to measure 3D position of operator's hand from depth sensor. However, Azure Kinect may not be able to track the hand position accurately due to the pose of the human body or occlusions. Figure 2 shows an example of a body tracking failure in Azure Kinect. In order to measure the hand accurately, this study also detects hand position from RGB image by MediaPipe and estimates 3D position based on corresponding depth value from depth sensor. Finally, we determine the operated shelf based on the hand position and known shelf position. Figure 3 shows hand landmarks detection in our study.

1. *3D Body Joints Measurement using RGB-D Camera*

This study places Azure Kinect above dispensing cabinet to measure the hand motion with less occlusion. The hand detection involves two steps. First, we determine the approximate position of the hand in the RGB image based on the wrist position obtained by body tracking in the Azure Kinect Sensor SDK. Next, we extract a Region of Interest (ROI) for each hand from the Kinect RGB image. These ROIs are used to detect 2D hand landmarks using the MediaPipe framework. Finally, the depth information from the Kinect's depth sensor is added to generate 3D hand landmarks.

2. *Drug Picking Activity Judgement*

The procedure for the decision algorithm is as follows. First, we calculate the hand position as the center position of the detected 3D hand landmarks as shown in Figure 3(b). This calculation enables a stable measurement of the hand position, especially when fingertips are hidden during the activity. Next, the distance between the hand position and each shelf position is calculated. Then, we identify the closest shelf from the hand. if both hands can be detected, we choose the shelf with the shorter distance. Finally, shelves that have been detected for

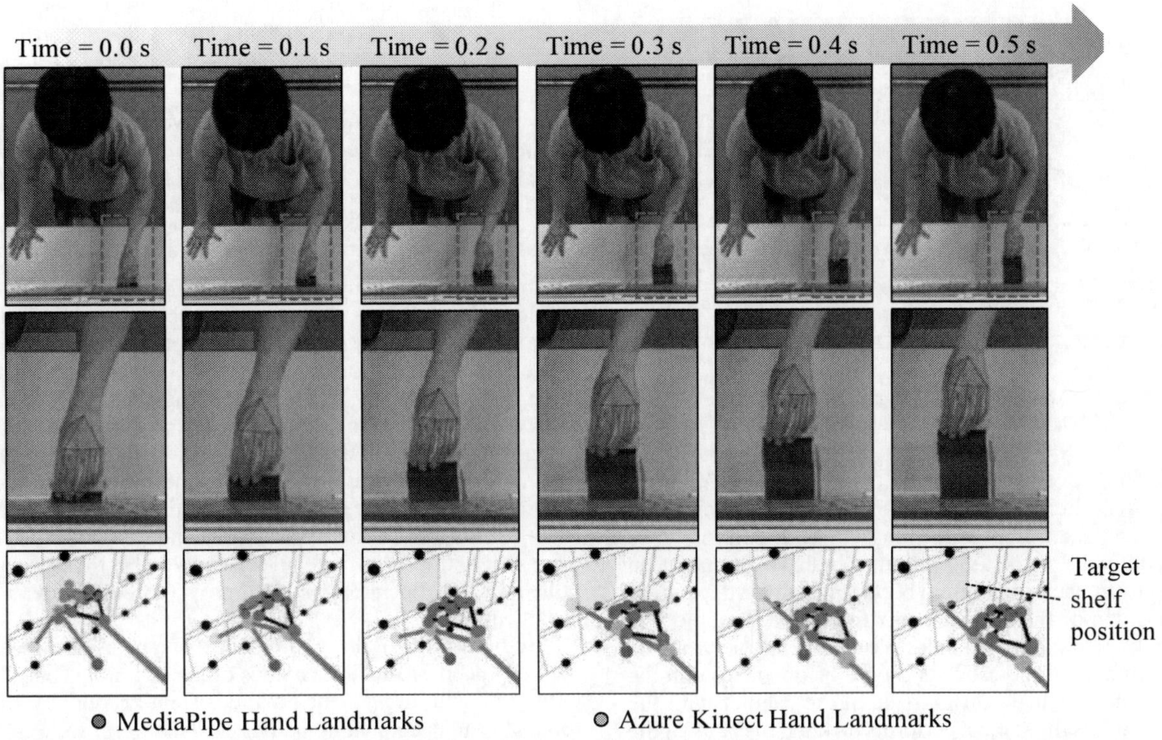

Figure 6. The result of proposed hand joint measurements in our study.

TABLE I. JUDGEMENT ACCURACY USING EACH LANDMARK.

	Landmark		
	Azure Kinect		MediaPipe
Subject	Wrist	Hand	Hand
A	43%	99%	100%
B	18%	89%	99%
C	32%	90%	99%
D	63%	93%	98%
E	30%	79%	99%
All	37%	90%	99%

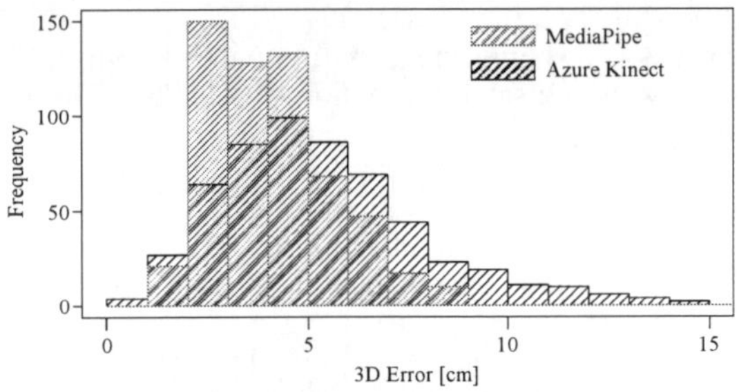

Figure 7. The Histogram of error distribution between 3D hand and target shelf when subject pick it.

more than 0.5s are judged as "operated shelf". If more two shelves are determined, the shelf with the longer time is adopted. In this study, the drug picking activity is defined as "pulling out the target shelf". We do not consider that whether the actual drug is obtained or not.

IV. EXPERIMENTS AND RESULTS

We evaluated the proposed framework in terms of judgement accuracy and suitable hand landmarks. First, we measured the drug picking activity by subjects to verify our framework's judgement accuracy. Second, we measured the center of each hand landmark of the Azure Kinect and the MediaPipe, and compared the distance between each hand position and the target shelf in order to clarify which hand landmark is suitable for the judgement. Figure 4 shows the arrangement of the dispensing cabinets used in this experiment and the index corresponding to each shelf. The dispensing cabinet used in this experiment can hold 63 shelves (7 rows by 9 columns). The shelf's size is 9.4cm×10.6cm×13.3cm. We aligned two cabinets side by side and put them 85.5cm above the floor. The Azure Kinect is installed at 92cm above the cabinets. The resolution of the color camera is 1920×1080px, the field of view is 90° ×59°, the resolution of the depth sensor is 512×512px, and the field of view is 120° ×120°. We collected five healthy subjects (A~E) for the experiments.

1. Our Framework's Activity Judgement Accuracy

The procedure of our experiments is as follows. First, we asked the subject to stand in the center of the cabinets. This position is defined as initial position. Next, we randomly

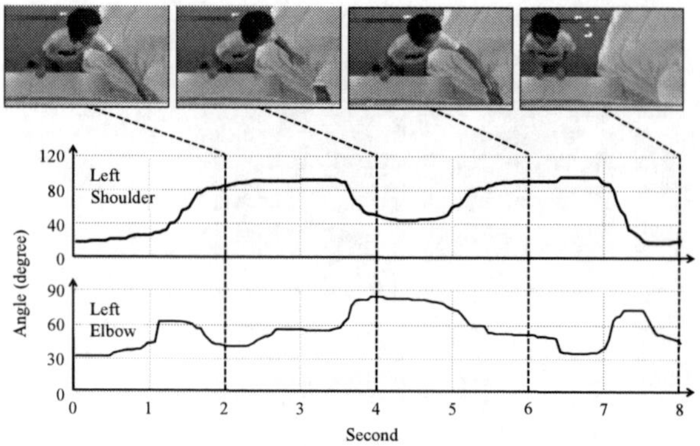

Figure 8. Left shoulder and Left elbow joint angle during subject A pick shelf, A-1.

displayed an index of shelves to choose from on a monitor set up above the shelves. Each subject is asked to pick the corresponding shelf after confirming its ID. Figure 5 shows the procedure of drug picking activities in this experiment. In order to prevent the activity from becoming uneven depending on the position of the subject at the time, we ask subject to return back the initial position after each picking action. The shelf on left side of the cabinets should be operated with the left hand, whereas that on right side of the cabinet with the right hand. When the subject performs picking, the back of the hand should face upward. Finally, we judge the activity based on our frameworks. For the experiment, the subject performs the picking activity only once per shelf. After this measurement, the experimenter confirms the activity. If subject picked a wrong shelf, this action was excluded from this evaluation.

In this experiment, we compared the picking accuracy using different human body landmark: the Azure Kinect's wrist, the center of hand landmarks of the Azure Kinect, the center of hand landmarks of the MediaPipe. Table 1 shows the resulting judgement accuracy. The hand landmarks of the MediaPipe were able to judge the activity with highest accuracy. Figure 6 shows the measurement result of the drug picking activity on shelf F-8 by subject E.

2. Comparison of Azure Kinect hand and MediaPipe hand

We verified whether the hand landmarks of Azure Kinect or MediaPipe are more suitable for judging the picking activity. First, we manually obtained the hand position when subject grasps target shelf. Next, we calculated 3D Euclidean distance between the hand position and the target shelf. Finally, we tested difference between the distance to the target shelf for both landmarks using Welch's t-test. A significant difference was found in the scores for the hand landmarks of MediaPipe (M=4.1cm, SD=1.5cm) and the one of Azure Kinect (M=5.3cm, SD=2.5cm); $t(902.46) = 9.95$, $p < 0.001$. There results suggest that the hand landmarks of the MediaPipe is better than Azure Kinect for the judgement. Figure 7 shows that the histogram of the 3D distance to the target shelf for the hand landmarks.

V. Discussion

In this study, we have constructed a framework to judge drug picking activities using the Azure Kinect. Compared to BCMA system and ADS, our framework does not require scanning of bar-code each time, as well as no capital investment or the high cost of installing LEDs or AR markers on dispensing cabinets. Our experiments show that our framework can accurately judge the picking activity by hand tracking at low-cost.

In order to further improve the judgement accuracy of drug picking activity, the following can be considered. First, improvement of body tracking from depth image is important to increase the detection of body joints. In this study, we have measured operator by Azure Kinect installed the top of the dispensing cabinet to capture operator's hand with less occlusion. However, the tracking will fail if the operator's body is leaning forward or closed to the cabinet. In order to solve this problem, we consider an additional training data for body tracking from the upper part of human body. Second, using the Azure Kinect's depth sensor to detect the target shelf pulled by the operator could improve the accuracy of the judgment.

Body tracking of the Azure Kinect can be used to measure the body position and joint angles of the operator. This allows us to calculate movement traveled, angular velocity of the joints during drug picking activities. Therefore, we think our framework has a potential to extract characteristic movements in the activity and the evaluation of the activity load. Figure 8 shows the joint angles of the subject A's left shoulder and elbow in shelf A-1 operation.

In order to verify effectiveness of our framework for judging drug picking activities, we enforced several constraints on the subject's movements during the experiment. In practice, however, operators can perform their drug picking activities without these constraints and use different types of shelves. In the future, we intend to evaluate the activities without such constraints, but with the Azure Kinect, we believe we can measure the reference position of each shelf of different sizes.

VI. Conclusion

In this study, we have proposed the judgement framework for drug picking activity. Our framework uses the Azure Kinect to evaluate the activity easily at low-cost. In addition to use body tracking of the Azure Kinect, we utilize hand tracking from an RGB image to track operator's hand for more stable. Our experiments show that the proposed framework enables accurately judge the activity by hand tracking taken advantage of the Azure Kinect and the MediaPipe. In the future, we will improve the accuracy of the activity judgement and measure the activity without constraints and analyze the movement of the operator.

References

[1] Pharmaceutical Safety and Environmental Health Bureau, "The state of dispensing operations", https://www.mhlw.go.jp/content/000498352.pdf [retrieved: July, 2021] (in Japanese)

[2] C. Han et al., "The assistance for drug dispensing using LED notification and IR sensor-based monitoring methods," 2018 9th International Conference on Awareness Science and Technology (iCAST), pp. 264-267, Sept. 2018, doi:10.1109/ICAwST.2018.8517168.

[3] E. G. Poon et al., "Effect of bar-code technology on the safety of medication administration,", The New England Journal of Medicine, Vol 362, pp. 1698-1707, May. 2010, doi: 10.1056/NEJMsa0907115

[4] J. Bonkowski et al., "Effect of barcode-assisted medication administration on emergency department medication errors," Academic Emergency Medicine, vol. 20, pp. 801-806, Aug. 2013, doi: 10.1111/acem.12189

[5] C. Chapuis et al., "Automated drug dispensing system reduces mediaction errors in an intensive care setting," Critical Care Medicine, Vol. 38, pp. 2275-2281, Dec. 2010, doi: 10.1097/CCM.0b013e3181f8569b

[6] J. G. Dib et al., "Effects of an automated drug dispensing system on medication adverse event occurrences and cost containment at SAMSO," Hospital Pharmacy, Vol 41, No. 12, pp. 1180-1184, Dec. 2006, doi: 10.1310/hpj4112-1180

[7] AIOI SYSTEMS CO., LTD, "Projection Picking System," https://www.hello-aioi.com/en/solution/digital_picking/projection/pps/ [retrieved: July, 2021]

[8] J. Martinez, R. Hossain, J. Romero, and J. J. Little, "A simple yet effective baseline for 3d human pose estimation,", pp. 1-10, Aug. 2017, arXiv:1705.03098

[9] G. Moon, J. Y. Chang, and K. M. Lee, "Camera distance-aware top-down approach for 3d multi-person pose estimation from a single RGB-image," pp. 1-15, Aug. 2019, arXiv:1907.11346

[10] F. Zhang et al., "MediaPipe hands: on-device real-time hand tracking," pp. 1-5, Jun. 2020, arXiv:2006.10214

[11] Microsoft Azure, "Azure Kinect DK," https://azure.microsoft.com/en-us/services/kinect-dk/ [retrieved: July, 2021]

[12] Ultraleap, "Leap Motion Controller, " https://www.ultraleap.com/product/leap-motion-controller/ [retrieved: July, 2021]

[13] Ultraleap, "Ultraleap Stereo IR 170," https://www.ultraleap.com/product/stereo-ir-170/ [retrieved: July, 2021]

[14] H. Fang, Y. Xu, W. Wang, X. Liu, and S. Zhu, "Learning Pose Grammar to Encode Human Body Configuration for 3D Pose Estimation," The Thirty-Second AAAI Conference on Artificial Intelligence, pp. 6821-6828, Jan. 2018, arXiv:1710.06513

[15] X. Chen, K. Lin, W. Liu, C. Qian, and L. Lin, "Weakly-Supervised Discovery of Geometry-Aware Representation for 3D Human Pose Estimation," Proceedings of the IEEE/CVF Conference on Computer Vision and Pattern Recognition (CVPR), pp. 10895-10904, Jun. 2019

Development of a Flexible 3D Pointing Device with Haptic Feedback

Koma Yoshikawa, Yuta Ono, and Oky Dicky Ardiansyah Prima
Graduate School of Software and Information Science, Iwate Prefectural University
152-52 Sugo Takizawa, Japan
email: {g231s035, g236s001}@s.iwate-pu.ac.jp, prima@iwate-pu.ac.jp

***Abstract*—With the increasing trend toward diversification of display devices, the development of displays with curved, folded, or spherical surfaces, has become popular in recent years. At the same time, a new Three-Dimensional (3D) pointing device is required to provide effective user interaction for 3D displays. This study attempts to develop a new 3D pointing device with an Inertial Measurement Unit (IMU) sensor, a flexible mechanism, and haptic feedback. For the haptic, we adopt both active and passive haptic feedback. Here, we perform experiments with the prototyped device to verify the effects of the flexible mechanism and haptic on 3D pointing. Experiments confirmed that the haptic has a significant impact on 3D pointing, enabling more accurate input operations. However, the flexible mechanism was not significantly assisting the adjustment of the input to the depth.**

Keywords-haptic feedback; flexible interface; stylush pen; IMU.

I. INTRODUCTION

The use of virtual contents has become common in recent years, regardless of the field or application, such as entertainment, industry, and education. With the increase in the variety of displays, the interaction with virtual contents is becoming more extensive. Augmented Reality (AR) contents that can be viewed with commonly used mobile terminals, AR glasses, and head-mount displays are attracting attention. These devices have dedicated controllers with motion tracking capabilities and hand tracking that enable users to input operations intuitively without losing the sense of reality of the contents.

In addition to AR devices, multi-view 3D displays are also being developed. These displays create the illusion of 3D content as if it exists in real space. Looking Glass [1] is the first personal holographic flat display that allows 3D content to be viewed at an effective viewing angle of approximately 40-50°. The spherical display [2] uses motion parallax to project 3D images onto the 360° surface of the sphere and renders the images according to the viewing direction to achieve the same effect as the Looking Glass. Unlike AR devices, the surface of these displays can be touched directly, allowing for the adoption of input methods, such as touch and pointing interfaces.

For the input interface of a multi-view 3D display, the use of existing mouse and touch interfaces in its original form is not intuitive. This is due to the limited information that can be input by these input interfaces, which is limited to Two-Dimensional (2D) information, making it difficult to manipulate the contents in depth. Although the 3D pointing device proposed by Prima et al. (2020) was developed for 3D spherical displays, it is difficult for users to sense how much input they are making when performing 3D pointing to depth [3]. Therefore, a mechanism to enable input to the depth is necessary for this pointing device.

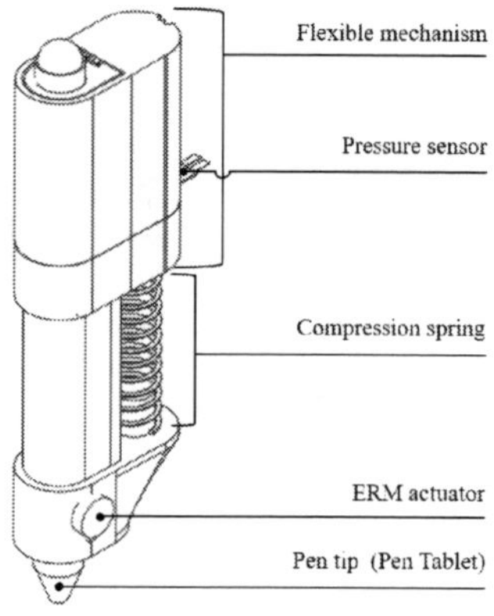

Figure 1. The configuration of the 3D pointing device in this study.

This study aims to develop and evaluate a stylus-type 3D pointing device with a flexible mechanism and vibration actuators for intuitive input. Giving a haptic input sensation is expected to enable more accurate input for 3D pointing to depth. In addition, the introduction of a flexible mechanism is expected to make it easier to adjust the depth input.

The rest of this paper is organized as follows. In Section II, we describe the related works of 3D input interfaces. Section III introduces our approach to implement the pointing device. Section IV describes our experiment results. Section V discusses about the further enhancements to the proposed pointing device. Finally, Section VI presents our conclusions and future works.

II. RELATED WORKS

Haptic devices play an important role in human-computer interaction [4]. These devices are often used as interfaces to convey virtual tactile sensations to users using vibration, temperature, and pressure.

There are two types of haptic devices: active and passive [5]. Active Haptic Feedback (AHF) uses the movement of computer-controlled actuators as feedback. The advantage of AHF is that it can be flexibly realized according to the content, such as reproducing the texture of an object or the sensation of collision through vibration. High performance actuators and

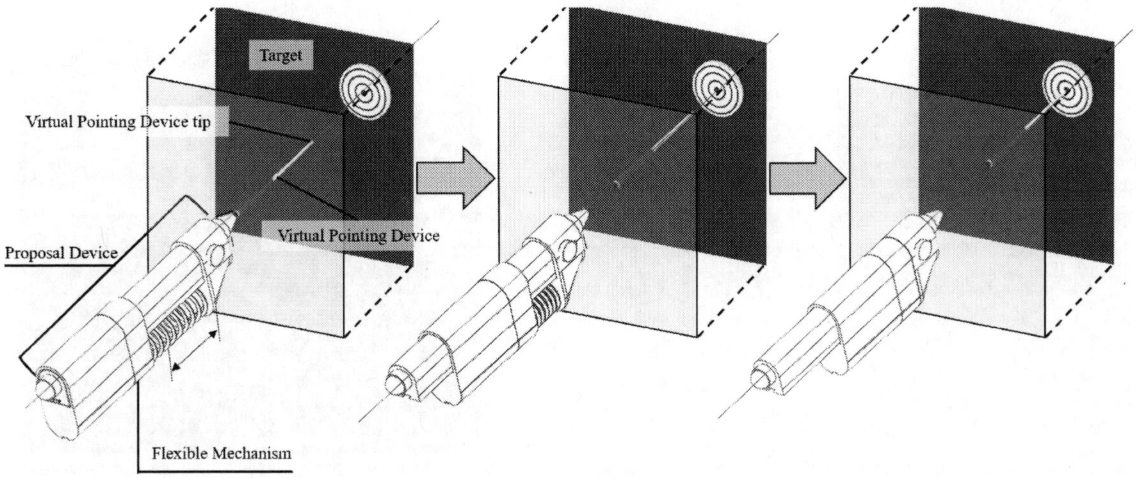

Figure 2. Depth input operation by pushing the pointing device with the flexible mechanism.

complex controls can be used to generate high quality sensory feedback. In contrast, Passive Haptic Feedback (PHF) is a haptic that uses a real object to provide haptic feedback. The advantage of PHF is that it can easily generate high-quality sensory feedback at a lower cost than AHF because it uses physical properties such as the shape and weight of the object. However, it has the disadvantage of not being able to respond flexibly to content due to its strong dependence on physical properties.

A haptic stylus with a flexible mechanism was presented as an interaction device for manipulating small-sized virtual reality contents on mobile devices [6]. To manipulate 3D content, the stylus needs to be tilted and rotated. However, these functions are not implemented.

III. Flexible 3D Pointing Device with Haptic Feedback

In this study, we modified the stylus with flexible mechanism proposed by Choi et al. (2021) [6] and implemented AHF and pose orientation feedback to create a 3D pointing device. Therefore, our pointing device will have both AHF and PHF when manipulating 3D content in virtual space. To simplify the design of the device, we used Wacom Intuos Pros to detect the position of the pointing device tip relative to the touch point and the orientation of the device. The PHF is generated by the change in the length of the device due to the flexible mechanism and the repulsive force of the spring. AHF is implemented by Eccentric Rotating Mass (ERM) actuators that generate pulsing vibrations when the tip of the device touches a visual target in virtual space. PHF is intended to influence the perception of the amount of input, while AHF is intended to influence the perception of completion.

Figure 1 shows the configuration of the 3D pointing device in this study. The device vibrates the haptic motor to provide AHF to the user when the device tip hits with the 3D content in the virtual space. To implement the flexible mechanism, we used a spring and a pressure sensor. The pressure value changed by the compression coil spring when the user pushes in is treated as the input value to the depth. Figure 2 shows an example of depth input operation by pushing the pointing device with the flexible mechanism. Here, the pressure and AHF sensors are controlled by M5Stick-C, which communicates with the software via Bluetooth Serial. M5Stick-C and the AHF sensor is attached to the user's arm using a band. The total cost of the proposed 3D pointing device is about $100.

IV. Experiments and Results

The use of haptic feedback in input operations to virtual contents is expected to enable more accurate 3D pointing by improving the input sensation. In this experiment, we will evaluate to what extent the input sensation improves 3D pointing and verify the effects of the flexible mechanism and haptic on the operation. In this experiment, we measure the accuracy and precision of 3D pointing to a visual target using the proposed device and evaluated its stability for depth input. Figure 3 shows our experimental environment. The pointing system was implemented in Unity3D. The pen tablet was mounted on a wall and the touch coordinates were obtained so that the front of the real world was the front of the content.

Five subjects (male) between the ages of 23 and 27, participated in the experiment. Subjects were seated in front of a display while holding the proposed device. At first, the experimenter provided the subject with instructions on how to use the device to virtually touch the presented visual target. Next, subjects were given the opportunity to practice pointing the target using the device. The experiment was started after the subject were sufficiently familiar with the operation of the device.

Figure 4 shows the procedure of 3D pointing in this experiment. At first, the experimenter presents the visual target on the display. Next, the subject touches the tablet with the proposed device and adjusts its angle toward the visual target. After feeling that the angle has been adjusted properly,

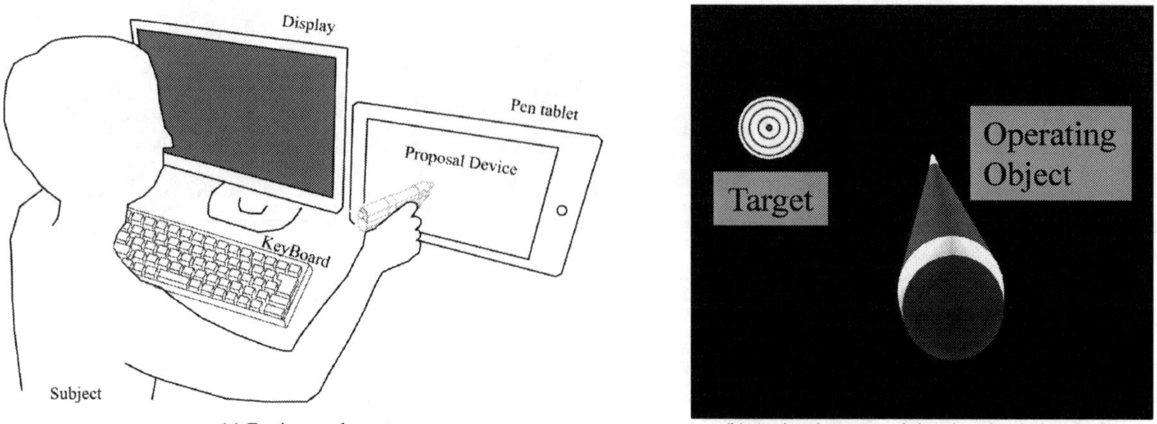

(a) Equipment layout

(b) A visual target and the virtual pointing device

Figure 4. Environmental experiment for this study.

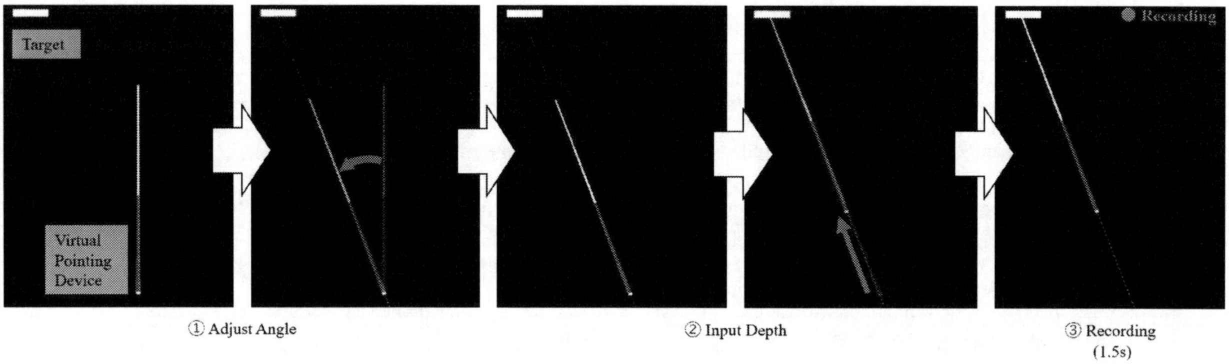

Figure 3. The procedure of 3D pointing in this experiment.

TABLE I. 3D POINTING PRECISION AND ACCURACY.

Condition	Mean [mm]	SD [mm]
None	7	5.3
PHF	8.2	6.3
AHF	4	3.3
PHF and AHF	4.7	4.3

the subject presses the device and make a depth input, trying to make the tip just touch the center of the visual target virtually. The subject records the position of the tip by pressing a button on the keyboard when he felt that this operation was successful.

In this experiment, 18 indicators were placed at equal intervals on the screen. During pointing, four patterns of combinations of with and without AHF and PHF were set up. The pointing precision and accuracy were evaluated with and without AHF and PHF. In case of using PHF, the pointing depth is adjusted by the flexible mechanisms of the device. On the other hand, when PHF is not used, the standard functions of the pen tablet are used for the input.

Table I shows the accuracy and precision of 3D pointing for each pattern of AHF and PHF. The results show that more accurate 3D pointing can be achieved by using AHF. Figure 5 shows a histogram of the resulting pointing z-scores for each pattern. Here, a negative Z-Error indicates that the pointing position is short, while a positive Z-Error indicates that the pointing position is longer than the target. Figure 5 (b) shows that the AHF allows pointing closer to the target. However, when both AHF and PHF were used, the pointing tended to be longer than when only AHF was used.

V. CONCLUSION

In this study, we have developed a flexible 3D pointing device with haptic feedback to evaluate the extent to which input sensation improves 3D pointing and to verify the influence of flexible mechanisms and haptics on the operation. Our experiment shows that the active haptic feedback enables pointing closer to the target.

In the future, we would like to install an IMU on the developed device to obtain rotation and stretching information by itself to be used in actual 3D displays.

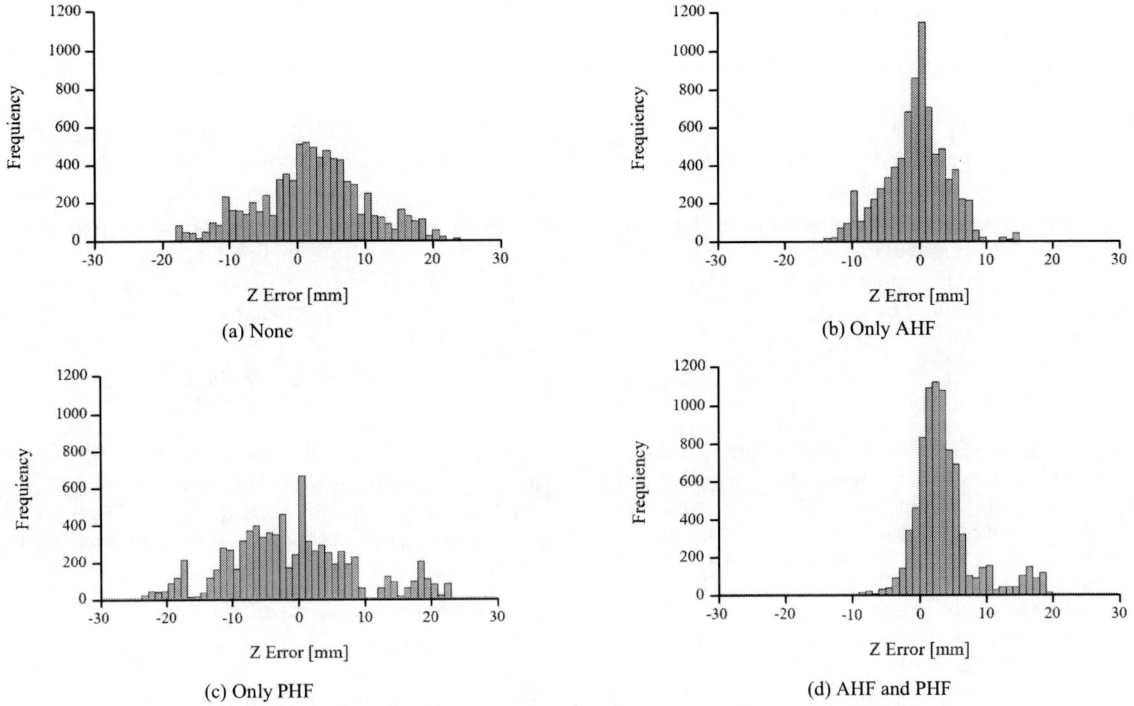

Figure 5. Histogram of the resulting pointing z-scores for each haptic pattern.

ACKNOWLEDGMENT

This work was supported by JSPS KAKENHI Grant Numbers 20K12123. We also thank to the Iwate Prefectural University of Japan, for funding this project. We also thank the editor and three anonymous reviewers for their constructive comments, which helped us to improve the manuscript.

REFERENCES

[1] Looking Glass, https://lookingglassfactory.com. [retrieved: June, 2021]

[2] J. Bolton, K. Kim, and R. Vertegaal, "SnowGlobe: A Spherical Fish-Tank VR Display," In Conference on Human Factors in Computing Systems - Proceedings, pp. 1159-1164, 2011.

[3] O. D. A. Prima, K. Hotta, R. Takahashi, and H. Ito,"A Pointing Device for 3D Interactive Spherical Displays," International Journal on Advances in Software, Vol. 13, No. 3 & 4, pp. 284-293, 2020.

[4] K. E. MacLean, "Haptic Interaction Design for Everyday Interfaces," Human Factors and Ergonomics Society. 2008, 4, pp. 149–194.

[5] K. R. Vaghela, A. Trockels, M. Carobene, "Active vs Passive Haptic Feedback Technology in Virtual Reality Arthroscopy Simulation: Which is Most Realistic?," Journal of Clinical Orthopaedics and Trauma, 16, pp. 249-256, 2021.

[6] D. S. Choi, I. H. Yun, T. H. Kim, S. Byeon, and S. Y. Kim, "Development of haptic stylus for manipulating virtual objects in mobile devices," Actuators, vol. 9, no. 2, 2020. https://doi.org/10.3390/act9020030.

Design of Interfaces for People with Blindness

Designing the Complete Learning Environment for Braille Users Studying Mathematics

Yvonne Eriksson
School of Innovation, Design and Engineering, division of Information Design
Mälardalen university
Eskilstuna, Sweden
email: yvonne.eriksson@mdh.se

Björn Westling
School of Innovation, Design and Engineering, division of Information Design
Mälardalen university / Swedish Agency for Accessible Media
Eskilstuna, Sweden / Malmö, Sweden
email: bjorn.westling@mtm.se

Abstract—**Digital platforms are not automatically accessible for people with blindness, it must be designed for multimodality, both regarding the architecture and the interface. With the point of departure in the Nine Laws of Cognition we focus on complex content such as mathematics and how it could be accessible for Braille readers. The aim of this paper is to highlight and to discuss what is required from digital platforms to support mathematic Braille. The situation for Braille users learning mathematics is not at all very satisfactory. When using the ASCIIMath format (a mathematical markup language) in digital reading and writing, Braille users practice a format not in use by teachers or sighted peers. What we are aiming at here, is to identify the functionality and the technical infrastructure needed to make the design of a truly usable learning environment possible.**

Keywords; EPUB3; ASCIIMath; Braille digital platforms.

I. INTRODUCTION

The digitalization of society makes it possible to design computer interfaces accessible for people with blindness and low vision. Digital platforms are not automatically accessible for people with blindness and low vision, it must be designed for multimodality, both regarding the architecture and the interface. In this paper, we will focus on complex content such as mathematics and how it could be accessible for Braille readers. Not by simplifying the complexity but to make it accessible. The aim of this paper is to highlight and to discuss what is required from digital platforms to support mathematic Braille.

When it comes to e-books a technological shift is ongoing. A pilot study was initiated by the Swedish Agency for Accessible Media, MTM (MTM = Myndigheten för tillgängliga medier), in which EPUB 3 (EPUB = electronic publication) was introduced for users with blindness. EPUB 3 is an e-book file format and a technical standard for production and consumption of digital books, and for other various publications. It is not specifically aimed for users with print impairments, but with the ambition to be accessible for all users [1]. The EPUB 3.2 specification states that "EPUB 3 defines a distribution and interchange format for digital publications and documents. The EPUB format provides a means of representing, packaging, and encoding structured and semantically enhanced Web content—including HTML [HyperText Markup Language], CSS [Cascading Style Sheets], SVG [Scalable Vector Graphics] and other resources—for distribution in a single-file container" [2].

A. *Complex content for Braille users*

Braille consists of a cell containing six dots that could be combined in 64 different ways. Even though Braille has specific combinations of dots representing the various letters in the alphabet, and though the Braille cell combinations are not based on letter sign similarities but on other principles, Braille needs to be considered as a unique writing system with its own writing principles. Braille is used for various kinds of notations, text, phonetics, music, mathematics, and science. With the use of certain Braille patterns as composition signs, it is possible to vary the meaning of the following braille cells, and thus creating a very large number of character representations in Braille. An example is given in Figure 1 showing how letters are discriminated from numbers.

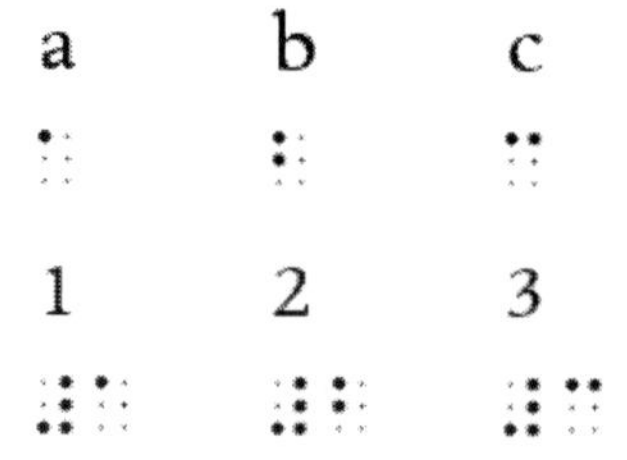

Figure 1. Braille letters with the special composition sign for numbers change meaning to numbers.

However, this ability of Braille in representing various notations is not in itself enough to make it possible accessing complex content in digital form, such as mathematics.

Complex could be defined as something consisting of many different and connected parts. Mathematics is complex and denoting or involving numbers or quantities containing both a real and an imaginary part. The notation systems for mathematics are also complex and in more advanced mathematics many kinds of expressions exist built on known and unknown variables. Expressions are often notated in print in a two-dimensional form, e.g., fractions and square roots. For a Braille reader, all this will be presented in a linear form as shown in Figure 2.

$$z = \frac{\frac{7x-6y}{5x+8y}}{\frac{7x-6y}{8y+5x}}$$

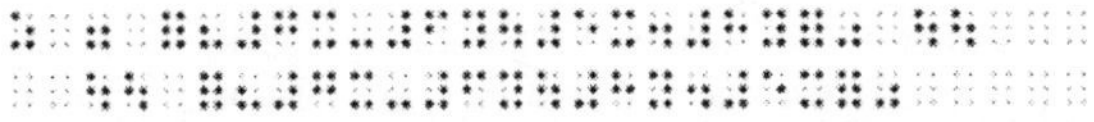

Figure 2. Mathematics in Braille is mainly linear, here an example of a complex fraction in Swedish Braille.

The principles for how to represent mathematics in Braille (Braille standards) vary considerably between languages and countries. In Swedish Braille, a mathematical expression may be written within a regular text, whereas in an English text special Braille signs are needed indicating that the content is mathematical. In Figure 3 this difference is shown with a simple mathematical example.

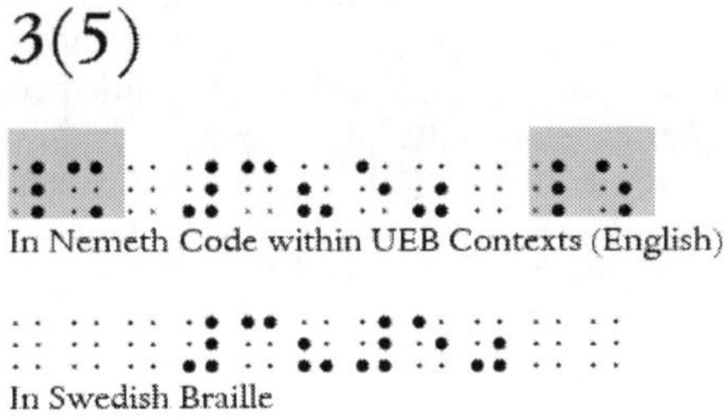

Figure 3. The Nemeth code for mathematics uses "switch indicators" for when the user should interpret Braille signs as mathematics – here marked in grey. In Swedish Braille no such indicators are used.

B. From Library for the blind to Agency of Accessible Media

In 1980 the library of the Swedish Association of the Visually Impaired was reorganized, becoming the core of the then founded Swedish Library for Talking Books and Braille, a governmental agency. The mission for the Swedish Library for Talking Books and Braille was to make already existing, published books and music notations accessible for Braille readers and readers of talking books. The content ranged from fiction, poetry, popular science to books for children, but also course literature for students at universities. The target group were people with blindness or low vision. That group expanded over the years to include people with different kinds of reding disabilities, such as dyslexia, cognitive disabilities, diseases causing spasms, and other problems when reading printed books. The disability could be permanent or temporary. Because of the expanded target group and the variety of media due to the digitalization, the Swedish Library for Talking Books and Braille, made a shift in their focus and became the Swedish Agency for Accessible Media (MTM) in 2013. MTM produces and distributes literature and magazines in accessible formats for people with reading disabilities and actively participates in the development of accessible media.

A simplified definition of media is literature and magazines made by MTM. Accessibility of these media includes talking books, Braille books, e-textbooks, literature in sign language, tactile picture books, Braille calendars, the easy-to-read news magazine *8 sidor* (8 pages), and easy-to-read books. The ability to make media accessible rests on theories about our senses, how they work individually and in combination. The interest for how different senses work and in which way a loss of one sense affects an individual has a long history. Much of the research regarding blindness has focused on the relation between vision and touch [3] [4]. What kind of information could be replaced by touch when someone has lost their eyesight? Research has been in relation to Braille reading, and tactile pictures, but also on spatial understanding and blindness [5] [6]. A study from 1965 contains both an extensive literature review on reading of talking books and a study that compared sighted students with students with blindness in relation to what they have comprehend of the content [7]. This study is representative for research from the first decades of the use of talking books, since the focus for the early studies was not on comparing Braille reading and talking books, but on making comparisons between sighted and non-sighted reading talking books. Talking books were introduced during the 1930s, e.g., in 1934 by the National Library Service at the Library of Congress, and in 1935 by the Royal National Institute for Blind (RNIB), and further developed during the following decades. The first talking book was recorded on disc and was played on special designed turn tables and it was not until tape recorder were developed in 1950s it was spread to a larger audience with blindness. To begin with, there was an over-reliance on its ability to replace Braille. This could partly be explained by the enthusiasm for the technology and partly by a simplified production of talking books compared to Braille. The Braille books were manually copied by people that had knowledge in Braille while recording talking books could be made by anyone that had some reading aloud skills. The development in technology and reading devices for recorded books has been striking from tape recorder to cassette recorder, to Walkman, MP3 (a coding format for digital audio), Daisy players (Daisy = digital accessible information system) and smartphones. The development of accessible Braille has followed the same noticeable development, with refreshable Braille displays for computers, Braille printers, and refreshable Braille displays to use in combination with smart phones. However, later discussions have brought up the necessity of access to the written language for people with blindness, the necessity of access to Braille. Both for learning outcome and for democratic reasons literacy is important.

In section II, the cognitive processes in relation to accessing platforms that support problem solving in mathematics are explored. In section III, multimodality is discussed, and in section IV, the focus is on usability and technical development, the challenges and what ought to be developed to improve the usability for Braille readers studying mathematics. In section V, we suggest further research and development in order to progress in the creation of a complete, flexible, and usable learning environment for Braille users learning mathematics.

II. Cognitive Processes

The cognitive psychologist Barbara Tversky presents The Nine Laws of Cognition in her book, *Mind in Motion: How Action Shapes Thought* (2019). These laws serve as a basis for discussion in this book, combined with socio-cultural perspectives. The laws are as follows:

1. There are no benefits without costs.
2. Action molds perception.
3. Feeling comes first.
4. The mind can override perception.
5. Cognition mirrors perception.
6. Spatial thinking is the foundation of abstract thought.
7. The mind fills in missing information.
8. When thought overflows the mind, the mind puts it into the world.
9. We organize stuff in the world the way we organize stuff in our minds.

These laws illustrate how the mind gets involved as we navigate the world and interpret our environment. Even though our mind and senses are dependent on physiological conditions, the way we think, the emotional condition we are in and how we organize 'stuff' in our mind are also highly dependent on the cultural traditions that we belong to, as well as on our living conditions. It is a relationship between cognitive aspects and a socio-cultural perspective, which is a combination of culture, cultural traditions, socio-economic conditions, and societal aspects. These aspects need to be taken into consideration when designing for people with blindness and low vision.

A. There are no benefits without costs

The lack of one sense will causes challenges for a person, to make something accessible does mean that some effort is needed. To make a platform or a software accessible for a Braille reader means it could be usable with a Braille display or by synthetic speech. Synthetic speech will require more strain on working memory than using the Braille display. Since a Braille display only show one row at the time it does not give the same overview as screen display.

B. Action molds perception

Perception is not something that comes to us, we need to be active to perceive the environment. To be able to perceive the Braille letters motion is needed, one must move the fingertips on a display or a printed sheet to recognize the letters. However, how the movement goes and how many fingers that are involved, if both hands are used or not, depends on the individual [8]. The same goes for audio information, one can hear a sound, voice, or noise, but to perceive the content or identify what is causing the noise we must listen actively.

C. Feeling come first

If we are not motivated to read, learn, or do something, we do not gain either understanding or knowledge. The feeling is often affected by what supports or hinders the use of a platform or a software. By designing for accessibility there is chance that the user feels addressed and by that motivated to take the effort to use the platform.

D. Mind can override the perception

Seeing is something we learn, and we continually learn to do it [9]. When we have something in front of us, it could be an object or a view, we do not always look at what we see since memory overrides perception. For a person with blindness, it is not always that they perceive what they touch or hear, since they are occupied by previous experience that works as a grid between them and the environment. We experience the world from our own bodies, that involves previous experience and memory that are involved in all perception.

E. Cognition mirrors perception

What we see, touch, and hear, influences our mental images, and our mental images influences the perception of the environment [10]. Like sighted people, blind people learn to touch and hear continually. It is a way to learn about the environment, or as Tversky [11] puts it: "Mental spatial frameworks can be used to store and organize ideas, any kind of idea..." She argues that spatial mental frameworks can organize ideas, and mental image is not necessarily created in relation to pictures, it could as well be created from words [11].

F. Spatial thinking is the foundation of abstract thought

Much of our thinking is ordered in space and time, we think of the future or the past, where we have put things and how to organize our desk or files in the computer. Spatial thinking is also a part of spatial awareness. Spatiality could be discussed on both micro and macro level. On micro level we could discuss various phenomena, such as design of a text, a computer interface or Braille book. Spatial thinking includes logic, something that could be communicated. Platforms and interfaces aiming to support people with blindness need to have a spatial and hierarchical structure that follow the logic of the content and the intended use.

G. When thought overflows the mind, the mind puts it into the world

Like sighted people, blind people need to take notes, or jotting in textbooks to remember important parts. Printed Braille books do not allow jotting in the book, the notes need to be made separate as text or voice memos. A possibility to integrate jotting and the writing of exercises within a teaching material, creating an interactive textbook, should be possible within an EPUB 3 publication, but is not commonly spread yet. For the time being, exercises are made in parallel, e.g., as MS Word documents.

H. We organize stuff in the world the way we organize stuff in our minds

In early 2000s Lev Manovich [12] argued that for an interactive multimedia program to be interactive, the user needs to go into the head of the programmer, that is to understand his or her logic. This is still the case in many situations, but most of us has been trained in how to find out the logic of the designer of a program. To make complex content accessible such as mathematics and science for people with blindness, a user involvement is necessary.

III. Multimodality

The term modality could be defined either as a sense or as a medium such as text, picture, or sound. Often when we talk about multimodality, we include both definitions, since a multimodal process involves the use of various senses when we are watching a movie or read a book that includes text and pictures. However, a single media can involve a multimodal process, we read about an environment and imagine how it looks like, or we read about a specific sound and hear it inside the head. To design for multimodal experience among people with blindness, and low vision, it is necessary to have knowledge in how tactile perception works, how audio input can support activities, and the principles for Braille reading.

We perceive and understand our surroundings through our senses. Many researchers believe that the ability to interpret the impressions we get through our senses are innate, others that we through experience learn to interpret the various sensory impressions we get through sight, hearing, feeling, taste, and smell [5]. There is also an extensive discussion as to whether our senses conflict with each other or interact, and if so how. Too much input from different modalities can lead to cognitive load [13]. An individual who is either congenitally blind or that later acquires an injury, will not obviously develop the other senses to compensate for the missing. Instead, it can work the opposite way. It is therefore important to stimulate and activate, for example, a child with blindness so that he or she really utilizes touch, smell, and hearing.

The orientation system is fundamental to the others which are: the visual, the auditory, the haptic and the taste-smell system. The basic orientation system interacts with the other systems and constitutes a frame of reference for these [14]. It can be assumed that people with blindness become better at interpreting tactile information than sighted. Not because there is a special one sensitivity, but because you concentrate and practice in a different way than sight needs to do. The tactile perception is very limited. We can only feel one small area at a time, the sense of touch does not function as seeing where one can get an overview of a large area at the same time. What can be perceived by touch is what we are in direct contact with.

Auditory input, such as read out text or synthetic speech, is common for people with blindness, and function as a support or supplement to Braille. However, when studying mathematics, a combination of braille and audio is necessary since it requires too much cognitive load to use audio only.

IV. Usability and Technical Development

During 2021 MTM is performing a shift to EPUB 3 as the overall production format for various media types, leaving DTBook (DTBook = Digital Talking Book), a Daisy XML production format (XML = Extensible Markup Language). Daisy is an international standard designed to be a complete audio substitute for print material and is specifically designed for use by people with blindness, low vision, and dyslexia. Based on the MP3 and XML formats, the Daisy format has advanced features in addition to those of a traditional talking book. MTM is furthermore planning to use EPUB 3 as distribution format for talking books (with text and recorded sound). The present distribution format is called Daisy 2.02. This change has been prepared and expected for many years and is a part of a global shift in electronic publishing and in accessible publishing for persons with print disabilities.

Driving forces in the development of industry standards for accessibility, in both mainstream publishing and in specialist accessible publishing by organizations for people with a print disability, has been the Daisy Consortium [15], the International Digital Publishing Forum (IDPF) [16], the World Wide Web Consortium (W3C) [17], and others. This technological shift will lead to accessibility improvements for Braille readers. To be noted here, and of importance, is the use of standard internet technologies in EPUB 3, such as HTML5 and CSS3.

EPUB 3 publications will in most cases have built in accessibility features, such as:

- Being readable with assistive technologies.
- Having text that fits all screen sizes.
- Having adjustable text (font, color, font size and line spacing).
- Being navigable by chapter, section, page, sentence and more.

A. Pilot study of EPUB 3

But accessibility does not come by itself, to prepare for the coming shift to EPUB 3 as a consumer format at MTM a pilot project was performed in 2018. The overall purpose was to "create increased usability for customers at MTM and SPSM (The National Agency for Special Needs Education and Schools) by the transition to a more modern consumer format for various digital products which today are delivered in the Textview format [a local e-book format] and in the Daisy 2.02-format". The pilot project produced a requirements document for a usable digital reading experience by Braille users, based on a survey with 7 Braille users and 10 teachers/counsellors working with visually impaired. A thorough study of current recommendations and best practices in accessible digital publishing was carried out and a first draft of production guidelines was created. These guidelines are today in active use. A production process for creating valid and accessible EPUB 3 files was established. A sample book for testing purposes was created, as well as a set of feature tests based on the gathered requirements. Testing was performed with Braille users [18].

The need to fulfill certain prerequisites before introducing EPUB 3 as a distribution/consumer format were observed, including the following:

- EPUB 3 reader software and screen readers must function well together. This means, e.g., that keyboard shortcuts are coordinated and does not have competing functions in the reader software and in the screen reader respectively. Information must be sent to the refreshable braille display and to the speech synthesis equally.
- Access to original pagination/page numbering when available to enhance navigability.
- Skippability or escapability, i.e. the possibility to escape from certain content such as tables, and to continue to read the main content.

Concerning mathematics in EPUB 3, the pilot study stated that, since the EPUB 3 specification allows the embedding of mathematical markup with MathML (Mathematical Markup Language), it is very likely the best choice to handle mathematics in digital master files. The need for development of support for the Swedish language for MathML was therefore highlighted, both for output in braille and in speech synthesis.

B. Usability challenges for Braille users learning mathematics

The Swedish Braille Authority is the official language caring authority for Swedish Braille under the auspices of MTM. It has been noted and expressed by the Swedish Braille Authority, that teaching material and teaching methods for students learning mathematics using Braille have a large potential to be improved.

The current learning materials produced by SPSM and MTM for Braille users contain mathematic content in the ASCIIMath format. This is a practical and useful choice by the agencies since the Braille users may by themselves write mathematical expressions in the ASCIIMath format using a normal computer keyboard.

The situation for Braille users learning mathematics is not at all satisfactory though. When using the ASCIIMath format in digital reading and writing, Braille users practice a format not in use by teachers or sighted peers. This means that Braille users cannot present their exercises in a format that teachers and peers are familiar with.

Braille users may also get paper Braille teaching materials from SPSM and from MTM. The Braille standard for writing mathematics on paper is very much different from reading and writing digitally in the ASCIIMath format. We can see here that Braille users need to be acquainted with several alternative mathematical formats, which is not expected from their sighted peers – their cognitive load is hence comparatively heavier.

The possibility to use Braille as input, to write mathematical expressions by using a Braille keyboard, is not present. Neither is the possibility to choose the paper Braille standard for mathematics as output format, nor speech input or output for Swedish.

The choice to produce mathematic content in the ASCIIMath format seems to have been the least bad choice, meaning that it has provided the Braille user with some functionality, but not at all satisfactory in usability. What we now imagine is that the technical development has created a possibility to go beyond present and earlier technical barriers.

Current testing in 2021 at MTM has used MathJax software embedded in the EPUB 3 book to render mathematical expressions. The MathJax project is an open-source software product that provides support for mathematical markup directly in HTML source code, such as LaTeX (a document preparation system), MathML, and ASCIIMath markup. As output MathJax may produce HTML and CSS, SVG, or MathML. The MathJax software seems to be in the forefront in current technology for producing or rendering mathematics.

V. DISCUSSION

The vision is a complete, flexible, and usable learning environment for Braille users learning mathematics by providing all complementary input and output possibilities that are relevant for Braille users, for the individual to choose from.

The result from the EPUB 3 pilot study indicated that the readers would benefit from the multimodal input where Braille and synthetic speech could be combined simultaneously. Since the EPUB 3 presupposes a text to be well-structured in markup, it supports a spatial and hierarchical structure that follow the logic of the content and the intended use. That reduces the cognitive load which influences the way people learn [13]. For people with blindness this is important, as they are limited to senses (touch and hearing) that do not allow an overview of the material they are reading.

The EPUB 3 format supports spatial thinking [11] since it offers the possibility for good navigation in the book, enabled by a strict hierarchical structure in markup. Navigation in relation to page numbers is not guaranteed though, it depends on page numbers being present in the source material and if the EPUB reader software has the functionality to render page numbers. The possibility to skip parts in a text such as figure and tables is enabled through supporting markup.

The ability to make use of the various parts of a flexible learning environment, such as Braille keyboard, speech, ASCIIMath and MathML (with regular keyboard) enhances multimodality. Since multimodal processes are involved in learning situations it is important that people with blindness have access to several modalities. Such flexibility will motivate the Braille reader since it gives a feeling of freedom [11].

The various output modes required for a flexible learning environment are similar but have more variants: refreshable Braille devices, speech, Braille embossers, ASCIIMath, MathML, and SVG for images. The ability to emboss mathematical content in paper Braille is an important feature for Braille users, just as printing is for print users.

Image output (e.g., the SVG format) is crucial for Braille users, e.g., when delivering exercise assignments to sighted teachers. The possibility to send images with mathematical content to refreshable Braille devices that can reproduce images and graphs in a tactile mode, such as the Graphiti from Orbit research, would enable Braille users yet another way to interact and explore mathematical content. That will support the ability to get spatial overview and support spatial thinking since it is the foundation of abstract thoughts [11].

The future complete, flexible, and usable learning environment would rely on the EPUB 3 format and on current technology for producing and rendering mathematics, most notably the MathJax software. The development of the software should preferably be made with consideration to multimodality and the cognitive aspects that are presented in the Nine Laws of Cognition. We have identified what is needed for people with blindness to have access to complex content in Braille:

- The possibility to write in Braille, to input Braille – note that there are fundamental differences in how Braille standards for mathematics are constructed in various languages and countries.
- Conversion between Braille and MathML/ASCIIMath/LaTeX needs to be developed.
- The possibility to output Braille to various devices including embossers.
- Conversion between MathML/ASCIIMath/LaTeX and Braille needs to be developed and/or adapted to various languages, such as Swedish.
- An individual choice in input and output settings.
- Software that can display mathematics visually using MathJax and HTML5, both within and outside the EPUB 3 context.
- Software that can display mathematic content written by Braille users.
- Interaction with refreshable Braille devices that are able to produce images and graphs, such as the Graphiti, an interactive tactile graphics display from Orbit research.

VI. CONCLUSION

The conclusion is that more knowledge is needed when designing the interfaces for a future learning environment for Braille users learning mathematics. What we are aiming at, is to identify the functionality and the technical infrastructure needed to make the design of a truly usable learning environment possible. Central is the possibility to use Braille as input and output mode, to switch freely between the available input and output modes, and the possibility to make these choices individually. Crucial for the motivation in Braille users to learn mathematics is an interface that is designed with regard to cognitive aspects and taking available modalities into consideration, that is touch and hearing.

A. Future research

The Swedish Braille Authority has identified the need of performing several investigations or knowledge overviews in preparation of the creation and design of a more complete, flexible, and usable learning environment for Braille users learning mathematics:

- A knowledge overview of teaching materials/resources and methods for sighted learners in mathematics. What are the various teaching materials/resources and methods? Which of them works, and which does not work, for Braille users? Why does certain teaching materials/resources and methods work well?
- A knowledge overview of the learning situation in various countries for students learning mathematics using Braille.

REFERENCES

[1] The World Wide Web Consortium (W3C). *EPUB Accessibility 1.1: Conformance and Discoverability Requirements for EPUB Publications*. [Online]. Available from: https://www.w3.org/TR/epub-a11y-11/ 2021.07.01

[2] The World Wide Web Consortium (W3C). *EPUB 3.2: Final Community Group Specification 08 May 2019*. [Online]. Available from: https://www.w3.org/publishing/epub3/epub-spec.html 2021.07.01

[3] D. Katz, The world of touch,, L.E. Kreuger, Ed. A Psychology Press Book, Hillday, New Jersey: Routledge, 1989.

[4] Y. Eriksson, Tactile Pictures. Pictorial representations for the blind 1784–1940. Diss. Acta Universitas Gothoburgensis, 1998.

[5] J. M. Kennedy, Drawing and the Blind. Pictures to Touch. New Haven: Yale University Press, 1993.

[6] S. Millar, Space and Sense. Oxford: Routledge, 2008.

[7] F. J. Crowley, A Comparison of the Listening Ability of Blind Students and the Listening Ability of Sighted Students in the Intermediate Grades. Bronx: Fordham University, 1965.

[8] Y. Eriksson and K. Fellenius, Interaction between Braille and tactile pictures for a deeper understanding. Terra Haptica. Tactile picture, Cognition, Education, 2014, pp 55–65.

[9] Y. Eriksson, Bildens tysta budskap. Interaktion mellan bild och text [The silent message of the image. Interaction between image and text]. Lund: Studentlitteratur, 2017.

[10] N. Mirzoeff, How to See the World. UK: Pelican Books, 2015.

[11] B. Tversky, Mind In Motion, How Action Shapes Thought. New York: Basic Books, 2019.

[12] L. Manovich, The Language of New Media, Cam. Mass.: MIT Press, 2001.

[13] G. Cooper, Research into cognitive load theory and instructional design at UNSW. In: Retrieved October 22 (1998), p. 2003.

[14] J. J. Gibson, The Ecological Approach to Visual Perception, Houghton Mifflin Harcourt, 1979.

[15] The DAISY Consortium. [Online]. Available from: https://daisy.org/ 2021.07.01

[16] International Digital Publishing Forum. [Online]. Available from: http://idpf.org/ 2021.07.01

[17] The World Wide Web Consortium (W3C). [Online]. Available from: https://www.w3.org/ 2021.07.01

[18] From Textview to EPUB 3 – a Swedish pilot project for the introduction of EPUB 3 as consumer format at MTM and SPSM, final report, Stockholm: MTM, 2018.

The COSMO@Home Application – Iterative Development and Implementation of the Learning Goals

Marie Sjölinder, Olov Ståhl, Erik Einebrant, László Sall Vesselényi, Niels Stor Swinkels
RISE
Stockholm, Sweden
e-mail: marie.sjolinder@ri.se, olov.stahl@ri.se, erik.einebrant@ri.se, laszlo.sall.vesselenyi@ri.se, niels.stor.swinkels@ri.se

Barbara Weyn, Marjolein Verly, Sam Geuens, Jessia Nijs, Marlies Treunen
KU Leuven, UZ Leuven
Leuven, Belgium
e-mail: barbara.weyn@kuleuven.be, marjolein.verly@kuleuven.be, sam.geuens@uzleuven.be, jessica.nijs@uzleuven.be, marlies.treunen@kuleuven.be

Anas Abdelrazeq, Samira Khodaei Dolouei, Kathrin Hohlbaum
RWTH Aachen University
Aachen, Germany
e-mail: Anas.Abdelrazeq@ima.rwth-aachen.de, samira.khodaei@ima.rwth-aachen.de, Kathrin.Hohlbaum@ima.rwth-aachen.de

Sanne Nauts, Privender Saini, Ozgur Tasar, Annerieke Heuvelink
Philips
Eindhoven, Netherlands
e-mail: sanne.nauts@philips.com, privender.saini@philips.com, ozgur.tasar@philips.com, annerieke.heuvelink@philips.com

Abstract—This work describes the design journey in the development of an edutainment application for children. The aim of the application was to prepare children for an MRI scan. The COSMO@Home mobile application is based on a number of learning goals that are conveyed by a set of mini-games aimed at teaching and preparing children for the magnetic resonance imaging (MRI) scanning procedure. Each mini-game addresses one or more of the learning goals identified by the project as being important to prepare children for the procedure. The learning goals were: 1) Learn about the MRI procedure, 2) Familiarization with MRI sounds, 3) Familiarization with the size of the MRI scanner, 4) Practice the timings, 5) Practice lying still, 6) Learn about accessories such as earplugs and head coil, and 7) Understand that metal is not allowed in the MRI room. During the iterative development, initial tests to explore the general concept were conducted with children without a planned MRI scan and outside the hospital. In a second phase, more complete versions of the prototype were tested with children at the hospital. During the last phase, the application was tested in a real context with children in their homes. The main outcome of the iterative development and the testing was an application that, overall, seemed to convey the learning goals. However, the tests also revealed challenges in addressing the most important learning goal of lying still.

Keywords-design for children; educational software; gamification; game design.

I. Introduction

This work describes the design journey in the development of an edutainment application for children. The aim of the application was to prepare children for an MRI scan. The COSMO@Home mobile application is based on a number of learning goals that aim to teach and prepare children for the MRI scanning procedure. The application consists of a number of mini-games that provide the child with general information about the MRI procedure and about the MRI scanner. In the mini-games, the child receives information about what is allowed and not allowed during the procedure and is also able to practice some of the important things to remember. Each mini-game addresses one or several learning goals that were identified, in expert workshops, as being important to prepare children for the procedure. The learning goals were: 1) Learn about the MRI procedure, 2) Familiarization with MRI sounds, 3) Familiarization with the size of the MRI scanner, 4) Practice the timings, 5) Practice lying still, 6) Learn about accessories, such as earplugs and head coil, and 7) Understand that metal is not allowed in the MRI room.

The aim of this paper is to describe the design journey of developing a set of mini-games that successfully contribute to children achieving the learning goals. Design targeting children is briefly described in Section 2, and the developed application is presented in Section 3. Sections 4, 5 and 6 present the user tests that were conducted in the different stages of the iterative development. The paper ends with a discussion and conclusions (Section 7) about the design process towards incorporating the learning goals in the mini-games and in the application.

II. Designing for Children

Researchers have argued that games are a unique way to engage and motivate people in learning and education [1][2]. There are several advantages of using games for learning. Because a game can be used to model parts of the real world, it makes it possible for people to play around with and visit an abstract reality of a real-life setting or place, but in a simplified form [3]. A significant motivation for using educational games in learning is the engagement and joy they bring to the user [4]. As in learning, games also use typical techniques that can be found in educational psychology. Techniques such as rewards, feedback, and encouragement to collaborate are common practices for teachers as well as typical elements of a game. What gamification adds to learning is, according to Kapp [3], another layer of interest that both engages and motivates the player to learn.

Applications aiming at educating and preparing children require consideration of several design aspects. When designing educational games, both motivation to use and achievement of intended learning goals are important aspects. Guidelines regarding games, educational games, and child–computer interaction are all well-documented areas [5]-[9]. Winn [6] stated that the intended learning goals should be central and clearly set before the development of a game is started. Setting these goals can then help the designer throughout the development phase as they provide a practical way of measuring the intended learning outcome. Clear goals and rules within the game are important for the player, and they are also important for creating motivation [9]. If the player does not know what to do or if the goals of the game are unclear, it creates frustration and becomes unmotivating. Feedback is another important tool for learning through games and it can optimize learning by directly giving the player tips and tricks with respect to the performance and actions within the game [9]. Rewards are typical components of games and are a good way of encouraging and motivating the player [4][7][10].

With respect to instructions, it has been suggested that in-app tutorials should be avoided, since there is a tendency for children to not read or remember instructions given in this way. A better solution is to provide guidance through which the user can be active [7]. Further, Chiasson and Gutwin [10] suggest that the interface should be intuitive enough to be used without instructions, or that child users are given guidance until the intended task is understood [10]. An alternative to written text and instructions is graphical metaphors and interfaces in which minimal use of text is required, especially for the youngest users. Giving instructions in speech with corresponding pictures and animations can also help the users to both remember and understand the instructions [10].

In the process of selecting hardware, Chiasson and Gutwin [10] found that touchscreen devices rather than computers are better and more appropriate tools for children. Yet while touchscreen devices are a good choice for child users, there are limitations to the interaction in terms of the child's motor skills.

Based on existing design recommendations and on adaptations towards the specific context, the application in the project was developed in an iterative way.

III. THE COSMO@HOME APPLICATION

A novel preparation protocol called COSMO has been developed to help enable successful MR scans to be conducted on children without the use of sedation. COSMO is designed to achieve MRI examinations with awake children as young as four years of age in a time- and resource-efficient manner without lengthy preparation procedures or repeated hospital visits. The children are prepared by immersing them in an imaginative, child-friendly and engaging story, which is told and performed by trained hospital staff. The aim of the COSMO@Home project is to scale up the COSMO protocol by creating a digital COSMO tool that can be used by children and parents to prepare for the scanning sessions at home. Such a tool will limit the need for dedicated staff members and, as such, is far more scalable and cost-effective than the current approach.

The application consists of a framework or a starting page where different mini-games and other functionalities can be accessed. The app is built around a space theme, and the players are told they need to train to become an astronaut who can fly to space in a rocket. As part of their training, they will need to complete space missions, which means they need to build a rocket and fly it to a distant planet. When they return to Earth, they need to start training for their next space mission. This training is carried out by playing mini-games. Each mini-game is designed to teach the player something about the MRI procedure. The idea is that while training to become an astronaut, they will at the same time learn different aspects of MRI.

The starting page or the "home page" of the application is the space campus from which six mini-games can be reached (Figure 1). The app includes four 3D games: the Memory game, the Metal game, the Scanning game and the Balance game, and two augmented reality (AR, a real-world environment that has been enhanced by computer-generated perceptual information) games: the AR Comparison game and the AR Scaling game.

Figure 1. The space campus with game and activity buildings.

The user can collect rocket parts in each game, and when all games have been completed one time, the player has gathered all the rocket parts and can go to the launchpad and put together a rocket. When this has been done, the player sets off for space. During the space journey, there is a space game in which the player can collect stars. After the space game, the player reaches a planet and meets an alien. The player hands over a gift to the alien, and in return gets a mystery item that can be scanned once back at the space campus. There are five space missions that the player needs to complete in order to become a full-fledged astronaut, and in each one they will visit a different planet and meet a different alien. After completing these five missions, it is possible to continue playing and fly to space, but when doing so the existing planets will be revisited. The training and space mission loop is illustrated by Figure 2.

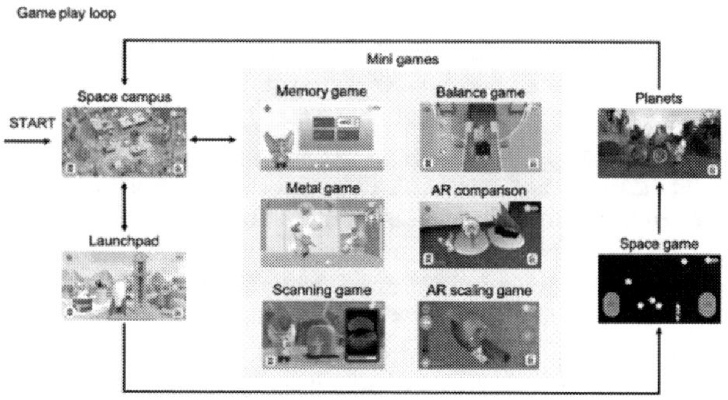

Figure 2. The game play loop, consisting of mini-games and space missions.

Space campus and buddy character: The space campus, or "Home page," consists of a number of buildings. Each building represents an activity or mini-game that the player can engage in. When the player clicks on a building, the camera zooms in and the application then switches to a view from inside the building, where the game or activity starts. The player is accompanied by their buddy character, Ollie. Ollie speaks to the children via voiceover audio, explaining to them all they need to know about their training to become an astronaut and giving them feedback and encouragement when they are playing games or participating in other activities. Ollie is a fully animated 3D character, and the children will see him move around in the scenes, making various kinds of gestures such as waving, pointing, and cheering

Memory game: The aim of the Memory game is to convey knowledge about the sound of the MRI scanner. The player sees a board with a number of cards. When they click on a card, it opens and plays an MRI sound and provides an animation of that sound. The goal for the player is to find cards with matching sounds, which are then removed from the board until the entire board is eventually cleared. The number of the cards increases with each higher level.

Metal game: The aim of the Metal game is to teach the player that metal objects are not allowed in the MRI room. In the game, a set of objects are moving around and the player should remove (click on) the ones that are made of metal. While the game is running, the player sees Ollie walking slowly towards the MRI room, and the goal is to remove all metal objects before he gets there. If Ollie reaches the MRI room before all the metal objects have been removed, the round fails and the player needs to try again. At each level, the number of objects and the speed of Ollie and the moving objects increase.

Scanning game: The aim of the Scanning game is to increase the player's understanding of the MRI procedure and of the duration of a scan session, which can be long. The player places "mystery objects" in the scanner and waits for them to be scanned. While scanning, the player can see a scan image being revealed, and once the scan is complete, they need to guess the true identity of the mystery object. The game uses scanned images of real fruits, and afterwards, the player is presented with a selection of fruits and they need to identify the one that matches the MRI image.

Balance game: The aims of the Balance game are to increase understanding of the MRI procedure, and learn about accessories (different types of coils), as well as to provide information about the need to lie still and to practice lying still. The child selects a coil and then Ollie's scan starts. During the scan, the player needs to hold the phone still; otherwise, the phone starts to vibrate and the scan image starts becoming distorted. After the scan, the resulting scan image is added to the adventure journal, where the player can look at it again later.

AR Comparison game: The aim of the AR Comparison game is to help children understand the size of an MRI scanner by asking them to guess which of two visible objects (an MRI scanner and a random object) is bigger. AR technology is used to make the objects appear in 3D in the physical room. The AR tracking is based on a marker that needs to be placed on a flat surface, for example a table. The child can then scan the marker and the game starts. There are several rounds of comparing the MRI scanner to objects such as a cake, a house or even fantastical objects such as a T-Rex. The objects appear from a magical hat that needs to be pressed. The child receives stars after completing each comparison.

AR Scaling game: The aim of the AR Scaling game is to help children understand the size of an MRI scanner. Additionally, an extended learning goal is introduced in order to allow the discovery of different parts of the MRI scanner. The AR technology is used in order to make the MRI scanner appear in full 3D size in the room. After placing the marker on the floor, the MRI scanner appears in a small size. With plus and minus buttons, the children can increase or decrease the size of the MRI scanner. Once the right size is found, the game proceeds to the extended learning goal, where the children have to discover different question marks on the MRI scanner and also can collect stickers.

During development of the prototype, feedback was gathered iteratively in the different stages through participatory observation of professionals and through questionnaires. In the first phase, the concept of a few mini-games was tested with 15 children (6 in Sweden and 9 in Germany) outside the hospital. In the second phase, a more mature version was tested with 17 children at the University Hospitals Leuven, although still under supervision of the investigators. In the third phase, the application was tested with 13 children using the application independently at home. In total, 45 children participated in the tests during the iterative development of the application. The different phases are shown in Table 1.

TABLE I. OVERVIEW OF THE DIFFERENT USER TESTS

Location	Date	Aim	Participants
Initial tests – concept and functionalities			
RISE Sweden	August - September 2019	Get a first impression of how the app was perceived by children of different ages.	6 children, 3-15 years old
RWTH, Germany	October 2019	Feedback on first mini-games and on the use of AR.	9 children, 6-9 years old
Tests at the hospital			
KU Leuven, Belgium	November 2019	Feedback on improved version of the prototype with further features. How the learning goals were conveyed.	9 children, 4-10 years old
KU Leuven, Belgium	April/May 2020	Feedback on improved version of the prototype, entire app with all the mini-games and the reward system. How the learning goals were conveyed.	8 children, 4-9 years old
Tests in the home environment			
KU Leuven, Belgium	October - November 2020	Practical aspects related to home usage, feasibility, and inclusion in hospital workflow.	13 children, 5-11 years old

IV. Initial Tests – Concept and Functionalities

The first phase of the development was supported by initial tests with users. These tests were conducted in Sweden and Germany with children that were not associated with a hospital. The aim of these tests was to get a first impression of how the app was perceived by children of different ages, and also to get feedback on the mini-games and the concept.

A. First Feedback on the Concept

The first test was conducted at RISE in Gothenburg, Sweden in August and September 2019. This first version of the app consisted of two mini-games: the Memory game and the Metal game. The aim of this study was to get a first impression of how the app was perceived. Regarding the youngest children, the goal was to get feedback about to what extent they understood the concept. For the older children, the aim was to get an initial understanding of how to motivate this user group. Six children in a wide age range between three and fifteen years old participated in this study. An introduction was given about the MRI testing, the app, and the purpose of the test. After that, the participants tried the app and played the games. Questions were asked about what they liked about the app and about what they did not like about the app. Observations of usage were made by the test leader in regard to engagement, understanding of the concept, and navigation, as well as in relation to the learning goals.

Result: The overall idea of an app with mini-games seemed to work well, as did the space theme. The metaphorical connection between preparing for MRI scans and preparing for space travels felt meaningful to the children. However, the oldest children felt that the app as a whole was somewhat too childish for their age. It was not obvious to the youngest children that it was possible to access the mini-games by clicking on the buildings. However, when they had received instructions about this, navigating into and back out of the buildings was no problem. The gameplay purpose of the mini-games (i.e., collecting rocket parts) was very unclear without visiting the launchpad as a first step. The younger children did not pay attention to the entire MRI movie, which was something that the older children did do. The older children also felt that the most important part was when the child in the movie was shown as happy or at least undisturbed during the MRI scan. Experiencing someone else's positive experience of the procedure was encouraging.

All of the children figured out how to play the memory game. The learning goal of becoming familiar with the sounds of the MRI scanner, in the Memory game, was very clear to the children. For the younger children, it was not clear to the children which sounds were related to the MRI scanning procedure. The game concept of the Metal game was unclear to the children, and the learning goal (to not bring metal objects into the MRI scanner) was also somewhat unclear. It was not clear which items a player should or should not press. However, most of the items seemed to be recognized. The children expressed that the narration did not emphasize well enough that metal was completely prohibited from being taken into the MRI room. However, when asked specifically, the children had a good idea of what they could and could not bring into the room from among the things the children were wearing at the time. During the user tests, it became clear that it was more challenging than anticipated to achieve a strong connection between the different games and the learning goals. As a result, one mini-game (a Tetris-inspired game) was removed/replaced. Finally, these tests also explored the use of VR for applications targeting small children. Insights gained during the tests resulted in a change from the use of VR to AR due to difficulties for small children to wear the VR equipment.

B. Feedback on the Mini-games and on the Use of AR

The second test during this first stage was conducted by RWTH Aachen University in Germany in October 2019. In this version, an additional mini-game (the Scanning game) had been included and one AR game (the Scaling game). The aim of this test was to get feedback on the improved version with more mini-games, and to test a new AR mini-game. Initial feedback regarding on-boarding (getting into the game) and narrative (spoken information and voiceover) was also gathered. Nine children between the ages of six and nine participated in this test. After an introduction, the children played all of the mini-games by themselves and the test leader only intervened when necessary. During and after each mini-game, the child was asked questions about what they thought about the game (fun/boring, fast/slow, easy/hard, childish/mature), and about what they liked and did not like. They were also asked about what was hard and easy to understand, and if they had understood the purpose of the game. During the sessions, observations were made regarding whether the app seemed engaging and whether the concept of the space campus was understood. The test leader also tried to get an understanding about to what extent the children gained knowledge based on the learning goals.

Result: Almost all of the children were excited about the game as a whole and thought it would be helpful for children to understand what an MRI is. They liked the space scenario, but the connection between MRI and space was still not always clear. Almost all of children knew what a magnet was afterwards, and they could recall what not to take to an MRI. The children also recalled that an MRI is "noisy and takes pictures". Afterwards they also could tell that they learned not to move, and to lie still during the scan. The environment seemed easy to navigate, but the connection between each building and the game that was accessed by clicking on it was not clear. The children thought it was fun to watch the video, and they were able to answer the questions in the video (for example, "Can you hear the noises?").

All the children easily got familiar with the Memory game, and it was easy to get started. The increasing degree of difficulty in the levels seemed to be good, but younger children needed some guidance. After a while, when they had got the gist of it, they did not care about the sounds. The children knew intuitively what to do in the Metal game; they easily found all the objects and were able to transfer this knowledge to reality (the instructor asked them if they, for example, could bring a watch or bracelet to the MRI, and all of the participants were able to say "NO" and explain why). For small children, it was difficult to know if certain objects were made out of metal or not. The aim of the Scanning game was understood, but it needed further explanation. The participants found it nice that there was something in the box (but all of them thought at first that it was a rocket part). With respect to the AR Scaling game, for the youngest children it was difficult to navigate using the phone. Some of them dropped the phone multiple times in excitement. The game was difficult, and the children needed a lot of explanation and support. However, some of the older children found it exciting to walk through the machine. Afterwards, children were able to "walk the size" of an MRI scanner within the room.

V. Tests with Children at the Hospital

In this phase of the development, tests were conducted with children at the University Hospitals in Leuven. In these tests, the aim was to get feedback on improved versions of the prototype, including new features. At the end of this phase, the entire application, with all the mini-games and the reward system, was tested. In these studies, it was also examined how the learning goals were conveyed.

A. First Test at the Hospital

The first test at the University Hospitals in Leuven, Belgium took place in November 2019. The aim of this test was to gain feedback on the improved and extended version of the prototype, which consisted of five mini-games clearly connected to the learning goals. The mini-games included in this version of the prototype were: the Memory game, the Metal game, the Scanning game, the Balance game and the AR Scaling game. This version also had a coherent narrative from playing the mini-games to getting rewards and completing the game. This test included a first approach towards investigating to what extent the learning goals were conveyed. This test was built up around a number of modules, depending on how much time the child could spend on the test. Nine children between the ages of four and ten participated in this test. The tests were conducted in the waiting room at the hospital in Leuven. After playing the game, the children were asked general questions about the game and the character and after that more specific questions about the mini-game(s) they had played. These questions were conducted to find out what they thought about the game and if they understood how to play it. The children were also asked if they understood the purpose of the mini-game(s) and about what they learned from each game. Observations were made regarding to what extent the children understood the concept and managed to navigate in the app, and to what extent they seemed to understand the learning goals.

Result: Overall, the children really liked the character Ollie, the game appearance as a whole, and the flying-to-space narrative. The navigation also seemed to work well, but it was still not clear that there were games in the buildings. Once the observers showed how to click on a building, the concept was understood. The goal of collecting rocket parts and building the rocket was not directly clear to all the children in the test. The older children seemed to understand the learning goals; however, it seemed that they gained most of their knowledge from the introduction movie even though several of the children found it too long. The younger children liked the application, but it was not clear that they understood the learning goals and they needed parental supervision. During this test, it also became clear that there were challenges regarding the most important learning goal (lying still). According to the health care professionals it was not practiced enough.

The Memory game and Metal game were the two most popular games. However, even though the sounds of the Memory game were more important to recognize than the images on the cards, the children often used the images, instead of the sounds, to find a matching pair. The Metal game was managed well by most of the children, and they seemed to understand the metal concept. The learning goal (understanding that a scan takes time) in the Scanning game was addressed by the fact that the child had to wait for an image. Some of the children in the test left this game since they thought the waiting was boring. With respect to the AR Scaling game, there were challenges; namely, that the actual size of the scanner became too large, which made the game difficult to play without parental support and a large physical space. Due to this, it was not clear if the learning goal of understanding the size of the MRI scanner was achieved.

B. Test of Complete Version at the Hospital

The next test in this phase was also conducted at the University Hospitals in Leuven, Belgium during April and May 2020. The aim of this test was to gain feedback on the improved version of the prototype, which consisted of a complete app with all the mini-games (Memory game, Metal game, Scanning game, Balance game, AR Comparison game and AR Scaling game) and the reward system. In this version, improvements had been made related to the size of the MRI scanner in the scaling game, and a tutorial had been added for first-time usage to provide a better understanding of what it was possible to do. This test was conducted using a tablet instead of a smartphone.

The feedback covered both usage and how well the learning goals were conveyed. Eight children between the ages of four and nine years of age participated in the test. All tests took place at the University Hospitals Leuven, either in the patient's room or in the waiting rooms of the children's hospital. In this test, the application was tested using a tablet. After an introduction with general questions, the children played through the mini-games, and it was also made sure that they played through the AR games. After they had played the mini-games, they were asked to put together the rocket and answer questions about the rocket and the space flight. Finally, the children were asked questions about the learning goals, and they also completed a questionnaire with questions about the character, the environment, and about which games they liked/disliked the most and about which games were the easiest/most difficult. During the session, notes were taken about what was easy/hard and about what seemed fun and motivating or boring.

Result: All games/game world looked good on the tablet and seemed to be easier to play on a tablet than on a phone. However, small children found the tablet heavy to hold. Most kids loved to play the game and liked to complete at least one round. Apart from some minor issues, the game world and navigating in the game world worked well, even for smaller children, and Ollie, the character, seemed to be a well-liked figure. The introduction movie was only possible to test with a few children due to a technical issue. However, it seemed to be liked and to convey the learning goals and it was educative.

The Memory game was very well liked and worked well. Even if it mainly was the images that were used for the pairing, it still conveyed the loud sound of an MRI scanner. In the Metal game, it was still a bit difficult for small children to differentiate which objects were made out of metal, and they often found them randomly. The Scanning game was a very well-liked game. The only thing that needed to be improved was the narratives, which needed to explain the waiting time better, and also to convey a stronger connection to the fact that it takes some time to scan an object or a person in an MRI scanner. The Balance game, which had the aim of showing the procedure and emphasizing the importance of lying still, was found to need some improvements. Better instructions were needed to explain the concept and better feedback was required on moving vs. holding the device still to be able to succeed. The AR Comparison game concept seemed to be liked a lot by some children, while others did not like it, which was probably due to issues with the technology. In this version of the application, the size of the MRI scanner was better and easier to handle. However, with younger children, assistance was needed to hold the phone still for the tracking. It was also difficult for younger children to grasp the concept of bigger/smaller objects, especially if they had not seen an actual MRI scanner before. At this stage, more testing was needed to understand if the learning goal was actually conveyed. For the AR Scaling game, the size of the MRI scanner was much better. However, the need for really large areas in which to play the game limits the usability. The game had potential, but the AR concept of the size of the MRI scanner was not always understood by young children.

The answers about what they thought of the games were few in numbers and varied from child to child, but the most-liked games were the Memory game, the Balance game and the Comparison game, and the most boring game was the Scaling game. The Metal game was considered to be the easiest game, and the Scaling game the hardest one, as shown in Table 2.

TABLE II. RESULTS FROM THE QUESTIONNAIRE, IN WHICH ONE GAME COULD BE SELECTED IN EACH CATEGORY

	Most liked	Most boring	Easiest game	Hardest game
Memory	2	1	0	0
Metal	1	1	3	1
Scanning	1	1	1	0
Balance	2	0	1	1
Comparison	2	0	2	1
Scaling	0	5	1	5

VI. USER TESTS IN THE HOME ENVIRONMENT

The aim of the last study during the iterative development of the application was to test the complete application with home usage and workflow around the usage. This test was also a pilot study for a forthcoming clinical trial. The study, which was approved by the ethical committee, was managed by University Hospitals Leuven in Belgium between September and December 2020. The usage of the app took place in the children's homes, and thirteen children between the ages of five and eleven participated in the study. Nine of them had had at least one MRI before and four of them did not have any experience with MRI procedures. One week before the start of test, the parents were contacted. A start package was sent to their homes at least four days before the scan. The package contained an introduction folder, a smartphone with installed app, a marker for the AR games and an informed consent form. At the time of the scan, the children answered questions about which game they liked/disliked the most and which game they thought was the easiest/most difficult. The children also answered questions about general likeability of the app and about their desire to play the app again, and both children and parents also answered questions about anxiety related to the scanning procedure.

Results: The answers about what they thought of the games were, in this test as well, few in numbers and varied from child to child. However, they were in line with the results from the previous test, with the most-liked games being the Memory game, the Balance game, and the AR Comparison game. With respect to the most boring game, answers were spread out between all the games. In this test, the Memory game and the Scanning game were considered to be the easiest games, and the Metal game the hardest one, as shown in Table 3. Again, it is important to point out that the answers were few and spread throughout the different games, and also that the aim of these questions was just to identify if any of the games were too difficult and/or too boring to be included in the app. In general, all the games seemed to work well, but the Memory game seemed to be really liked and easy to play, and the Metal game and the Scaling game might need further adjustments.

TABLE III. RESULTS FROM THE QUESTIONNAIRE, IN WHICH ONE GAME COULD BE SELECTED IN EACH CATEGORY

	Most liked	**Most boring**	**Easiest game**	**Hardest game**
Memory	3	2	3	2
Metal	1	1	2	4
Scanning	1	2	3	1
Balance	2	2	2	1
Comparison	2	2	1	2
Scaling	0	2	0	2

In the question in which the children rated the overall likeability of the app on a scale ranging from 0-10, the average was m=7.69. A further measurement on how well the app was liked was the question about the desire to play the app again. On this scale (0-10), the average was m=6.77, which is quite in line with the extent to which the participants liked the app. After the app usage but before the scanning procedure on the day of the scan, both children and parents were asked (0-10 VAS scale) about their anxiety related to the scanning procedure. The reported anxiety for children dropped, compared with a baseline, from 2 to 1 (mean anxiety). For the parents, the reported mean anxiety dropped, compared to a baseline, from 5 to 3. This is a positive trend, indicating that after app usage the children were less anxious on the day of their scan. The observations made on the scanning day also showed that the children had fewer questions and that they were much better prepared. Only in a very small group of children was additional training needed. With respect to the learning goals and the need for additional training, the most important learning goal to address further was the lying still goal. All other aspects seemed to be sufficiently addressed at home and needed no additional training in the hospital. With respect to the entire context in terms of home usage and workflow, the app could be used at home without the supervision of a researcher and it worked well within the clinical workflow. However, further testing is of course required to draw definitive conclusions.

VII. CONCLUSION

In one of the tests at the hospital, the app was used on a tablet. All the games and the game world looked good on the tablet and seemed to be easier to play on a tablet than on a phone. However, small children found the tablet heavy to hold, which is line with Chiasson and Gutwin [10], suggesting that while touchscreen devices are a good choice for child users, there are limitations to the interaction in terms of the child's motor skills. During the development of the application, important motivational features and rewards were included in the application [4][7][10]. These were used for general motivation to increase the learning [3]. Since very young children were a part of the target group, instructions were mainly based on graphics and spoken explanations according to previous work and/or guidelines [10]. What was noted in the tests was that even though the aim of the spoken explanations was to keep them short and simple, in some cases they had to be further shortened to enable getting the message through to the youngest children as well. It has been suggested that in-app tutorials should be avoided, since there is a tendency for children to not read or remember instructions given in this way [7]. The tests that were conducted during this development showed the opposite. Since the application consisted of a quite complex path through the environment, with games, rocket parts, building a rocket and going to space, a tutorial describing this path had to be added. This was especially needed for the younger age groups, which might not already have the game literacy that older children might have.

With respect to the learning goals of *learning about the procedure* and *learning about accessories such as earplugs and head coil*, the introduction movie and the Balance game were aimed at conveying these learning goals. In the tests, it was shown that the children gained much of their knowledge from the introduction movie. However, it was also shown that the older children, to a greater extent than the younger ones, finished watching the entire movie. The learning goal of *understanding that metal is not allowed in the MRI room* was addressed in the Metal game. One insight during the tests was that it was, to some extent, difficult to understand what the objects represented and to differentiate between metal and non-metal objects, especially for the youngest children. The learning goal of *practicing the timings* was addressed in the Scanning game and in the Balance game. The challenge regarding the design in this case was to both convey the concepts of a long period of time and waiting, and at the same to create a game that is not boring. The aim of the Memory game was *familiarization with MRI sounds*. This game was very well liked and easy to play. It might have been the case that the pairing was mostly done using the images instead of the sounds. However, the game still contributed to making the MRI sounds more familiar. The learning goal of *familiarization with the size of the MRI scanner* was addressed by the AR Comparison game and the AR Scaling game. Using an AR technique with paper-printed markers could to some extent be complicated, especially for young children. Both physical and digital interaction with "walking around" a large object could also be a challenge, as in the case with the Scaling game. This game requires both a large physical space and quite demanding interaction. In general, the tests showed that AR gaming is still quite difficult for young children as it requires a lot of additional knowledge, the ability to hold the phone still while pressing buttons, and the attention capacity needed to look at the phone while moving around. It could be advisable to further develop AR games for children in more cooperative ways that allow playing with a parent or older sibling. Despite these challenges, at the end of the development process, the understanding of the size of the MRI scanner seemed to be understood by most of the children. Finally, the learning goal of *practicing lying still* was addressed by the Balance game, where the child was supposed to keep the device still during the scan procedure. Based on feedback from nurses at the hospital, this was the most important learning goal, but the task in the game too weakly resembled actually lying still in a real context. As a result of this, one further AR game, the Box game, was developed. The aim of this game is to train children to keep their heads lying still during an MRI scan. This game consists of a physical box asset that enables the children to experience being in a head coil. The game requires some set-up before the gameplay, which is why it is advised in the beginning to get help from a parent. During the gameplay, the child navigates through a narrow canyon with a rocket. The head movement of the child is tracked and the less the child moves their head, the faster the rocket flies and reaches the goal. Additionally, there are phases in which the children are allowed to move their head, indicated visually with clouds and auditive sounds. While they can't move their heads, the MRI sound is loud and the rocket flies through the canyon. This new, lying still, game has been included in the latest version of the application and will be tested with children in the forthcoming tests.

In general, most of the learning goals that were set up seemed to be conveyed successfully by the application in these smaller tests that were conducted as a part of the development. The learning goals and the effect of using the application will be further evaluated in a forthcoming larger clinical study.

ACKNOWLEDGMENTS

This work was conducted within the COSMO@Home project that is funded by EIT Health. The authors would like to thank all the participants in the tests, and all the employees at University Hospitals Leuven who contributed to the work.

REFERENCES

[1] S. Kelle, R. Klemke, and M. Specht, "Design patterns for learning games," Int J Technol Enhanc Learn, vol. 3, pp. 555-569, 2011, DOI: 10.1504/IJTEL.2011.045452.ß

[2] A. Amory, "Game object model version II: A theoretical framework for educational game development," Educ Technol Res Dev; vol. 55, pp. 51-77, 2007, DOI: 10.1007/s11423-006-9001-x

[3] K. Kapp, The Gamification of Learning and Instruction. Pfeiffer, 2012.

[4] A. Abdul Jabbar, and P. Felicia, "Gameplay Engagement and Learning in Game-Based Learning: A Systematic Review," Rev Educ Res, vol. 85, pp. 740-779, 2015, DOI: 10.3102/0034654315577210

[5] W. Wolfgang, M. Barret, and D. Görlich, "Design, Dynamics, Experience (DDE): An Advancement of the MDA Framework for Game Design,", in Game Dynamics, pp. 27-45, Springer, 2017, DOI: 10.1007/978-3-319-53088-8_3.

[6] B. Winn, "The Design, Play, and Experience Framework," in Handbook of Research on Effective Electronic Gaming in Education, pp. 1010-1024, 2009, DOI: 10.4018/978-1-59904-808-6.

[7] N. Soni, A. Aloba, K. S. Morga, and P. J. Wisniewski, "A framework of touchscreen interaction design recommendations for children (TIDRC): Characterizing the gap between research evidence and design practice," Proc 18th ACM Int Conf Interact Des Child IDC 2019, pp. 419-431, 2019. DOI: 10.1145/3311927.3323149.

[8] H. Gelderblom, and P. Kotzé, "Designing technology for young children: What we can learn from theories of cognitive development," ACM Int Conf Proceeding Ser, pp. 66-75, 2008 DOI: 10.1145/1456659.1456668.

[9] S. B. Linek, "As you like it: What media psychology can tell us about educational game design, in Handbook of Reseach on Improving Learning and Motivation through Educational Games, pp. 606-632, 2011, IGI Global.

[10] S. Chiasson, and C. Gutwin, Design Principles for Children's Technology, Interfaces 7, 28, 2005.

Sign Language Conversational User Interfaces Using Luminous Notification and Eye Gaze for the Deaf and Hard of Hearing

Takashi Kato*, Akihisa Shitara†, Nobuko Kato*, and Yuhki Shiraishi*
*Tsukuba University of Technology, Japan
Email: {a203101,nobuko,yuhkis}@a.tsukuba-tech.ac.jp
†University of Tsukuba, Japan
Email: theta-akihisa@digitalnature.slis.tsukuba.ac.jp

***Abstract*—We investigate the design of a user-friendly natural user interface for the deaf and hard of hearing (DHH). Voice-based conversational user interfaces (CUIs), such as Amazon Alexa and Google Assistant, are becoming increasingly popular among consumers. DHH users may not be aware of notifications from CUIs, may not be able to obtain response information, and may have difficulty waking up the CUIs. In this study, we designed a system that adds luminous notifications and sign language to the CUI and conducted Wizard of Oz experiments to investigate whether the system can provide an optimal user experience for DHH users. The results suggest that luminous notifications improve the usability and make notifications easier. After assessing the necessity of sign language/text display, we found that people with longer sign language histories tend to use sign language, and all people require the use of a text display. The percentage of DHH users who gazed at the system before entering commands into the system (93.4%) also suggests that gazing can be an effective way to wake up the system. Our findings provide guidance for future CUI designs to improve the accessibility for DHH users.**

Keywords*—*Deaf and hard of hearing, sign language, accessibility, user interface.

I. INTRODUCTION

The recent proliferation of voice-based interaction devices has created new accessibility barriers for many deaf and hard of hearing (DHH) users. In this paper, we propose a conversational user interface (CUI) to improve the accessibility for DHH users. In recent years, human-computer interaction (HCI) researchers have begun to evaluate sign language processing technologies from an interdisciplinary perspective [1], and as a result, this topic was addressed at a workshop on user interfaces [2]. Accessibility studies of CUIs by DHH users have reported that sign language is more suitable than gestures and text as an alternative input method to speech [3]. It has also been reported that the use of sign language is preferable to touch screens as an input method [4]. However, both of these studies substitute sign language for speech in voice user interfaces (VUIs) and do not consider the physicality of DHH users who mainly use visual information. There are few research reports on such CUIs, and HCI researchers are not working on devising or implementing design guidelines [1]. We therefore need to design CUIs accessible to DHH users, including notification methods, information transmission methods, and eye gaze.

We can classify the output of the CUIs into two patterns: the system notifying us of an "Alarm Notification" or a "Phone call," and the system describing the "Weather" or "News" that the user has requested. In the former case, DHH users do not notice the notification from the CUI, and in the latter case, they do not notice when the CUI has ended its response. In other words, it is essential to investigate the best output method of the system for DHH users, instead of the voice output provided by CUIs. By contrast, luminous notifications are familiar in deaf culture. For example, DHH users use intercoms, alarms, and fire alarms with luminous notification functions in their daily lives [5]. In addition, a luminous device that transmits the direction of the sound source of the surrounding alarms to DHH users with light has been developed [6]. In this study, we investigate whether luminous notifications can improve usability for DHH users.

Subtitling has recently become an accessibility feature for CUIs with displays [7]. Even if DHH users use this feature, there is a concern that the user experience will be lower if the system outputs subtitles. This is because an interaction will mainly be in sign language if the sign language input from the user is enabled. With devices such as Alexa entering the home, there have been reports of increased hands-free interaction with devices placed in the kitchen or living room [8]. Therefore, it is conceivable that people will be more likely to interact while doing other things. DHH users should also be able to capture responses from CUIs while doing other things. Here, it is essential to clarify whether the sign language/text output method of the system affects the user experience of DHH users, based on the difference between flowing and remaining signs for a certain period. Moreover, whereas designers must translate into the speaker's language in the case of television and the Web, CUIs are transmitted by a computer, and thus the language can be adjusted to suit the recipient. In other words, the designer should consider the output method of sign language/text, considering the user's preference in terms of attributes. Therefore, we investigate the preferences of DHH users for sign language and subtitles under the condition of parallel work when CUIs provide not only subtitles but also sign language.

To initiate a dialog with a VUI, users need to use wake words, such as "Alexa" for Amazon Alexa, "OK, Google" for Google Assistants, and "Hey, Siri" for Siri. Although studies on the waking up of personal assistant devices have compared the methods preferred by DHH users [9], they have not examined the use of eye contact, which is essential for

TABLE I
LINGUISTIC MODALITIES OF HEARING AND DHH INTERACTION WITH CUIS.

Type / User	Conversation		Call	
	CUI → User	User → CUI	CUI → User	User → CUI
Hearinng	Voice		Voice	
DHH	Sign Language / Text **		Luminnous *	Eye Gaze ***

"*": RQ1, "**": RQ2, "***": RQ3.

starting a conversation in interpersonal communication with DHH signers [10]. The authors believe that eye gaze allows for a natural interaction without an explicit wake-up and increases user satisfaction. Therefore, we investigate the possibility of using an eye gaze in a CUI.

In this study, we devised the following research questions to improve the accessibility of CUIs by DHH users.

- RQ1: Does the light-based response of the CUI improve the usability for DHH users?
- RQ2: What is the best sign language/text display method for CUI for DHH users?
- RQ3: Is eye gaze an effective method of waking up to CUI for DHH users? If yes, what kind of gaze input is effective?

As shown in Table I, RQ1–RQ3 are research questions that cover the mutual input/output modalities that DHH users want to achieve when interacting with CUIs.

DHH users use sign language/text modalities when interacting with CUIs (RQ2). They use the luminous notification modality when calling from CUIs to DHH users (RQ1). By contrast, when DHH users call to (wake up) a CUI (RQ3), they use the eye gaze modality. We investigate whether using these mutual input/output modalities in CUIs can improve the user experience of DHH users.

This study contributes empirical knowledge regarding the preferences and concerns of DHH users, such as notification, sign language/text display methods, and whether eye gaze is practical for waking up a device, thereby guiding future system designers.

In Section II, we describe related studies on CUIs and eye gaze. In Section III, we provide information on the participants, the device architecture, and the experimental procedure. In Section IV, we describe the results obtained from the experiment. In Section V, we provide a discussion of the research questions. Finally, in Section VI, we give some concluding remarks and areas of future work.

II. RELATED WORK

A. Conversational User Interface

In recent years, research on natural user interfaces, which enable natural and intuitive operations in humans, has been progressing. For greater convenience and prosperity, a "conversational" interaction with users is required that enables an intuitive operation and mental support [11]. Advances in speech recognition, speech synthesis, and natural language processing have enabled humans to interact naturally with user interfaces [12].

The VUI is an interface that uses the auditory and vocal organs and utilizes their functions as a language. With the improvements in voice recognition and natural dialog technology, VUIs are attracting attention and are becoming more popular because they can be used as hands-free devices without interrupting the user's work flow [13]. However, it is difficult for DHH people to use a VUI [14], [15].

Gestural user interfaces are those that use visual and physical functions, such as arms, fingers, and facial expressions. Example applications include motion sensing in Google Pixel 4 [16] and drones. However, gestures do not have linguistic properties, and thus their expressive power is limited.

We believe that optimal sign-language-based CUIs for DHH people should be an interface that utilizes body language, including vision, arms, fingers, facial expressions, and language. In addition, because hearing is a more passive and subconscious stimulus than sight, as long as others are nearby, speech can easily be noticed in any direction [17]. Therefore, we expect that our sign-language-based CUIs will solve the privacy problem of VUIs in an office space. Moreover, because it does not require speech recognition, it does not cause recognition problems in noisy environments. In addition, we expect sign-language-based CUIs to help overcome the problems of gestural user interfaces [18], such as reduced expressiveness and increased memory load, because they use natural language for interaction. By contrast, through the technology of sign language recognition advancement, HCI researchers have begun to consider user interfaces that can interact with sign language [19].

B. Eye Gaze in Sign Language

The preferred wake-up techniques of DHH users in descending order of preference are the use of the ASL sign-name of the device, waving in the direction of the device, clapping, using a remote control, using a phone app, and fingerspelling the English name of the device [9]. However, the comparison provided in this study does not include eye gaze. By contrast, interpersonal communication of a DHH signer requires the other person's attention when calling out to them in comparison to those with hearing [20]. In addition, when initiating a conversation with a DHH user, it is necessary to make eye contact, which can be done by tapping the user on the shoulder or waving a hand [10]. With this background in mind, this study investigates through a Wizard of Oz experiment whether eye gaze is essential for DHH users to operate a CUI.

III. METHODOLOGY

A. Participants

Using a mailing list, we solicited the cooperation of 12 DHH students in their 20s to participate in the experiment.

We also investigated the characteristics of the participants to analyze the effect of their attributes on the results of the

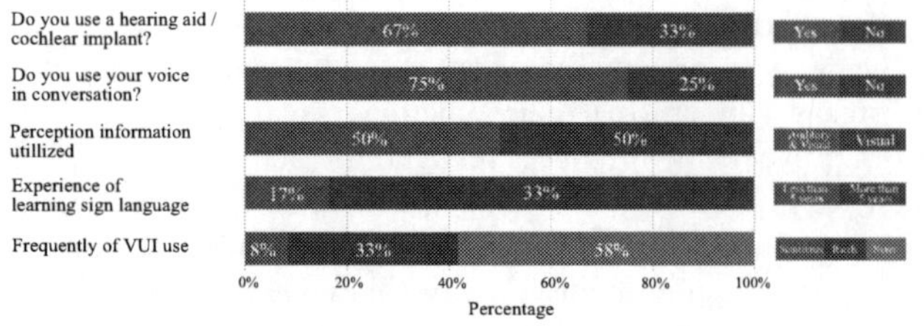

Figure 1. Graph of prior experience with voice user interfaces for 12 participants.

experiment. Specifically, we conducted a preliminary questionnaire survey on the age, gender, and cochlear implant/hearing aid use of the participants to determine whether they use their voices when communicating, whether they mainly use auditory or visual communication, and whether they use both, as well as their sign language history and their experience using VUIs. Figure 1 shows the results. The age of our participants, 8 male and 4 female, ranged between 20 and 24. We asked the participants to rate their experience of using VUIs on a 4-point Likert scale (1 = usually, 2 = sometimes, 3 = rarely, and 4 = never). The results showed that the response of one participant was 2 = sometimes, four participants responded 3 = rarely, and seven participants responded 4 = never. The majority of the participants commented that "they could not have their voices recognized" or that "they lived a life where they did not speak using voice." Research mentioning that a minimal number of DHH users use personal-assistant devices [21] indicates a similar trend to that of the participants in this experiment.

This study was approved by the Research Ethics Review of Tsukuba University of Technology, where the experiment was conducted. The duration of the experiment was 90 min, and the honorarium paid to the participants was 1,305 yen (approximately $12).

B. Device Architecture

The basic configuration of the system built in this experiment was an iPad, a Meross Smart Wi-Fi LED Bulb (LED Bulb), and a GoPro HERO9 camera. Figure 2 shows the appearance and operation of the system. We set four tasks that the system can perform: "Phone call," "Alarm settings and notifications," "Checking the Weather," and "Checking the News." An Apple iPad simulated Alexa, and the display was created using Microsoft PowerPoint 2019 and combined with the signer's video. To switch screens remotely, the remote function of Keynote was used. LED bulbs can be set to any color (16 million RGB colors) and a blink cycle, and it can be controlled remotely from a smartphone app. An LED bulb flashes yellow when the system notifies the user of a "Phone call" or "Alarm notification" and light green when the system provides "Weather" or "News" to the user. In addition, the GoPro camera views the sign language input from the user.

C. Procedure

The recognition rate in a real-life continuous sign language recognition system developed in 2019 was 39.6% [22]. Therefore, it is impossible to conduct experiments incorporating sign language recognition technology to interact with a user interface using sign language. The Wizard of Oz method [23], [24] is a solution to this problem. With this method, a human called a wizard pretends to be the system and interacts with the user. In the Wizard of Oz method, even if the entire system is not yet complete, the wizard can complement the undeveloped parts of the system and make it work. To verify RQ1–RQ3, we conducted an experiment based on the Wizard of Oz method. Figure 3 shows the experimental environment. In this experimental environment, we assumed that the participants interacted with the system while working on their PCs. Therefore, we placed the system on the left side of the desk in front of the participants at 45 degrees and the work PC in front of them. We tried to make the participants aware of the system response while the system was operating so that they did not have to constantly look at the system. We also aligned the system at the eye level of the participants. The instruction device prompted the participant to issue commands to the system at certain times. We incorporated a program in PsychoPy (v2021.1) [25] to display numbers and/or English letters at random positions on the screen. In addition, the frame rate of the installed camera was 50 fps.

The critical points for the participants and the experimenter (Wizard) in this environment are as follows.

Participant

1) Owing to the nature of the Wizard of Oz method, the participants assume that there is a sign language recognition system and do not know that a person (wizard) is operating the system.
2) During the experiment, the participant has to continuously work on the task of "entering numbers/English letters displayed at random positions on the work PC screen with the keyboard as they appear."
3) The participant commands the system using sign language commands for "Setting the alarm," "Checking the weather," and "Checking the news." The participant presses the button as soon as the end of the description

Figure 2. System prototype.

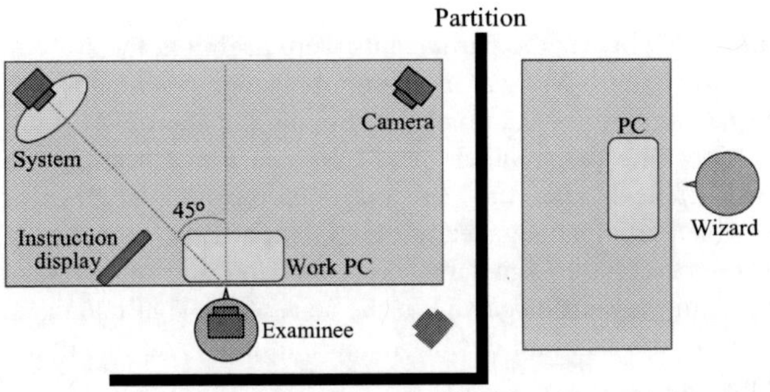

Figure 3. Experiment setup.

of "Weather" or "News" from the system is noted.
4) During the work, the participant uses sign language commands to stop the "Alarm notification" and "Phone call" sent by the system.
5) During the experiment, the user wears a GoPro attached to a head strap mount.

Experimenter (Wizard)

1) Owing to the nature of the Wizard of Oz method, the experimenter must not let the participants know that the experimenter is operating the system when performing the sign language recognition system.
2) During the experiment, the experimenter operates the system as well as the LED bulb.
3) When we asked the participants to conduct a specific task at an arbitrary time, we showed them the content of the task and an example of the command to be performed, and we immediately turned off the screen after confirming that the participants understood the task.

Before the experiment, we explained how to use the system and how the system behaves for each of the four tasks. In addition, to familiarize the participants with command execution using sign language, we gave them a practice session to perform a task equivalent to the real one before the actual experiment was conducted. The participants conducted each of the four tasks once and repeated them twice. To eliminate the order effects, the order of the tasks for each participant and the two conditions, "Luminous/Conventional," were counterbalanced.

D. Analysis Method

For the time analysis using video, we applied the ELAN [26] tool.

For RQ1, we used the system usability scale (SUS) [27], a widely applied evaluation index for a quantitative evaluation of usability, to examine the usability of "Luminous" and "Conventional." In addition, we believe that improved usability is also related to awareness. To evaluate the awareness of the notifications from the system, we measured by video the time between the notifications and when the participant noticed and reacted to them. We defined the reaction time for a "Call" as the time between the change in the display screen as the reaction start point and the users turning their eyes to the screen as the reaction endpoint. However, if the light turns on before the screen changes, the reaction start point is when the light turns on. We defined the reaction time for a "Response" as the time between the change in the display screen as the reaction start point and the user pressing the button as the reaction endpoint. However, if the light turns off before the screen changes, the reaction start point is defined as the time when the light turns off.

For RQ2, we examined the participants' need for sign language/text. After the experiment, we administered a questionnaire to determine the need for sign language/text using a five-point Likert scale (1 = agree, 2 = agree a little, 3 = neutral, 4 = disagree a little, and 5 = disagree).

For RQ3, we examined whether the participants gazed at the system before giving a command in sign language. For this purpose, we measured the percentage of the total number of times the participants gazed at the system at least once in the 5 s before the sign language command and the time between the start of the gazing and sign language using video. For the data to be analyzed, there was a scene during the experiment in which the system responded to an "Alarm notification" or "Phone call," and the user was given a command to stop the system. The user looks at the response screen before making a sign language command and does not provide analysis data to investigate whether the user gazed at the screen before the sign language command. The data for analysis are the three tasks for which the user actively gives a sign language command, i.e., "Setting the alarm," "Checking the weather," and "Checking the news."

IV. RESULTS

A. System Usability Scales

Figure 4 shows the results of the SUS investigated after the experiment. The mean SUS value of "Luminous" was 80.67, with a standard deviation of 7.62, and that of "Conventional" was 68.96, with a standard deviation of 14.6. As a result of the Wilcoxon signed-rank test, "Luminous" was found to be significantly higher ($p < .05$).

B. Reaction Time

Figure 5 shows the results of the reaction time. The mean reaction time to "Alarm notification" and "Phone call" of

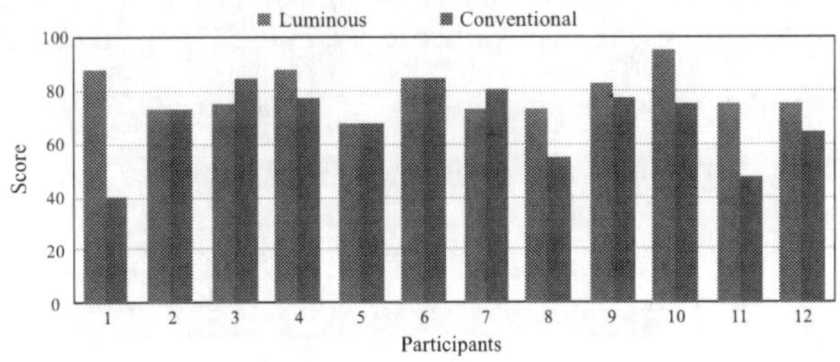

Figure 4. SUS score for each participant (N = 12).

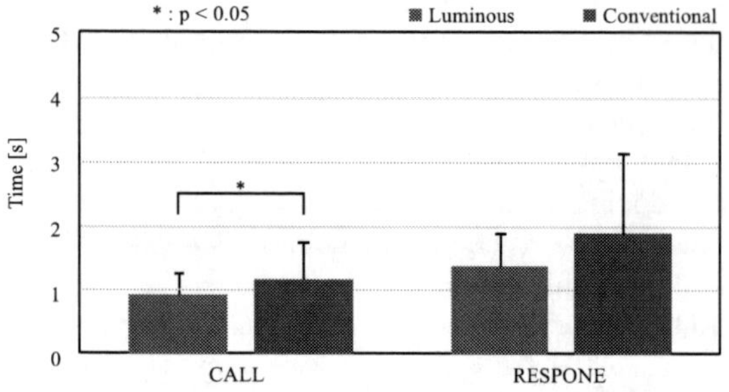

Figure 5. Reaction time for each feedback from the system.

"Luminous" was 0.91 s with a standard deviation of 0.35 s, and the mean value of "Conventional" was 1.19 s with a standard deviation of 0.57 s. The Wilcoxon signed-rank test showed that the reaction time was significantly shorter for "Luminous" ($p < .01$). The mean reaction time to the end of "Weather" and "News" for "Luminous" was 1.37 s with a standard deviation of 0.50 s, and the mean value of "Conventional" was 1.91 s with a standard deviation of 1.22 s. The Wilcoxon signed-rank test showed no significant differences between "Luminous" and "Conventional" ($p = .36$).

C. Necessity of Sign Language/Text

Figure 6 shows the results of a 5-point Likert scale to assess the need for sign language and text for the 12 participants, respectively. In terms of sign language, we found the following: 1: "Agree" was reported by four participants. 2: "Agree slightly" was reported by two participants. 3: "Neutral" was reported by three participants. 4: "Disagree slightly" was reported by two participants. 5: "Disagree" was reported by one participant. There were three participants who did not need sign language (4,5), and their sign language experience was, in order of shortest to longest, three years (1st), five years (2nd), and fifteen years (5th). By contrast, for text, "1 = Agree" was reported by nine of the participants, and "2 = Agree slightly" was reported by three of the participants.

D. Eye Gaze

During the experiment, a pattern occurred in which the experimenter turned off the screen of the instructional device late, indicating the task to be performed, and the participant gave a sign language command while reading. We removed these data from our analysis because they were unsuitable for examining whether the participants were gazing at the system. The participants (N = 12) input sign language commands into the system 69 times: 23 times for "Setting the alarm," 24 times for "Checking the weather," and 22 times for "Checking the news." Table II lists the percentage of the total number of times the participants gazed at the system at least once during the 5 s before the sign language command and the average time from the start of gazing to the start of the sign language, as well as the standard deviation and minimum and maximum values.

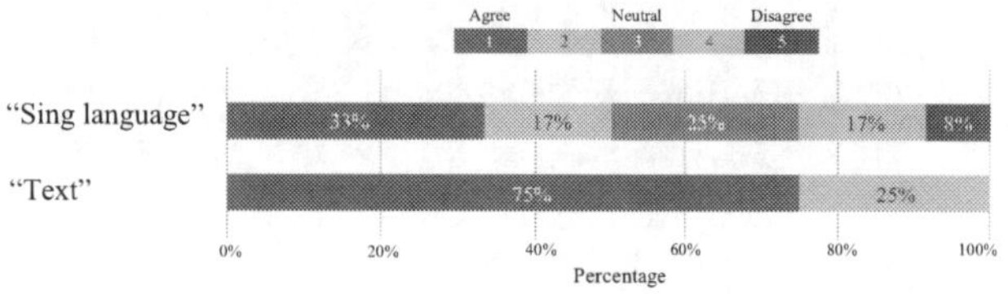

Figure 6. Necessity of "Sign language" / "Text".

TABLE II
PERCENTAGE OF EYE GAZE, MEAN AND STANDARD DEVIATION OF TIME OF EYE GAZE

Task	*Percentage (%)*	*Mean±SD (s)*	*Min (s)*	*Max (s)*
Alarm	100	0.76±0.61	0.20	3.18
Weather	100	0.43±0.23	0.10	1.08
Alarm	86.4	0.59±0.44	0.20	2.08
Total	93.4	0.59±0.47	0.10	3.18

A high percentage of the total number of users gazed at the system before using the sign language commands.

Three participants, P3, P8, and P9, waived before applying the sign language. These three participants had experience using VUIs and knew that they should use a waking command. The interviews also revealed that they thought it was necessary to take explicit action before talking to the system during this experiment.

V. DISCUSSION

A. RQ1: Efficacy of Luminous Notification

The results described in Section IV-A suggest that luminous notification improves the usability of DHH users in noticing notifications from the CUI. In addition, the reaction times to "Alarm notification" and "Phone call" were significantly shorter when using a luminous notification, suggesting that it is easier to notice such notifications from the system.

Participants commented, "I am familiar with luminous notification methods, such as the intercom system in my house, which notifies me by light, so it would be more impressive to add light to the system as well. I can notice the light notification even when I am concentrating on my work." However, there were also comments such as "I feel uncomfortable with the luminous notification because I live my life relying on sound. Therefore, the system may not be suitable for people who use their daily hearing functions.

From Figure 4, we can see that the usability of P3 and P7 decreases with a luminous notification. They commented that they did not feel the need to use a luminous notification because they only noticed the change in the system screen. This may be because there were cases in which DHH users could respond to conventional methods [28]. In this experimental environment, the system was placed on the left side of the desk in front of the user at a 45 degree angle and within the peripheral vision. During this experiment, we placed the system within the peripheral vision of the front of the user, and thus some of the subjects noticed changes in the screen without looking at the system.

By contrast, there were no significant differences in the reaction time to the end of the "Weather" and "News" responses when using the luminous notification, as described in Section IV-B. However, some of the participants commented positively that "it was convenient to know when the response ended without having to look at the system." By contrast, others commented negatively that "luminous notification was not necessary for information (weather and news) that I wanted," and "the light was too bright." As a result, the usability of the system can be improved by reducing the light exposure and improving the luminous notification method, although the noticeability remains the same.

A participant commented that it is preferable to increase the brightness of the display, as in ON AIR, instead of directly informing us with LED bulbs. For a luminous notification, we used LED bulbs, which were initially used as lighting fixtures. Therefore, we need to consider a way to change or blink the brightness of the display directly instead of using external LEDs.

In this study, we incorporated a luminous notification as a means of responding to DHH users. However, some participants commented, "I think it would be easier to notice if there was a notification method using vibration as well as light." In the future, we believe that it will be necessary to conduct a verification experiment that includes a vibration notification. In addition, because we placed the system at the front of the participants in this experiment, we need to find a way to make them aware of the notifications from the rear.

B. RQ2:How to Suitably Display Sign Language/Text

From Section IV-C, we can see that all of the participants need to display text regardless of the user attributes. By contrast, the necessity for the sign language display varies from participant to participant. In addition, we can see that those who have not signed for a long time tend not to believe that sign language is necessary.

The participants who did not need sign language commented that they did not understand sign language and had trouble processing information when both sign language and text were output simultaneously. By contrast, the participants who needed to use sign language commented that the sign language display made it easier for them to remember the system responses. Some of the participants commented, "When I look at the task screen while working, the remaining text is better than the flow of the sign language."

For hearing users, interaction with VUIs has the advantage of being eyes-free [13]. Therefore, users frequently interact with CUIs while conducting other tasks. However, in the case of DHH users, the advantage of eyes-free interaction is lost because they cannot acquire audio information and instead gaze at the screen. To complement this, we anticipate that DHH users will need text information that they can recognize, even if they look away for a moment. One possible solution to this problem is to stop the sign language when the user looks away and start again when the user looks back.

C. RQ3:Efficacy of Eye Gaze

Section IV-D shows that the participants tend to gaze at the screen before speaking in sign language.

During this experiment, we did not provide instructions on how to wake up the device. Nevertheless, the participants naturally gazed at the system with a high probability.

By contrast, 3 of the 12 participants did not gaze at the system but made hand gestures instead. When DHH users use waving as a wake-up method, there is a concern that signs made while talking to another person may be recognized as waving at unexpected times, such as during a "Phone call" or "Alarm notification." In addition, we believe that gazing is a more natural way of interacting than waving every time a command is used. These results suggest that gazing is a compelling wake-up method.

When Alexa waits for a response from the user, there is a time limit of 8.0 s [29]. From Table II, the maximum time between gazing at the system and the start of sign language was 3.18 s. In other words, when DHH users use gazing as the wake-up method, they can use commands within the system's waiting time.

D. Limitations

In this study, the age range of the participants was low, and the sample size was small, with all participants being university students. In addition, 92% of the participants had little or no experience using VUIs. During this experiment, we did not present a line of sight from the system. In other words, the user cannot judge whether the system and the user's gaze coincide.

VI. CONCLUSION AND FUTURE WORK

In this study, a system was designed that adds a luminous notification and sign language to CUIs to provide an optimal user experience for DHH users. We surveyed DHH users (N = 12) to determine the optimal input and output modalities of the CUIs.

We tested the effectiveness of a luminescent modality applied to call from the CUIs to DHH users using the SUS and found that the usability of the system was improved using a luminous notification. The reaction time of the luminous notification to the call from the system (0.91 ± 0.35 s) was significantly shorter than that of the conventional system (1.19 ± 0.57 s). After assessing the necessity of sign language/text display, 50% of the participants answered that they needed to use sign language for the display method of CUIs, and 100% of the participants answered that they needed to use text. We also found that people with longer sign language histories tended to use sign language. As a result of the experiment on whether the gazing modality is effective for DHH users to wake up the CUIs, the percentage of times they gazed at least once in the system during the five seconds before the sign language commands was as high as 93.4%, suggesting that gazing is a compelling wake-up method.

Future studies will include a more diverse group of people such as children and the elderly. We also plan to conduct an evaluation experiment after using a system entirely accustomed to the participants. We are also planning to conduct an evaluation experiment to determine whether gaze can be used as a wake-up command.

We expect that our findings will become one of the design guidelines used for CUIs suitable for DHH users.

ACKNOWLEDGMENT

This work was partially supported by JSPS KAKENHI Grant Number #19K11411 and the Promotional Projects for Advanced Education and Research in NTUT. We would like to thank Editage (www.editage.com) for English language editing.

REFERENCES

[1] D. Bragg et al., "Sign Language Recognition, Generation, and Translation: An Interdisciplinary Perspective," Proceedings of ASSETS '19: The 21st International ACM SIGACCESS Conference on Computers and Accessibility, pp. 16–31, NY, USA, Oct. 2019.

[2] D. Bragg et al., "Sign Language Interfaces: Discussing the Field's Biggest Challenges," Proceedings of CHI EA '20: Extended Abstracts of the 2020 CHI Conference on Human Factors in Computing Systems, pp. 1–5, NY, USA, April 2020.

[3] G. Evan, K. Raja S., R. Jason, V. Christian, and W. Brittany, "Accessibility of Voice-Activated Agents for People Who Are Deaf or Hard of Hearing," Proceedings of CSUN '19: 34th Annual Assistive Technology Conference Scientific/Research, vol. 7, pp. 144–156, San Diego, 2019.

[4] W. Gilmore et al., "Alexa, Can You See Me?" Making Individual Personal Assistants for the Home Accessible to Deaf Consumers," Proceedings of ASSETS '19: 35th Annual Assistive Technology Conference Scientific/Research, vol. 8, pp. 16–31, San Diego, 2020.

[5] J. Berke, [retrieved: June 30, 2021], "Assistive Listening Devices for the Deaf and HOH, https://www.verywellhealth.com/assistive-listening-devices-1046105

[6] A. Matsuda, M. Sugaya, and H. Nakamura, "Luminous Device for the Deaf and Hard of Hearing People," in Proceedings of the Second International Conference on Human-Agent Interaction (HAI '14), pp. 201–204, Oct. 2014.

[7] Amazon, [retrieved: June 30, 2021], "Hearing Communicate and stay connected with Alexa." Available: https://www.amazon.com/b/ref=ods_afe_hop_hp?node=21213721011

[8] F. Bentley et al., "Understanding the long-term use of smart speaker assistants," Proceedings of the ACM on Interactive, Mobile, Wearable and Ubiquitous Technologies, vol. 2, no. 91, pp 1–24, Sept. 2018.

[9] V. Mande, A. Glasser, B. Dingman, and M. Huenerfauth, "Deaf Users' Preferences Among Wake-Up Approaches during Sign-Language Interaction with Personal Assistant Devices," Proceedings of CHI EA '21: Extended Abstracts of the 2021 CHI Conference on Human Factors in Computing Systems, no. 370, pp 1–6, May 2021.

[10] SignGenius, [retrieved: June 30, 2021], "Do's & Don'ts - Getting Attention in the Deaf Community." Available: https://www.signgenius.com/info-do's&don'ts.shtml

[11] R. Byron and N. Clifford, "The Media Equation: How People Treat Computers, Television, and New Media Like Real People and Places," Bibliovault OAI Repository, University of Chicago Press, pp. 18–36, 1996.

[12] H. Candello et al., "CUI@CHI: Mapping Grand Challenges for the Conversational User Interface Community," in Extended Abstracts of the 2020 CHI Conference on Human Factors in Computing Systems (CHI EA '20), pp. 1–8, NY, USA, April 2020.

[13] C. Pearl, "Designing Voice User Interfaces: Principles of Conversational Experiences," O'Reilly Media, 2017.

[14] J. P. Bigham, R Kushalnagar, T. K. Huang, J. P. Flores, and S. Savage, "On How Deaf People Might Use Speech to Control Devices," in Proceedings of the 19th International ACM SIGACCESS Conference on Computers and Accessibility (ASSETS '17), NY, USA, pp. 383–384, Oct. 2017.

[15] A. Glasser, "Automatic Speech Recognition Services: Deaf and Hard-of-Hearing Usability," in Extended Abstracts of the 2019 CHI Conference on Human Factors in Computing Systems (CHI EA '19), no. SRC06, New York, USA, pp. 1–6, May 2019.

[16] verizon 2020 [retrieved: June 30, 2021], "Google Pixel 4 - Motions and Gestures." Available: https://www.verizon.com/support/knowledge-base-228703/

[17] National Institutes of Health (US); Biological Sciences Curriculum Study, "NIH Curriculum Supplement Series," [Internet], Bethesda (MD): Information about Hearing, Communication, and Understanding, 2007.

[18] M. Henschke, T. Gedeon, and R. Jones, "Touchless Gestural Interaction with Wizard-of-Oz: Analysing User Behaviour," in Proceedings of the Annual Meeting of the Australian Special Interest Group for Computer Human Interaction (OzCHI '15), New York, USA, pp. 207–211, Dec. 2015.

[19] A. Glasser, V. Mande, and M. Huenerfauth, "Accessibility for Deaf and Hard of Hearing Users: Sign Language Conversational User Interfaces," in Proceedings of the 2nd Conference on Conversational User Interfaces (CUI '20), New York, USA, no. 55, pp. 1–3, July 2020.

[20] A. M. Lieberman, "Attention-getting skills of deaf children using American Sign Language in a preschool classroom," Applied Psycholinguistics, vol. 36, no. 4, pp. 855–873, July 2016.

[21] A. Pradhan, K. Mehta, and L. Findlater, "Accessibility Came by Accident: Use of Voice-Controlled Intelligent Personal Assistants by People with Disabilities," in Proceedings of the 2018 CHI Conference on Human Factors in Computing Systems (CHI '18), New York, USA, no. 459, pp. 1–13.

[22] R. Cui, H. Liu, and C. Zhang, "A deep neural framework for continuous sign language recognition by iterative training," IEEE Trans. Multimedia, vol. 21, no. 7, pp. 1880–1891, July 2019.

[23] N. Crook, [retrieved: June 30, 2021], "Wizard of Oz testing – a method of testing a system that does not yet exist." Available: https://www.simpleusability.com/inspiration/2018/08/wizard-of-oz-testing-a-method-of-testing-a-system-that-does-not-yet-exist/

[24] N. Fraser and N. Gilbert, "Simulating speech systems. Computer Speech & Language," vol. 5, pp. 81–99, Jan. 1991.

[25] J. Peirce and J. R. Gray, "Simpson, S. et al. PsychoPy2: Experiments in behavior made easy," Behavior Research Methods, vol. 51, pp. 195–203, Feb. 2019.

[26] The Language Archive, [retrieved: June 30, 2021], "ELAN." Available: https://archive.mpi.nl/tla/elan

[27] J. Brooke, "SUS: A quick and dirty usability scale," Usability Eval. Ind., vol. 189, pp. 1–7, Nov. 1995.

[28] D. Bavelier et al., "Visual attention to the periphery is enhanced in congenitally deaf individuals," The Journal of Neuroscience: The official journal of the Society for Neuroscience, vol. 20, no. 17, pp. 1–8, Sept. 2000.

[29] Developer documentationamazon alexa, [retrieved: June 30, 2021], "Alexa Design Guide." Available: https://developer.amazon.com/en-GB/docs/alexa/alexa-design/available.html

Immersive Learning with AI-enhanced Virtual Standardized Patient (VSP) to Improve Dental Student's Communication Proficiencies

Aadithya Gowthaman, Linda Kirova, Bingyu Li, Patrick Molen, Ines Said, Jordan Smith, Austin Stanbury, Markus Santoso PhD
Digital Worlds Institute
University of Florida
Gainesville, Florida. United States
markus.santoso@ufl.edu

Cortino Sukotjo DDS, PhD
Restorative Dentistry Department
University of Illinois at Chicago
Chicago, Illinois. United States
csukotjo@uic.edu

***Abstract*— COVID-19's lockdown policy is causing the dental schools to halt their preclinical curricular and clinical activities, including a learning session with Standardized Satient (SP) to train student's communication proficiencies. In this project, we developed Virtual Standardized Patient (VSP): an immersive learning with Artificial Intelligence (AI)-enhanced Virtual Standardized Patient to improve dental student's communication proficiencies. Augmented Reality (AR) was used to immerse the virtual patient into user's space, user also has an option to switch to Virtual Reality (VR) to fully immerse the user with the digital environment. AI element facilitates a seamless communication between virtual patient and user, and we also added an adaptive storytelling to allow student to explore several discussion's options.**

Keywords-virtual standardized patient; immersive learning; artificial intelligence; adaptive storytelling.

I. Introduction

Dental practitioners require not only psychomotor skills but also communication skills. Previously, an immersive technology was developed as an alternative solution to drill psychomotor skills in preclinical education [1]. As part of this paper, authors explored faculty perceptions about related project and faculties enjoyed the immersive experiences and suggested that the virtual set-up provides a holistic and realistic view of a dental operatory for students.

Other research group developed a conversational Virtual Standardized Patient to enable students to practice history-taking skills [5]. Their project allowed students to take a history of a VSP, develop a differential diagnosis, and document the encounter in the electronic medical record [5].

In this paper, authors introduced an immersive technology application to increase dental student's communication proficiencies. Traditionally, dental schools provide a face-to-face sessions between student and Standardized Patient (SP) to mainly focus on improving their communication skills.

SP is a 'patient-actor' who has been trained to consistently portray a specific patient role, outlined by a script devised by topic content experts [4]. SPs have been used in dental curricula to address skills in working with tobacco cessation counseling, emergencies, interprofessional skills, and complete denture treatments [2]. The individualized experience of having a student work with a SP to develop communication skills has been an effective means of teaching communication, data-gathering, promoting interpersonal skills, and cultural sensitivity [7].

Conventionally, this learning sessions take place on-site and required in-person interaction between student and actor. However, lockdown caused by COVID-19 pandemic has forced most of schools to close and suspend their academic activities including the face-to-face session between student and SP. The motivation of this paper is to introduced our project: Virtual Standardized Patient (VSP). VSP is an immersive learning module that utilize an AI-enhanced virtual standardized patient to overcome the limitation of SP's conventional approach.

This paper will be structured into several sections. Section 1 will cover about project's introduction. In section 2, authors will discuss about the main project, Virtual Standardized Patient, including assets and the technology behind it such as the AI-Natural Language Processing, immersive technology (AR-VR), and adaptive storytelling feature. In section 3 we will conclude our discussion by discussing about limitations and future plan for this project.

II. Virtual Standardized Patient

To offer a digital simulation that replicates the traditional learning session, VSP project employed an user with the learning modules. We also implemented an AI's Natural Language Processing (NLP) to facilitate a seamless communication between user and virtual patient. Furthermore, VSP also added an adaptive storytelling approach to allow student to explore different answers and observe difference patient's responses. Assets (Environment and Virtual Patient)

The discussion between patient and dentist most of the time happened inside the dentist's room. To replicate this situation, we prepared similar assets that inspired from the real objects starting from the color tone, layout, and others. The assets includes dental room and chair. The room is also completed with supporting objects including cabinets, sink, office desk, computer, and television screen as shown in Figure 1.

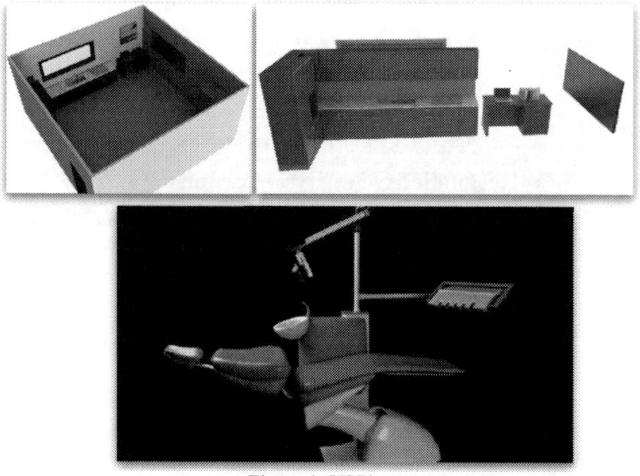

Figure 1. VSP's assets.

A. *Virtual Patients*

In this project, we included two virtual patients that represent different races and communities, as shown in Figure 2. The virtual patients wear casual dress code and they are rigged and animated following the prepared dialogue.

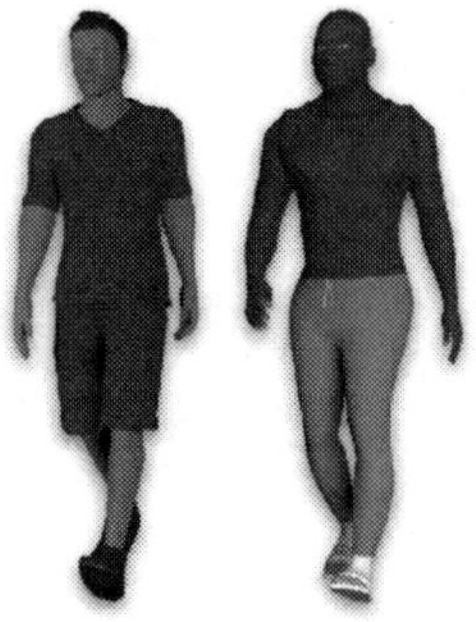

Figure 2. VSP's Virtual Patients

B. *Markerless-AR & VR session*

VSP project is an immersive learning platform that employed both AR and VR technology. AR is a technology that allow user to see the real worlds, with virtual objects superimposed upon or composited with the real world [4]. Furthermore, AR is a system that have the following three characteristics: combines real and virtual, interactive in real time and registered in 3D [6]. For VSP's AR session, we applied a markerless experience powered by Google ARCore Software Development Kit (SDK). With ARCore, user could scan their room, place the virtual patient on the designated spot, and the virtual patient will be immersed onto user's real space without any printed marker as shown in Figure 3.

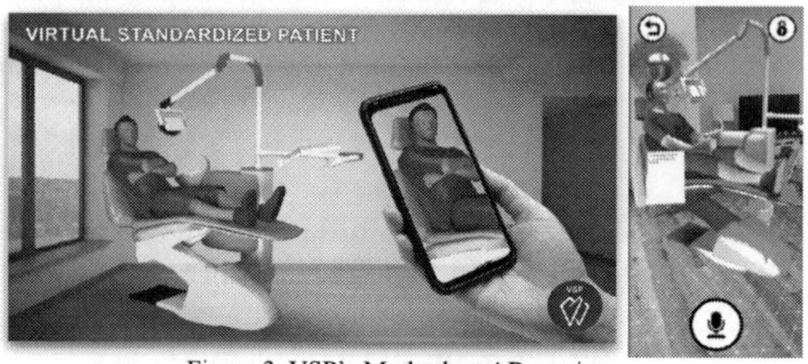

Figure 3. VSP's Markerless AR session.

VR is defined as a computer-generated digital environment that can be experienced with as if that environment was real [3]. In VSP project, user has an option to switch from AR to VR mode. In this session, they will be fully immersed into the dentist room and interact with the virtual patient there as shown in Figure 4.

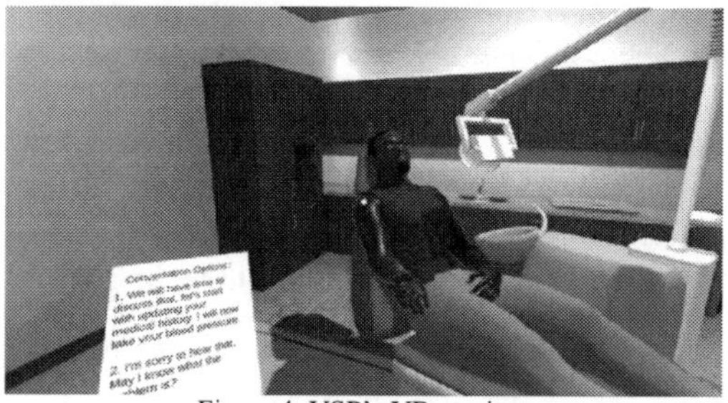

Figure 4. VSP's VR session.

C. *Seamless Communication & Adaptive Storytelling*

Improving user or student's communication skills is the main objective of VSP project therefore it is critical for them to be able to communicate verbally with the virtual patient. To facilitate a well-flow verbal communication, we implemented AI's NLP service provided by IBM Watson. NLP is the set of methods for making human language accessible to computers [3]. The speech recognition in NLP will convert an audio signal to text [3]; therefore, it will facilitate a verbal communication between the dental student and virtual patient.

Compared to the basic speech recognition, NLP allow the system to identify the appropriate word, phrase or response by using context clues and this feature is essential in VSP to offer a smooth communication flow between user and virtual SP. In this project, we trained the AI system to detect user response and give an appropriate feedback including the ability to understand several phrases and detect it as 'greeting'.

Virtual simulation allow us to offer many scenarios that sometime could not be offered in conventional learning sessions. In VSP project, we implemented an adaptive storytelling to allow student to explore several answers to observe possible patient's responses therefore they could be more prepared when they handle the real patient. Figure 5 showed the diagram of VSP's adaptive storytelling.

III. CONCLUSION

Real time speech interaction in immersive environment between real user and virtual character has been implemented including for Human Resource (HR) training purposes and for general medical student training. However, our VSP project that mainly focus for the dental student is a novel application of immersive learning platform. COVID-19 lockdown mandate also shows a demand for dental learning module that mobile and less site-dependent. VSP could be a key breakthrough as an alternative solution that overcome the existing learning tool's limitation. Even though there were several VSP projects previously developed for the medical education, our project is novel since it explores the application of VSP for the dentistry education direction.

For current progress, VSP is still limited to one scenario: handling an angry patient and in the future we are planning to expand to another scenarios including delivering news to the young or child patient, educating senior patient about certain procedure, and others. We also plan to add supervision features both a real time supervision by faculty and including an AI-based supervisor. Our team also plan to run a quantitative study with potential user to learn about their perception about this project.

REFERENCES

[1] C. Sukotjo, S. Schreiber, J. C. Yuan, and M. Santoso, "Faculty perceptions of virtual reality as an alternative solution for preclinical skills during the pandemic," Journal of Dental Education, 2020. DOI: 10.1002/jdd.12499.

[2] C. T. McKenzie, K R. Tilashalski, D. T. Peterson, and M. L. White, "Effectiveness of Standardized Patient Simulations in Teaching Clinical Communication Skills to Dental Students," Journal of Dental Education, 2017; 81(10): 1179-86.

[3] J. Einstein, "Natural Language Processing," 2018.

[4] J. Jerald, "The VR Book: Human-Centered Design for Virtual Reality," 2015, ACM Books.

[5] K. Maicher, D. Danforth, A. Price et al. "Developing a Conventional Virtual Standardized Patient to Enable Students to Practice History-Taking Skills," Simul Healthc 2017; 12(2):124-31.

[6] R. Azuma, "A Survey of Augmented Reality," Teleoperators and Virtual Environments, 1997; 6(4): 355-85.

[7] R. C. Wiener, C. Water, J. Doris, D. W. McNeil, "Comparison of Dental Students' Self-Evaluation and Faculty Evaluation of Communication Skills During a Standardized Patient Exercise," Journal of Dental Education, 2018; 82(10): 1043-50

Figure 5. VSP's Adaptive Storytelling Diagram.

A Web-Based Communication Tool for Arabic-Speaking Newcomers to Canada

Fatma Ben Mesmia
dept. of Computer Science)
University of Regina
Saskatchewan, Canada
Fatma.Ben.Mesmia@uregina.ca

Malek Mouhoub
dept. of Computer Science
University of Regina
Saskatchewan, Canada
malek.mouhoub@uregina.ca

***Abstract*—The development of a communication aid tool for Non-English-Speaking newcomers to Canada is very important for their integration, self-reliance and contribution to the new society. Such a tool will indeed overcome the language barriers that the newcomers might be challenged with, which will ease their struggle in their first days in a foreign country. Following on a previous work extending the Pictopages software to address these challenges for the Arabic-speaking new comers to Saskatchewan, Canada, we propose a new web-based communication tool relying on a multilingual ontology. More precisely, the multilingual ontology is used to structure items, extracted automatically from Wikipedia via a Natural Language Processing (NLP) module. Our proposed communication tool allows newcomers to communicate and to interact with the target community via audio, text and visual symbols. In this regard, the tool includes several functionalities, such as a multilingual automatic speech-to-speech translation, localisation via Google Maps web mapping service, and important information and resources for newcomers. The latter are well-organized in a hierarchical manner, thanks to our proposed multilingual ontology.**

Keywords- Communication aid; Pictogram; Audio-visual strategy; Multilingual ontology; NLP.

I. INTRODUCTION

Communication aid tools that target people with intellectual or developmental disabilities have demonstrated their capability to help communicating successfully with others. The provided tools play a significant role to overcome communication issues as they are based on several technologies, including pictograms (clear symbols in black and white) and audio messages. Nowadays, it is important to make these communication aid tools available to newcomers. These tools will not only help to communicate but encourage users to engage a discussion in the new language. In other words, through a well-developed communication assistant system, newcomers will overcome their language barriers and be able to better share and transmit their opinions, ideas and thoughts. This will lead to improve their communication skills in the target language and facilitate their integration in the new society.

In [1], a new methodology has been proposed to develop a communication aid tool for Arabic-speaking new comers to Saskatchewan, Canada. The target tool extends the Pictopages software by attaching Arabic and English audio messages to a set of pictograms. More precisely, the user will communicate by selecting the appropriate pictogram symbol, which will output an audio sound in both languages (Arabic and English). Indeed, pictograms are symbols that express a clear and adequate visual representation of a given item, concept, location, service, etc. The methodology and the related tool do however have the following limitations. First, Pictopages software is only available for IPads, which limits its usability by newcomers. Second, while Pictopages allows the addition and customization of new pictograms, audio messages have to be produced and added manually. This is a tedious task especially given that users have different needs, over time, which will translate to a large number of items that have to be added dynamically. Finally, the methodology requires a face to face interaction with a set of participants to evaluate the new tool. This latter phase is not practical due to the current COVID-19 measures, among other challenges.

Our main goal in this paper is to follow up on the work in [1], and to address its limitations. More precisely, we propose a new Web-based communication tool for Arabic-speaking newcomers to Canada, meeting the following main objectives.

1) Facilitate the communication (of Arabic-speaking newcomers) in the two official languages of the host country (English and French),
2) improve communication skills in the two target languages,
3) encourage community engagement,
4) and accelerate newcomers integration, self-reliance and contribution to society.

Our proposed tool relies on a multilingual ontology, Wikipedia and Application Programming Interfaces (APIs). In addition to Arabic, English and French, our tool can be easily extended to other languages. Besides, different scenarios from a daily life/needs of a newcomer are represented and updated via a large set of items that are extracted automatically from Arabic Wikipedia. Also, these items are structured into a multilingual ontology created via an NLP module, and annotated through a Web Ontology Language (OWL) language. Indeed, the multilingual aspect is ensured by an API that extracts information from Wikipedia articles. Furthermore, audio messages associated with items are also recorded through an API. This latter API allows the recording of the same tone of a male or a female voice, and reads a word or a phrase based on its punctuation. Moreover, our proposed tool helps newcomers to find geographic locations of the important places that they might be looking for, such as hospitals, schools and grocery stores. Finally, the tool is linked to Websites for public services like emergency services, such as police and fire departments. The evaluation of the tool is conducted through a feedback survey component for end-users. This will help performing a perfective maintenance of the software.

The rest of the paper is structured as follows. In the next section, we present an overview of the different communication aid methods. In this regard, we will first present a classification of the known methods. Then, we present previous communication aids based on pictograms. Section 3 is dedicated to a related work that has been conducted to address the communication aid for non English-speakers, using Pictopages. In Section 4, we describe our proposed methodology. Section 5 provides the details of the multilingual ontology we have adopted. Section 6 presents the different components of our web-based application. Finally, concluding remarks and ideas for future works are listed in Section 7.

II. Overview of communication aid methods

A communication aid is a means of connection to help people who are struggling with troubles of speech and communication. Likewise, this aid assists individuals through facilitating their interaction and discussion with people around them. Besides, it allows them to share meanings more effectively [2]. Initially, a communication aid was just a simple letter written on a board. Nowadays, this communication aid has evolved to complex systems relying on sophisticated electronic devices.

A. Augmentative and Alternative Communication

Augmentative and Alternative Communication (AAC) is a generic term that refers to those communication methods supporting or replacing speech. AAC helps people to convey their thoughts and encourages them to express their needs. Moreover, AAC provides an opportunity for individuals to connect non only with family and friends but also to understand and interact with their environment, such as in a workplace or a shopping center [3]. AAC methods are classified into two main classes; the first one, named "aided AAC", comprises two sub-classes: "non electronic" and "electronic tools". The second class is called "Unaided AAC" as it does not require the use of material or equipment. In what follows, we will describe briefly each class and sub-class.

B. Unaided Communication

Unaided communication methods are based on sign language, gestures and body movements. This kind of communication methods are frequently used and understood by people. According to gestures and body movements, the majority of people are able to recognize facial expressions, communication through eye looking, and pre-verbal gestures such as pointing. However, a sign language is needed for individuals with hearing and speech impairment. Besides, a sign language has different types related to several cultures; among these languages, we quote American Sign Language and British Sign Language [3].

C. Aided Communication

Communication methods become sophisticated and as they keep pace with technological progress. In this context, we list aided communication methods, which are based on the use of equipment. Moreover, there are two sub-classes of aided communication methods; "Low-tech" and "High-tech". These sub-classes differ in terms of the used technologies. Low-tech methods use old techniques characterized by their simplicity. On the other hand, High-tech tools are based on modern techniques using advanced features. In what follows, we present each sub-class.

1) Low-tech communication aid: Low-tech communication aids use writing methods to transmit the information. These methods can be boards and books, which include significant symbols, meaningful letters or words and relevant pictures. Symbols could be described graphically as in Blissymbolics [4], which is a language containing thousands of symbols and in Boardmaker [5], which is a graphic database dedicated to make communication aids. The communication aids made via Boardmaker can contain thousand symbols translated into various languages. In this kind of communication aid, individuals can rely on eye-pointing to select a symbol or touch it directly through fingers or other movements, assuming they have the ability to move. Otherwise, symbol selection can be done by another person that follows the individual's instructions until getting the desired symbol [3] [6].

2) High-tech communication aid: High-tech communication aids allows to store and retrieve messages, having an electronic format, which helps individuals communicating through a speech output [7]. The High-tech communication aids can also be named SGD and VOCA, which stand respectively for Speech Generating Devices and Voice Output Communication Aids [8]. For these types of communication aids, the output speech can be generated through two manners, digitized and synthesized. According to digitized output speech, the devices play words or completed phrases, which are recorded. In general, these devices are the most understandable. For the synthesized output speech, the devices exploit a text to speech software for those who are not capable to spell words. High-tech communication aids have two categories of devices. The first one is called "dedicated devices" developed exclusively for AAC, while the second one ("non-dedicated devices") refers to computers running a software, to mimic AAC devices. High-tech communication aids can be classified into static and dynamic devices. Static devices, which can be modified manually, contain symbols having a position fixed on a paper overlays. On the other hand, dynamic devices contain symbols, which can be modified through a page linked to vocabularies and messages [7] [9].

D. Communication aids based on Pictograms

Pictograms are methods of communication that are considered as figurative and informative drawings. Pictograms can substitute written instructions to express information that can be quickly processed, such as road traffic signs. This kind of warning and mandatory information requires clear symbols acting as indicators. In addition, pictograms can provide a compromise between native and non-native speakers for a given language or between users with low level of literacy. Through pictogram symbols, old people suffering from visual impairment can interact with other people. Moreover, pictograms are useful for industries to spread legal information to their workers, such as the use of dangerous and hazardous materials [10] [11] [12]. In what follows, we present some previous communication aids based on pictograms.

In 1976, Maharaj S. developed a visual strategy based on pictograms, which aims to ensure the communication for non-verbal individuals. In 1980, Maharaj's pictogram application started to be used internationally. As a main goal, this application aims to offer a communication strategy for both children and adults with disabilities that impaired their verbal communication capabilities, such as cerebral palsy, autism and Alzheimer [13]. The provided symbols consist of a white symbol (corresponding to a simplified "picture") on a black background. The white symbol refracts light to provide the strongest impact for communication while the black background removes the possibility of figure ground confusions. The proposed symbols can illustrate objects, concepts or actions. They can also provide adaptive opportunities for communication especially for those who require such assistance for communicating with people around them, as well as providing a platform to create classroom materials for their benefit.

Similarly, low-tech to high-tech aids are available, from symbol-based communication boards (e.g., printable from software applications) to symbol and picture-based applications on mobile devices, as well as specialized, and dedicated messaging devices. Similarly, there has also been some use of pictograms to assist in the teaching of alternate languages [14], or in discordant language situations for specific needs (e.g., delivery of healthcare services) [15]. We also note some use of pictograms to help refugees to communicate in the language of their host countries [16] [17].

In [14], the author reports on a work using a method based on pictograms for teaching Turkish as a new foreign language. The proposed method uses both pictograms and sentences based on a context to build a new Turkish vocabulary. Besides, this work lists original pictogram patterns to show the value of this technique. In this regard, the author aims to help Turkish learners to use pictograms in a context to enhance their communication skills level in this target language. The proposed approach described uses a bold, high impact, text-based style of pictograms, where words are shown in a variety of fonts, sizes, alignments, and colors with added images, such as a leaf growing out of a letter, a cartoon drawing of a sad man sitting on a letter (with pools of tears below), a backdrop of a sun peeking above the clouds, letters with eyes and mouths, and "cold" blue letters (one with a toque) in what appears to be a snowfall. These teaching aids were intended for use in a classroom setting. It was reported that this approach was not only effective for teaching Turkish vocabulary, but it also increases the ease of learning and the vocabulary.

In [18], a teaching strategy is proposed for kindergarten students based on pictograms' assistance, which is based on mixing words with symbolic pictures. Indeed, the author believes that students can understand the relationship linking oral and written languages through learning how to recount, read and write short poems and rhymes in Spanish. Moreover, pictograms are used to illustrate poems and to ease not only students' understanding but to enhance their reading level so they become fluent. Pictograms, considered among the first writing forms, help boosting students' ability to learn and communicate (talking, listening, writing and reading). Furthermore, students start reading a poem with a short form, and identify pictograms in rhyme. Then, they practice the identified words and end up by composing and reciting their own poems.

In [15], the authors discuss the use of pictograms for health care in the context of US Navy exercises intended to provide training for humanitarian and disaster relief to U.S. military, Non-Governmental Organization (NGO), and other associated personnel. This work is motivated by the fact that communication between those providing medical care and those receiving it was problematic. This is due to either a lack of skilled translators or to translators who had little or no knowledge of medical terminology and practice. In most cases, it was not possible for English-speaking medical personnel to determine whether the message transmitted was correctly translated. In some cases where NGO translators were available to monitor local translators, it was found that the information was not being accurately delivered, with some of the information being highly inaccurate. Consequently, there was a need to provide medical staff with alternate methods of communication; additionally, those methods would require testing for effectiveness and validity before being put into practice. One potential method identified was the use pictograms representing common medical conditions and symptoms. To determine whether such pictograms would be capable of meeting the 85% level of accuracy specified by the American National Standards Institute (ANSI), thirty-six images (including three duplicates) were provided to medical personnel for interpretation. It was found that over 75% of the (unique) images met the ANSI criterion. This suggested that the use of pictograms could be a viable communication method when the medical staff and patients do not speak the same language.

Some research work have been conducted to manage the knowledge behind the graphic display of pictograms. By doing so, these pictograms could rely on an important semantic level of the associated vocabularies. In [19], the authors present an AAC device, called "Pictogrammar", to assist people with language impairments. Pictogrammar is based on two types of ontology. The first one, called Simple Upper Ontology (SUpO), is defined as a formal semantic ontology describing detailed knowledge of actualities. The latter can be simple words, with an important interest, to avoid and solve linguistic issues in order to automate the grammatical supervision. The second type, called PictOntology, is defined as an ontology developed to manage a set of pictograms linked to SUpO. Furthermore, PictOntology has four main properties. The first one is to share a common ontology for students, language pathologists, family and caregivers. The second property consists in implementing an effective predictive parser. Then, the third one is the motor planning overload, and the last property consists in generating a natural language, which is grammatically correct even if the input is not.

In order to encourage pictogram-based communication within medical settings, [20] developed a smartwatch application that offers a small number of pictogram's symbols that are designed specifically for emergency medical applications. The proposed application is developed through intuitive icons and interactive symbols. It is composed of four basic parts. The first one, Band aid, describes how to communicate a need for medical aid, while the second part is designated for moods and emotions via smiley face icons. Then, the third part is an apple icon to describe diet and allergy issues. Finally, the last one is a call out balloon for the chat.

In regards to developing health care applications, several research work on the use and evaluation of pictograms have been reported in the literature. In [21], the authors assess and investigate the impact of pictograms on the medication adherence through relevant articles from medical databases, such as PubMed and MEDLINE. The experimental investigation show that ten of seventeen studies have reported the significant role of pictograms, which complement the textual and oral information associated with medication. According to the reported studies, pictograms are efficient to illustrate graphically medical instructions and improve patient's understanding.

Following on the success in the pharmaceutical area, the impact of using meaningful pictograms is sill increasing. Besides, the graphical representations offered by pictograms are considered as an important means to convey clear and understandable messages. For instance, the target people, low-literacy patients, might need pictograms to remind them about the time to take a given medicine [22].

In the agriculture field, a new application based on pictograms is proposed in [23] to help low-literacy farmers. The proposed application allows farmers to manipulate complex machines. The authors relied on an artist to create graphics related to the instructions to operate the machines. In addition, the authors added some sketches following the work in [24].

Note that the use of pictograms is not the only approach adopted to develop communication aid. Smart devices are also used to assist in communication and engagement. In [25], the authors conducted an evaluation of a smartphone application, to assist individuals having intellectual, visual and motor disabilities, to use Whats-App messages, telephone calls, and access to leisure activities. The proposed application relies on a smartphone (Samsung A3) having an automated process via a MacroDroid application [26]. It has been found that, without this tool, the participants' performance is close to zero on communication and leisure activities. During the conducted experiment, the authors observe that the frequency of sending and receiving Whats-App messages and the use of leisure activities increases.

In [27], the authors evaluate an extended version of a smartphone aided application, which supports daily communication and leisure activities for individuals with intellectual and/or visual disabilities. The involved participants have participated in the program listed in [25]. In addition, the extended application depends on a new smartphone (a Samsung Galaxy J4 Plus device, which is operated by an Android 9.0 operating system and MacroDroid). This application relies on alternated periods dedicated for the participants to be engaged in communication and leisure with periods in which they were provided with instructions for daily activities. With the smartphone-aided application in [25], the participants were engaged in communication and leisure. However, they did not use any activity. It has been noted that, with the extended smartphone aided application, the participants maintain successful communication and leisure engagement. The participants also start carrying out activities with success.

III. Extending Pictopages for Arabic-speaking Newcomers to Canada

In [1], a methodology has been proposed to develop a communication aid tool based on Pictopages software to allow Arabic-speaking newcomers to select, from a list of pictrograms, the message to be communicated. Upon selection, the communication aid provides a recorded audio output of the corresponding word, phrase, or sentence in Arabic and English. Pictopages is available on iOS devices and has been commonly adopted for special needs individuals. The idea is to extend it to assist the Arabic-speaking refugees new community in Saskatchewan, Canada. The methodology and the related tool (extending Pictopages) has the following limitations. First, Pictopages software is only available for iPads, which makes it out of reach to newcomers. Second, Pictopages requires a manual addition and customization of new pictrograms. Moreover, audio messages related to the added pictograms have then to be manually produced and added. This manual process is a tedious task especially given that we will expect to add a large number of items meeting the users' needs and requirements. In [28], the authors highlight and criticize the manual aspect of creating pictograms, and consider this process as time consuming, and causing complicated navigation by the end-users. Moreover, the methodology in [1] for building and evaluating the tool requires the recruitment and face-to-face interaction with a set of volunteers, from the Arabic-speaking refugee community. These two tasks have been facilitated by the Regina Public Library (RPL), and initial meetings have been conducted to collect feedback on common interest areas (as shown in Figure 1). However, face to face interaction with the participants to evaluate the new tool is not currently possible due to the current COVID-19 measures. Regardless of the situation with the pandemic, the recruitment procedure is restricted to those individuals in connection with

RPL. This limits the diversity in terms of literacy level, English skills, age group and others.

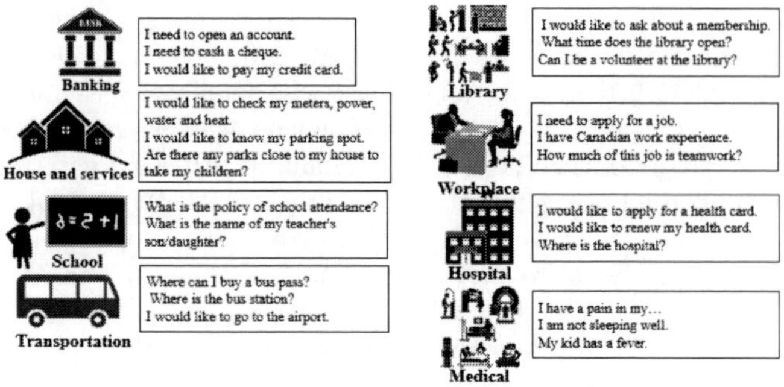

Fig. 1. Newcomers' areas of interest

IV. Proposed System

Our proposed system is meant to address the objectives and overcoming the limitations of the tool reported in the previous section [1]. More precisely, our ultimate goal is to facilitate the communication in the host country official languages (English and French), improve verbal communication skills, encourage community engagement, and accelerate newcomers integration, self-reliance and contribution to society. Therefore, our objective consists in building a web-based communication system that assists newcomers in different scenarios, such as daily routine, seeking a service, and when facing emergency situations. In this regard, we first start by gathering an initial study corpus containing more than 800 unstructured articles from Arabic Wikipedia. The corpus is then provided as an input to an NLP module to extract and annotate Arabic items, thanks to the Finite-State transducer formalism. Furthermore, all the established Finite-State transducers will merge extraction paths and annotation nodes, which defines the OWL syntax to generate a structured output. Besides, these Finite-State transducers are regrouped in a cascade acting on the study corpus in a precise order to reduce the execution time and to minimize the extraction and annotation errors. This way, the NLP process leads to the generation of an Arabic ontology that becomes multilingual by adding English and French (and other languages) via a translation API related to Wikipedia. Thereafter, all the annotated and structured items go through a process consisting in organizing them based on our multilingual ontology's levels and calling the adequate image and link to Wikipedia. The organization process is included in the creation of the Web pages composing our communication tool using Web design languages. Likewise, important functionalities, such as automatic audio message for each item's label in three languages, are also added. Finally, we propose new features, such as translation (text-to-text and speech-to-speech), text-to-speech conversion, speech recognition and localization via APIs. In what follows, we present the architecture of our proposed system.

Our proposed system evolves over time (according to users' needs) and can easily be extended, thanks to its dynamic multilingual ontology and other features. Moreover, our system follows a three-layer architecture, as shown in Figure 2.

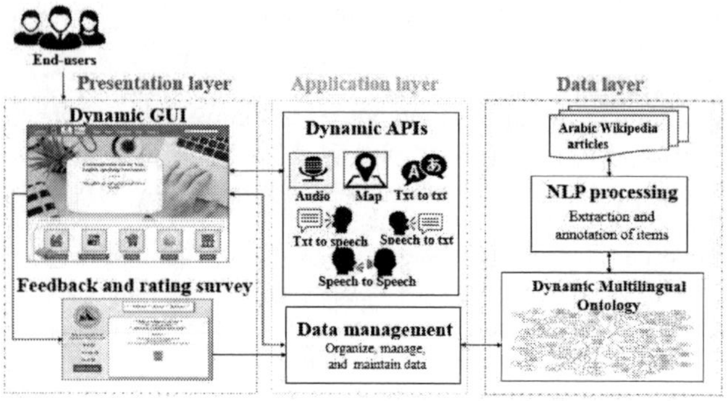

Fig. 2. Architecture of our proposed system

The first one (leftmost layer), called "Presentation", aims to present a Web-based GUI in an ergonomic view, in order to interact with users and collect their requests and feedback. The received feedback can be seen as a form of learning users' requirements and preferences, in order to achieve a perfective maintenance of our system. The second layer, called "Application" layer, is the heart of our system. This layer works behind the "Presentation" layer, and executes users requests through a communication with APIs and the "Data" layer.

V. Multilingual Ontology

Our proposed multilingual ontology has been created by following two main phases. In the first phase, an NLP process is conducted to extract and annotate Arabic items. Then, the second phase consists in translating these Arabic items in English and French, based on a Wikipedia API. The NLP process exploits a deep linguistic study that we have done using an Arabic Wikipedia corpus. Analyzing this corpus allows us to identify the candidate items through studying their forms or context, and to explore the related concepts and sub-concepts. Furthermore, the resulting conceptualization has an important level of granularity that increases based on the richness of the article content. A linguistic study has been performed to match the identified terms and their associated concepts with the OWL annotation syntax. This permits to specify the annotation path that will be exploited during the NLP process. Figure 3 describes our multilingual ontology with its concepts and sub-concepts.

After conducting the NLP process corresponding to phase one, we generate the OWL files from the semi-structured articles storing the extracted and annotated Arabic items thanks to an extractor that we have implemented in PHP. These generated OWL files are the input to the second phase, we described earlier for translating items from Arabic to English and French, to obtain the final multilingual form of our ontology. This translation process is also ensured by a PHP code that sends the queries to a Wikipedia API and organizes the obtained results to facilitate their integration in

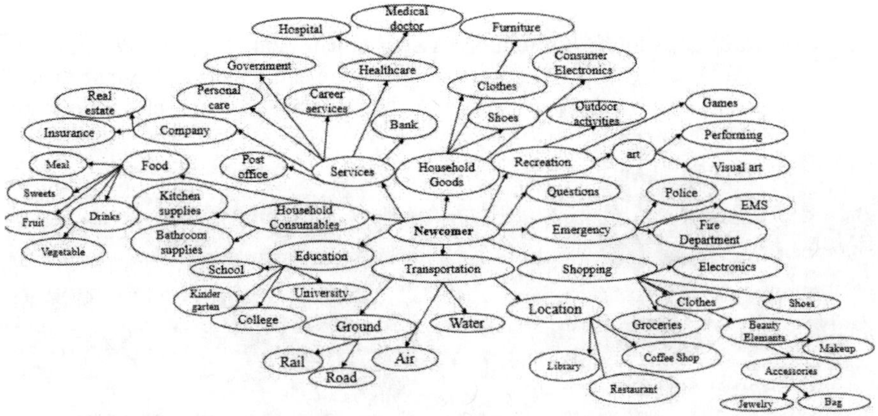

Fig. 3. Proposed Multilingual Ontology

our Web-based communication tool. Figure 4 illustrates an example taken from the OWL file associated with the sub-sub-concept "Fruits", which belongs to the sub-concept "Food". The latter belongs in its turn to the main concept "Household Consumables", as shown in Figure 3.

```
<owl:Thing rdf:about="#أناناس">
<rdf:type rdf:resource="#Fruits"/>
<rdfs:label xml:lang="en">Pineapple</rdfs:label>
<rdfs:label xml:lang="fr">Ananas</rdfs:label>
</owl:Thing>
<owl:Thing rdf:about="#تفاح">
<rdf:type rdf:resource="#Fruits"/>
<rdfs:label xml:lang="en">Apple</rdfs:label>
<rdfs:label xml:lang="fr">Pomme</rdfs:label>
</owl:Thing>
<owl:Thing rdf:about="#موز">
<rdf:type rdf:resource="#Fruits"/>
<rdfs:label xml:lang="en">Banana</rdfs:label>
<rdfs:label xml:lang="fr">Banane</rdfs:label>
</owl:Thing>
```

Fig. 4. Example of extracted items annotated in OWL

VI. Web-Based Application

Our proposed communication tool is a dynamic Web-based application, which belongs to the High-tech category. The related Web-pages are coded using HTML, PHP, JavaScript and CSS. The main page contains five main sections respectively describing; the tool's objective, the ten main items representing the topics of interest, the translation module, the map localisation module and the Contact us/Survey rubric. In what follows, we describe each section.

Figure 5 lists the ten main topics of interests. Upon selection of the chosen item, an audio message is generated to read the item's label in the appropriate language. To navigate, the end-user needs to click on the chosen topic to get the related subset of items, in a hierarchical manner. Figure 3 in Section V lists the hierarchy of the different items. Among the main items, we added new information related to the COVID-19 pandemic, as shown in Figure 6.

Fig. 5. Main items of our communication aid

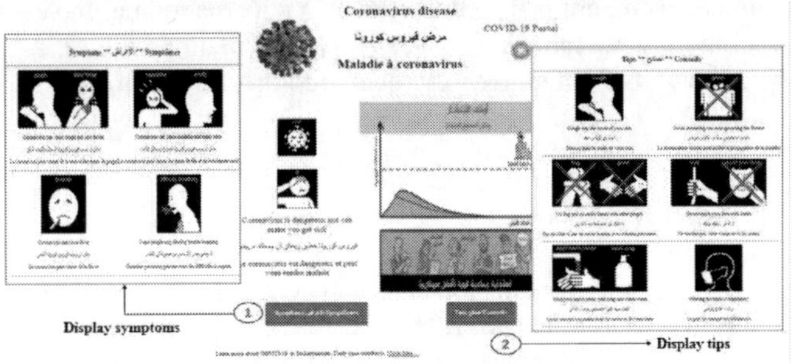

Fig. 6. Covid-19 information

These information are presented in an animated way, with audio messages, in order to attract users' attention. In this regard, we provided two links where the first one reports on daily information regarding the pandemic in Saskatchewan. The second link displays the disease's portal provided by Wikipedia.

A. Multilingual, Linked and Acoustic Items

Our communication aid contains items, which are associated with concepts corresponding to our ontology's levels listed in Figure 3. These items are represented by a colorful picture and buttons in three languages. We choose the 3D design to create these buttons in order to adapt our communication aid to new devices using touch screen features. Figure 7 shows an item called "air mattress", which belongs to the furniture's items.

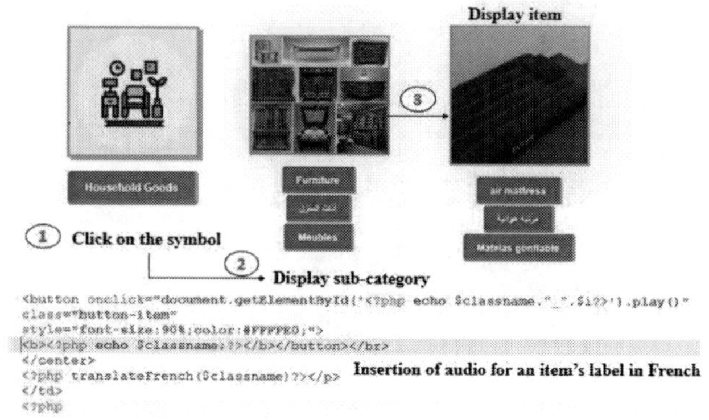

Fig. 7. Example of a multilingual item with audio output messages

The three labels related to this item are generated automatically via an API called MediaWiki API [29]. This API accepts several parameters, and the user can select the target language. We should mention that the generation of audio messages is done automatically via a Google API taking the labels as an input and generating an audio output. At first, we store this audio output after giving it a key in a hidden HTML tag. Then, we call the audio via a JavaScript instruction added to a "Onclick" function in the target button. The picture related to each item is linked to Arabic Wikipedia to help those newcomers who can read to get more information. Figure 3 also shows the difference between a colorful symbol and a picture, for recognizing a given item.

B. Translation and Speech Recognition

Translation is among the most important features for newcomers. Our tool provides three options for this feature: text-to-text, speech-to-speech, and text-to-speech. The first module, related to a text-to-text translation is illustrated in Figure 8.

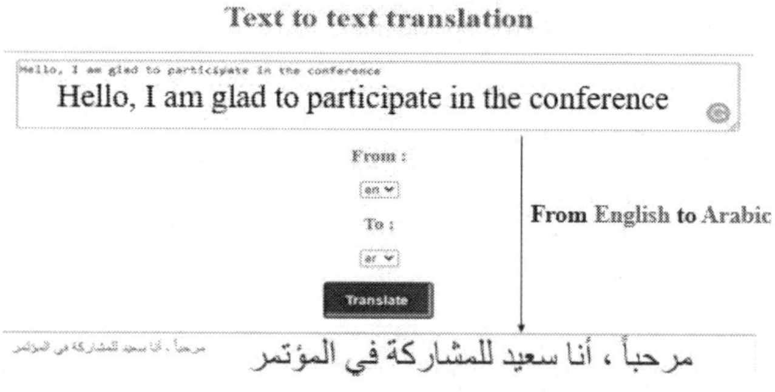

Fig. 8. Text to text translation

The second module, related to text-to-speech conversion, helps newcomers to learn and improve their pronunciation in English and French. This module can also be used to learn the Arabic language. The third module, related to speech-to-speech translation (see Figure 9), can be handy for those with visual impairment. This service allows users to speak into the microphone using their native language. The listener will then receive the translated speech in the target language.

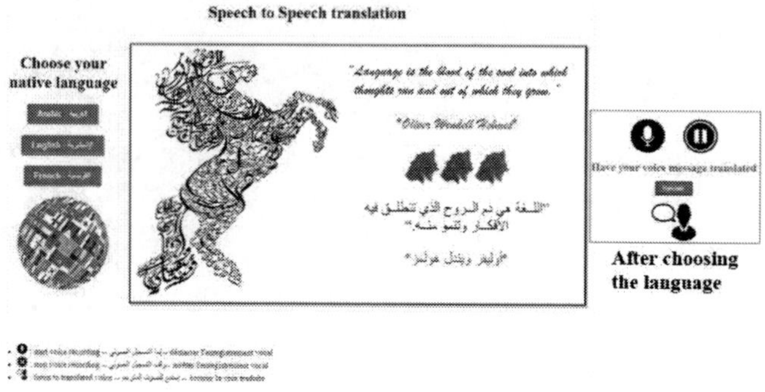

Fig. 9. Speech to speech translation

For each recognized language, we start by translating transcripts, thanks to the used API, into the target language. Then, we convert the translated transcript into a voice record. By doing so, the final audio message is added and ready to be played by the listener. Here, the voice recognition is ensured through a Speech Recognition API [30]. As mentioned earlier, the three modules can be extended to other natural languages.

C. Geographic Localisation

A localisation service is provided via Google Maps web mapping service. Through this feature, the user can see the map and locates the target destination before going out thanks to the street view option. Figure 10 illustrates the result for searching "University of Regina" using the localisation service that we provide.

Fig. 10. Geographic localisation of the University of Regina

D. Feedback survey

To collect users' feedback, we implemented a survey that allows to improve our tool's functionalities, features and services. This survey includes a set of Yes/No questions, and rating, in three languages. Figure 11 shows the survey form, which aims to measure the end-users' satisfaction. Feedback are anonymous so participants feel more comfortable, as their privacy is protected.

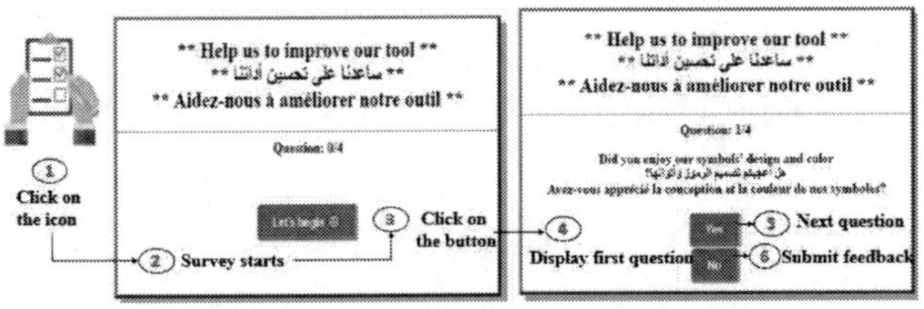

Fig. 11. Survey to collect users' feedback

VII. Conclusion and Future Work

We propose an extensible and dynamic Web-based communication tool for Arabic-speaking newcomers to Saskatchewan, Canada. Our communication tool follows a three-layer architecture designed to efficiently process end-users' requests. The top-layer ("Presentation layer") corresponds to a Web-based interface including five main sections, offering different services to the end-user. Among these services, a large set of items, corresponding to the main common information to newcomers, are arranged in a hierarchical manner, thanks to our multilingual ontology. These items are linked to Wikipedia, and are presented with text and audio sound messages, in three languages, generated automatically through an audio API. The other services include the speech/text translation module, the map localisation module, and a feedback survey. The speech/text translation module is particularly important as it allows a real-time verbal/text translation in the three languages. This can be a very useful communication tool for newcomers, especially in their first days in the host country.

In the near future, we plan to improve our tool's features and add new ones based on users' feedback. Then, we will enrich the textual communication of the chat-bot that we have implemented by adding an auditory option. This latter, aims to accelerate the time response and decision making, especially when the end-user has an emergent query requiring a quick response. Moreover, we will develop a learning module for young children in order to improve and develop their communication skills in the host country language(s). This will be done using known cartoon characters in animated conversations.

References

[1] M. Al-Ageili and M. Mouhoub, "Communication aid for non-english speaking newcomers," *arXiv preprint arXiv:2101.08319*, 2021.

[2] K. U. Rani, "Communication barriers," *Veda's Journal of English Language and Literature*, vol. 3, no. 2, pp. 74–76, 2016.

[3] I. E. Britannica. (1957) Encyclopædia britannica, incorporated 1957. [Online]. Available: https://www.britannica.com/., urldate = 2021-06

[4] Blissymbolics. (2021) Blissymbolics communication international. [Online]. Available: https://www.blissymbolics.org/

[5] Boardmaker. (2021) Boardmaker. [Online]. Available: https://goboardmaker.com/pages/boardmaker-online

[6] J. Scott, "Low tech methods of augmentative communication," *Augmentative Communication in Practice 2*, 1998.

[7] S. Glennen and D. C. DeCoste, *The handbook of augmentative and alternative communication*. Cengage Learning, 1997.

[8] R. Schlosser, "Roles of speech output in augmentative and alternative communication: Narrative review," *Augmentative and Alternative Communication*, vol. 19, no. 1, pp. 5–27, 2003.

[9] D. Jans and S. Clark, "High technology aids to communication," *Augmentative Communication in Practice 2*, 1994.

[10] C. Tijus, J. Meunier, B. Cambon de Lavalette, and J. Barcenilla, "Chapter 2: the design, understanding and usage of pictograms," *Written Documents in the Workplace,(Leiden, The Netherlands: BRILL, 2007) doi: https://doi. org/10.1163/9789004253254_003*, 2007.

[11] S. M. Otsubo, "A behavioral study of warning labels for consumer products: Perceived danger and use of pictographs," in *Proceedings of the Human Factors Society Annual Meeting*, vol. 32, no. 9. SAGE Publications Sage CA: Los Angeles, CA, 1988, pp. 536–540.

[12] T. P. A. of Pictogram, *Encyclopædia britannica*. Swedish Institute for Special Needs Education, 2001.

[13] S. MAHARAJ. (2017) Pictocom international. [Online]. Available: http://www.pictoworld.com/presentations.html

[14] N.-B. Takil, "Vocabulary acquisition with pictograms and contextual sentences in teaching turkish as a foreign language," *Turkish Studies International Periodical for the Languages, Literature and History of Turkish or Turkic*, vol. 11/3, no. 1, pp. 2133–2136, 2016.

[15] T. H. Clawson, J. Leafman, G. M. Nehrenz Sr, and S. Kimmer, "Using pictograms for communication," *Military medicine*, vol. 177, no. 3, pp. 291–295, 2012.

[16] M. Miller. (2016) A pictogram language designed for the displaced. [Online]. Available: http://www.fastcompany.com/3063452/a-pictogram-language-designed-for-the-displaced

[17] G. McNeill. (2015) Refugee communication board using symbols. [Online]. Available: http://www.callscotland.org/blog/refugee-communication-board-using-symbols

[18] A. Hart and S. I. Kindergarten, "Ancient forms of communication in the spanish immersion classroom: The use of pictograms and rebuses to promote the development of spanish language literacy," *Charlotte Teachers Institute*, 2015.

[19] F. Martínez-Santiago, M. Á. García-Cumbreras, A. Montejo-Ráez, and M. C. Díaz-Galiano, "Pictogrammar: an aac device based on a semantic grammar," in *Proceedings of the 11th Workshop on Innovative Use of NLP for Building Educational Applications*, 2016, pp. 142–150.

[20] K. Wołk, A. Wołk, K. Marasek, and W. Glinkowski, "Pictogram-based mobile first medical aid communicator," *Procedia computer science*, vol. 121, pp. 3–10, 2017.

[21] H. Sletvold, L. A. B. Sagmo, and E. A. Torheim, "Impact of pictograms on medication adherence: A systematic literature," *Patient Education and Counseling*, 2020.

[22] M. Montagne, "Pharmaceutical pictograms: a model for development and testing for comprehension and utility," *Research in Social and Administrative Pharmacy*, vol. 9, no. 5, pp. 609–620, 2013.

[23] W. S. Kisaalita and E. J. Sempiira, "Development of pictograms to communicate technological solution instructions (labeling) among low-literacy users," *Ergonomics in Design*, p. 1064804620959145, 2020.

[24] L. N. Ngoh and M. D. Shepherd, "Design, development, and evaluation of visual aids for communicating prescription drug instructions to non-literate patients in rural cameroon," *Patient education and counseling*, vol. 31, no. 3, pp. 245–261, 1997.

[25] G. E. Lancioni, N. N. Singh, M. F. O'Reilly, G. Alberti, V. Chiariello, C. Campanella, G. Grillo, and V. Tagliente, "A program based on common technology to support communication exchanges and leisure in people with intellectual and other disabilities," *Behavior Modification*, vol. 43, no. 6, pp. 879–897, 2019.

[26] MacroDroid. (2021) Macrodroid. [Online]. Available: http://macrodroid.com/

[27] G. E. Lancioni, N. N. Singh, M. F. O'Reilly, J. Sigafoos, G. Alberti, V. Chiariello, and S. Buono, "Extended smartphone-aided program to sustain daily activities, communication and leisure in individuals with intellectual and sensory-motor disabilities," *Research in Developmental Disabilities*, vol. 105, p. 103722, 2020.

[28] D. Schwab, P. Trial, C. Vaschalde, L. Vial, E. Esperança-Rodier, and B. Lecouteux, "Providing semantic knowledge to a set of pictograms for people with disabilities: a set of links between wordnet and arasaac: Arasaac-wn," in *LREC*, 2020.

[29] MediaWiki. (2021) Mediawiki api. [Online]. Available: https://www.wikidata.org/w/api.php?

[30] M. W. Docs. (2021) Speech recognition. [Online]. Available: https://developer.mozilla.org/en-US/docs/Web/API/SpeechRecognition

Mood Adaptive Display Coloring - Utilizing Modern Machine Learning Techniques and Intelligent Coloring to Influence the Mood of PC Users

Lukas Brodschelm, Felix Gräber, Daniel Hieber and Marc Hermann

Dept. of Computer Science
Aalen University
Aalen, Germany
Email: firstname.lastname@hs-aalen.de

***Abstract*—Humans are able to recognize a wide range of colors and interpret them in many different ways. Besides obvious effects like highlight and beautification, these colors can influence the emotional state of humans in a significant way. While this is no new information and color psychology is a heavily discussed topic in the psychological area, few research has been conducted in the human computer interaction area of this topic. Heavily relying on color in user interfaces of any kind the emotional aspect is often ignored and unwritten rules are applied. The gaming field provides many examples for such rules with red explosives and blue mana. Breaking with this trend, we present a novel mood adaptive display coloring approach. Utilizing psychological studies and state of the art machine learning technologies an intelligent coloring system is implemented. It is able to directly influence the emotion of human users, combating negative emotions and supporting positive feelings. Further a completely functional prototype is implemented. While fully working, there is much work left to refine and improve the project in this heavily neglected area.**

Keywords*—*Advanced Human Computer Interaction; Mood Adapting Coloring; Adaptive Display Coloring; Color Psychology; Emotion Recognition.

I. INTRODUCTION

Colors have been an important part of Human Computer Interaction (HCI) since the introduction of multi color displays. Nowadays, it is impossible to imagine software without them, the old default black and white is only used as a stylistic instrument. Even hardware is often produced with ambient lighting as a selling point. Colors are used as an important part of designs for Graphical User Interfaces (GUIs) in software like games, operating systems (OS) and business applications, helping players to get the required overview or leading workers through complex procedures with intelligent coloring.

However, the possibilities of colors do not end with highlighting certain things and improving the quality of life therefore, they can also be used to directly affect the user. Understanding the influence of color on the human user, clever coloring can increase the performance of a worker or calm him down during a difficult period. Such techniques can not only boost the productivity and improve emotional state, they can also have a beneficial effect on the health of users.

Color psychology is a highly disputed topic and the opinions heavily diverge about the facts and scientific evidence. However, thanks to this popularity of the topic much research is conducted in this area, allowing a solid foundation for further research in the HCI environment.

Using state of the art technologies, like facial recognition systems or intelligent devices such as smart watches, the mood of a user can already be recognized and measured quite precisely. The resulting information can be used to classify the emotions and start processes to reinforcing or combating these.

In this work, we introduce a novel approach to interact with users through decent adaptive coloring, providing emotional support and the best conditions to successfully master their current task. This is achieved through Mood Adaptive Display Coloring (MAD-Coloring), a framework to change the color of the display while exposing a generic API for clients to control the color according to the mood of the user. Further two simple clients will be implemented. While one of them provides a minimal boilerplate for further implementations, the second one utilizes state of the art machine learning techniques to recognize mood changes and provide the best suited coloring solution for the detected mood state.

The remainder of this paper is structured as follows: Section II provides background information for a better understanding of the work and introducing required secondary research. Section III describes the general concept of MAD-Coloring, while Section IV explains the currently implemented state of MAD-Coloring. Section V provides an overview of related works. Finally Section VI concludes the paper and lists further research options.

II. BACKGROUND

This section outlines the elementary information about color psychology and display coloring frameworks, as well as face recognition basics and a survey about the emotional effect of color, conducted during this work.

A. Color Theory and Psychology

While color is often accepted as an omnipresent thing without further questioning, it is actually a well defined construct which can be described accurately with its three components: hue, saturation and brightness. The emotional effect of color is closely linked to all three of those, therefore an adjustment of one of its values can lead to a completely different emotional reaction. This means e.g., a green with high brightness and saturation has a different emotional effect than a green with the same hue and saturation but low brightness.

Even though color psychology is highly disputed down to its fundamental theories, it is possible to elaborate some general statements which are used in this work. While many animals only see different shades of grey and some can even see with infrared or ultraviolet vision, humans have settled in the middle with a complex color perception. This has lead to the development of a society where colors play an important role in the day to day life, religion, work and freetime. Most people have a favorite color, and every kid, regardless of their origin, knows the red cross, star or moon provides them with help if needed.

While most humans see color the same way, it has quite different meanings for them. The context in which a color is experienced and from whom is fundamental for its interpretation. Age is an important factor, as studies prove, that children have different associations with certain colors than adults or elder people. Gender can also play a decisive role [1][2][3].

Elliot and Maier laid the theoretical base for contextual color psychology with their work in 2012 [1], highlighting six key properties of the psychological impacts of color:

- There might be psychological relevant associations with a color.
- Presentation colors might influence psychological operations, including but not limited to basic impulses such as attraction and avoidance.
- Associations with colors might trigger affective, cognitive or behavioral reactions. This happens subconscious or without intention.
- Color meanings and associations are influenced by both trained and inherited behavior.
- The relation between color perception and association is bidirectional. color perception has an impact on psychological processes and psychological processes have an impact on the way color is perceived.
- The psychological effect of color heavily depends on the context. The context is so important, that the influence of the same color might result in opposite effects for different contexts.

Those core statements are used by other research (e.g., [2]) in the field of color psychology and should be considered when targeting a psychological effect utilizing colors.

Li [3] gives a detailed overview over the preferences and effects with different groups of people in a medical context, more precisely during hospital stays. Children prefer brightly saturated colors and overall very colorful environments. These provide distraction from the tense situation and a calming effect, connected to the coloring, could be proven. Adults on the other hand tend to favor clean, cool colors like white, blue and grey. They associate these with a professional environment and thus a higher chance of a successfully treatment. There is also a connected calming effect. However, the effect is achieved through the impression of a professional environment, that evokes the feeling of a qualified treatment when seeking medical care. It is therefore only partially connected to the color and already an effect of the original feeling emitted by the color: professionalism. The author further states, that elder people tend to prefer warmer colors, although not as bright and less saturated than children. These colors help them to relax and effectively reduce anxiety. The professional, cool colors like white or grey even provide a negative effect on elders and sometimes children. This originates from the partly occurring associated with anxiety, loneliness and fear. The phenomenon is known in the color psychology as white scare.

Focusing on the target-context oriented effect of color, Maier et al. outline how the psychological impact of a color changes with the task domain [4]. Stated are the findings of different studies which point out that colors provide a performance enhancing effect in physical competitions. An example for this can be found in sports, where teams wearing red tricots win more games than those wearing any other hue. However, when it comes to an intellectual target-context the color red seems to have no, or even a negative effect, on the performance.

B. Emotion Recognition

Facial and Image Recognition is currently one of the most popular fields of machine learning. Elementary face detection is not a technical challenge anymore and a camera input can be analysed in realtime, with only a few dozen lines of code (e.g., [5]).

The popularity of such use cases provides us with the base for emotion recognition through feature detection in the mimic of peoples faces. Combining this technology with display coloring frameworks allows us to design systems which are capable of autonomously detecting emotions and correctly using different color overlays to improve and reinforce them.

Several models have been trained with a fairly high accuracy to detect emotion from images. These models focus on a combination of facial features to detect the emotional state behind pictures of faces. The model of Yang et al. [6] relies on the extraction of the mouth and eyes, achieve successful detection rates of up to 93% for certain emotions and a mean of 87%.

As emotions have a broad impact on the users behavior the detection is not only limited to image recognition. For a precise detection of emotions multiple sources of information can be used. Ghosh et al. suggests an approach to determine emotion based on speech recognition [7]. By combining multiple ways of emotion recognition detection accuracy can be improved even further. However, a background software with recording capabilities is rather problematic from a privacy point of view. Therefore, the improved recognition accuracy does not outweigh the privacy violation.

Other possibilities to increase the accuracy and therefore the value of automatic emotion detection could be provided by smart wearables like smart watches or fitness trackers. Measurements like the pulse could then be used to determine the stress level and provide other valuable insights. However, as the prototype should be as lean as possible this approach

TABLE I. EMOTIONAL CONNECTION TO COLORS SURVERY, RESPONDENTS = 522, VALUES IN %

Color	Ca	V	Sa	Co	M	St	H
red	3,79	14,86	13,38	7,32	9,37	**35,20**	8,45
orange	8,24	**19,41**	**18,09**	6,02	3,02	16,94	13,49
yellow	3,53	**21,15**	7,21	8,95	3,78	14,31	17,53
green	**22,09**	**18,34**	**15,44**	15,49	2,27	2,96	**24,72**
blue	**25,23**	9,64	**16,32**	**28,74**	7,55	4,77	14,25
violet	11,37	3,35	11,32	5,34	11,48	5,76	6,56
grey	11,11	0,40	5,44	13,08	**27,49**	3,95	2,27
black	12,81	2,68	10,29	13,43	**29,61**	6,74	4,41
pink	1,83	10,17	2,50	1,72	5,44	9,38	8,32

is not further considered in this work. The required multi machine solution with means of communication between devices would cause a too excessive codebase for the aspired simple prototype.

C. Emotional Effects of Colors - a Survey

As our excessive study of related research projects and studies could not provide a common interpretation of the concrete connection between emotions and colors, a simple survey was conducted. This survey however is only used to generate a default profile for the prototype, it is not scientifically representative. In the survey 522 people were asked to think of a color if confronted with an emotion. Multiple answers were allowed, this should allow the detection of patterns, e.g., all warm colors are connected with emotion X. The emotions which could be chosen in the survey were (Ca)lm, (V)italising, (Sa)fety, (Co)ncentrated, (M)elancholy, (St)ressed and (H)appieness. The possible answers consisted of colors which can easily be displayed on a display and provide strong contrasts to each other, allowing a meaningful implementation.

The surveys findings match well with the general statements from Rider [2]. While warmer colors (orange, yellow) have an arousing effect, cooler colors (blue, green) have a relaxing, calming effect. Rider further mentions the wide spread of possible emotions connected to green depending on brightness, saturation and context. As we only asked for the hue the subjects could not differentiate between different types of green. Therefore, green is strongly connected with most positive emotions, which, however, most likely refer to different types of green.

The survey results also concur with the findings of Kido [8], reinforcing the calming effect of green and blue. The deafening effect of red, determined by Kido, also matches the very strong association with stress by our survey.

The strong association of orange with safety, which cannot be found in other studies or surveys, most likely is caused by a bias of our survey. The poll was conducted on a group of people from the same community, where orange is a frequent and positively interpreted color, which could explain this behavior.

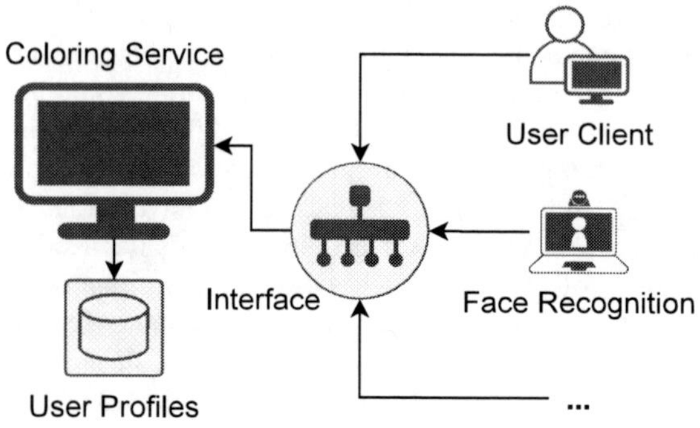

Figure 1. MAD-Coloring modular architecture concept.

D. Display Overlays

Display overlays are no new research topic and many refined products are available. In the gaming area they are omnipresent with the most popular example being steams ingame-overlay, other popular examples being the Nvidia Geforce Experience overlay, the Discord overlay or Overwolf. However, these are all limited to the gaming use cases and only Overwolf allows great modification freedom.

Other overlays with more modification freedome include OnTopReplica, Hudkit and pqiv. The pqiv image viewer is able to display transparent pictures and can easily be placed on top of other windows. Due to its implementation in Python, cross platform capabilities are provided. Missing click through support however requires extensive extension work to create a functional non blocking overlay.

OnTopReplica, a C# project, supports the display of selected windows on top of others on Windows systems. While it supports click through and adjustable opacity, it is limited to Windows and requires an additional overlay-window. This not only decreases the compatible systems but also increases the overhead significantly.

Hudkit is a C based framework with an exposed JavaScript-API [9]. The framework supports all Linux X-desktops and some OS X systems. It's main HTML page can be modified like Overwolf overlays using HTML and JavaScript. The page can then receive new input via established APIs like Websocket or WebGL and change the display accordingly. Multiple monitors and click through events are supported by default. Providing a powerful small footprint framework.

III. SOLUTION CONCEPT

This section provides insights in the architecture and concept for the MAD-Coloring prototype. The modular architecture approach is shown in Fig. 1.

The architecture is separated in 3 sections. The coloring service, the clients accessing and controlling the coloring and the interface, enabling communications between the clients and the display coloring.

The display coloring has to be able to project a color adjustable overlay on top of all connected monitors. To fully leverage the psychological effects the overlay must not be limited to gamma or brightness adjustments but must be able to display any color. The display must not reduce the productivity and therefore has to enable all actions which are possible without an overlay, e.g., right/left clicking or text selection. Further, the vision quality and readability of displayed content must not be reduced any further than necessary. This will be compared against the light constraints coming with night lights, e.g., reduced contrast and slightly changed colors. The coloring service further gets supplied with at least one user profile file. This allows users to adjust the color optimally for themselves and maximize the effect of MAD-Coloring.

The communication between clients and coloring should be kept as simple as possible to fit into the modular approach. This should enable easy access to the coloring service for new clients as well as the replacement of the Coloring implementation itself, e.g., if required by a change of the OS. To achieve this a simple interface should be created, supplying all required functionality for the coloring and client programms. New implementations could then simply use this interface and would be able to be used with the old clients/Coloring. This further enables the exchange of the communication framework with changes to only the interface itself. Clients and coloring would not be affected and could be used without any changes. The underlying communication framework should be chosen OS specific and use existing infrastructure rather than implementing something new. Therefore, reducing the implementation effort, requirements and overhead caused by MAD-Coloring.

Due to the interface, client programms can be created with minimal restrictions. For the prototype two client applications are planed. A manual user client, allowing the selection of moods by the user via text input, and a face recognition background service, detecting the mood via a webcam and changing the display coloring accordingly.

Thanks to the highly adjustable user profiles, changes or fine tuning of the color mapping in the implementation are always possible with little to none programming experience. This allows interested psychologists, therapists and doctors to use the MAD-Coloring on their own. Enabling them to adjust the system according to their own knowledge and research in the area of color psychology, highly tailored to their target group needs. Further, users trying the prototype on their own can adjust their profile as they most see fit, according to their own preferences.

IV. MAD-Coloring

This section gives insight in the implemented MAD-Coloring prototype for Linux systems, as well as the created simple user client and emotion detection client.

A. Interface

The interface is build on top of the D-Bus, as it represents the default solution for inter-process communication of most Linux desktop environments and therefore already is available on the system. This removes the need to install new software frameworks, perfectly fitting into the low overhead architecture of the solution concept.

The interface itself is separated into two parts. The main (top level) interface, providing simple python functions and a bottom level interface consisting of a D-Bus service and a corresponding client.

To ease the use of the interface, and allow easy interchangeability of the underlying system, the the top level interface has been implemented which only exposes the core functionality to client developers. It can be considered as a wrapper around the bottom level interface, providing the two required functionalities to implement new clients or a coloring service. These is a getter function, which is awaiting a new mood, and a setter function, to set the mood. Clients make use of the setter to specify the mood, while the coloring service uses the getter to detect mood changes originating from the clients.

While the top level interface is rather simple, the bottom-line D-Bus communication is more extensive. The D-Bus service specified by it exposes an interface with three methods on the D-Bus session bus. However, only one of the three methods is currently used in the top level interface, a setter for the mood. The other methods provide a getter for the currently active color code and the possibility to change the user profile on the fly, providing a boilerplate for coming extensions. For the top level interface setter function a connection to the exposed D-Bus interface is opened and the provided bottom level interface setter method is used to send the color change via the D-Bus.

It is up to the client if the communication is done via interface provided in this work or directly via the D-Bus. On the one hand the baseline D-Bus service provides a richer API and might be used with any programming language or due to some universal command line interface tools. On the other hand however using the Python interface instead is less complex and allows an easy exchange of the underlying D-Bus framework, which might be required due to the change of the OS. Requiring only the getter and setter pair at the top level interface allows an easy exchange of the base interface, as the new framework must only realize this two functions. When sticking to Linux Desktops the D-Bus provides more extensive functionality and grants the exchange of the programming language, but the provided python interface grants interchangeability of OS and base interface. Choosing the right interface is up to the developer and should be decided individually according to the needs of the implementation.

B. User Profiles

The profiles are implemented as .conf files. Using this well known and easy to use standard allows the modification of these files without any knowledge of programming. This is important, as for now the prototype provides no GUI to edit the user profiles and the users have to edit their profiles with a text editor on their own.

In the scope of the prototype, a default configuration is provided. The emotions and their respective coloring are

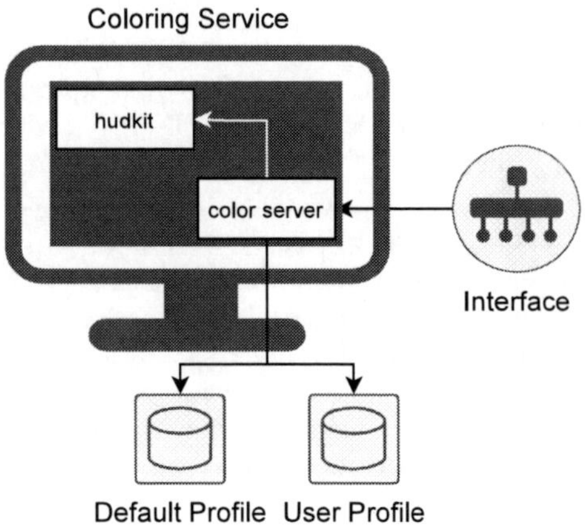

Figure 2. MAD-Coloring color service.

according to the survey in Section II. If the user wants to change the color of an emotion she can either change the default profile or create a new user profile. Following an override approach, the coloring service will always check the specific user profile first, if the emotion is not included the service will fallback to the default profile. This makes it quite comfortable to specify some custom mood/color pairs, while keeping default settings for most.

It is also possible to define new emotion/color pairs in the user profiles, wich are not defined in the default profile. However, in order to be used by the clients the emotions have to be added to their codebase as well.

C. Coloring-Service

For the coloring service a combination between a modified version of hudkit, introduced in Section II, and a self-made Python Color server is being used (Fig. 2).

Hudkit handles the display coloring. The color server provides the color services interface and control unit. This is achieved by implementing the earlier introduced Python interface and accessing the user profiles. Utilizing the Python interface, the server listens to changes of the mood send by a client. If a mood change is detected the server resolves the color according to the used profile. First the user specific configuration is read, if no entry for the specific mood is found the default config is read.

After resolving the color, the server sends a signal with the determined color to the hudkit webserver. Should a mood not be defined in the configuration files, the color server defaults to black with low saturation and displays an error. With this error handling a missing emotion does not lead to further problems durring the runtime, but clearly signals the user that a problem with the used client has ocurred. This error color will not be interpreted as an emotion by the user, as black is not used by the default configuration and we highly discourage the usage of black as it is mostly related to negativ emotions (cf. Table I). To counter possible negative emotions associated with black, the low saturation and higher brightness creates a grey overlay in the Hudkit server. This can be interpreted by users as boring, but will not trigger negative emotions.

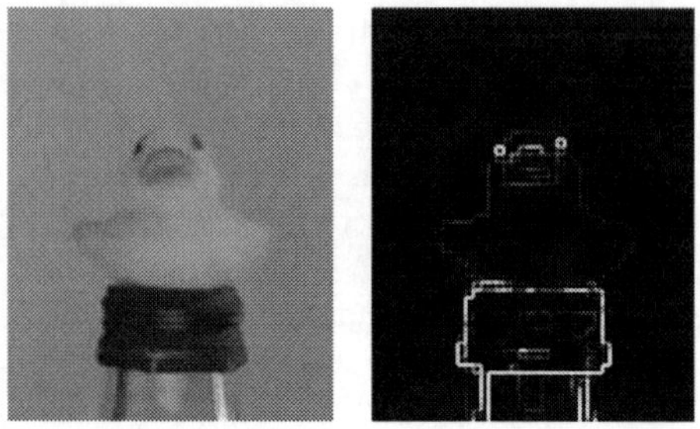

Figure 3. Face detection symbol image - feature highlighting.

D. Clients

The prototype includes two clients. A simple user client and a intelligent emotion detection client. The simple client provides a basic GUI to enter the current emotion and change the display coloring accordingly. It is implemented in Python and directly accesses the D-Bus instead of the Python wrapper interface.

The second client is an emotion recognition client, detecting the current emotional state of the user via image processing of a webcam feed. As a foundation the work of Rovai was used, creating a face recognition system utilizing a webcam with Python and OpenCV [5].

However, the final implementation differs fundamentally, as the client was extended to enable emotion recognition and connected to the Python interface to communicate with the coloring service. Further, a multi face detection was implemented, preventing a flickering color change if two or more faces are detected. As a result the client will not send emotional changes to the coloring service, until only one face is left in its field of view. A simplified version of the used feature detection can be found in Fig. 3. The eyes are clearly detected in white and the mouth in green. This allows the usage of the features in the neural network to determine the mood.

V. Case Study

Our current team solely consists of researchers from the IT domain, we have not yet consulted any psychological/medical experts. Thus we conducted a technical case study instead of a psychological evaluation of our prototype. The study was conducted on a Lenovo ThinkPad with 14GB RAM, an AMD onboard graphic chip, using a GNU/Linux operating system with a gnome X.Org desktop. During the test runs checks regarding usability impairments were conducted.

To pre-empt ethical concerns without the approval of an ethic-committee our test user simply controlled MAD-Coloring and rated possible concerns regarding the readability and usability of the desktop with activated MAD-Coloring. However, he was not exposed to the software for longer

Figure 4. MAD-Coloring in effect for moods A) neutral B) mad C) bored.

periods. The face recognition was triggered with prepared photos instead of live images of the test user.

As a scenario a computer science student with no prior experience of MAD-Coloring was instructed to start the MAD coloring client and conduct a manual color change via the simple user client. Afterwards the face recognition client had to be started. He was supplied with a computer which had a preinstalled MAD-Coloring service and the madservice's linux manual page.

The user was able to activate the service, change the color and start the face recognition client in less than a minute. All color changes and emotion detections worked without any problems. The user did not experience any problems regarding reduced readability, yet the usability in color sensitive applications like image editing was highly impaired because of MAD-Coloring's color overlay. However, this was an expected side effect as mentioned in our solution concept (cf. Section III). The effect of MAD-Coloring for some emotions can be seen in Fig. 4.

Following, we suggest a method for measuring the effects of MAD-Coloring in coming evalutions, which still needs to be reviewed by psychological experts. Since MAD-Coloring is designed to be used in daily routines and any kind of test scenario might cause indifferences, we strongly recommend to evaluate MAD-Coloring integrated in the daily life of subjects.

To quantify MAD-Coloring, we introduce the concept of an mood diary where subjects record their emotional condition, and whether they are able to concentrate for work or not. The subjects might write this mood diary for a reasonable period (2-4 weeks). Afterwards, based on these diaries, basic emotional profiles can be created for all subjects.

In the second phase we recommend to split up the subjects into three groups. Group A will be working with our MAD-Coloring and the preconfigured color profile (based on scientific work from the color psychology domain and our own survey). Group B is working with MAD-Coloring as well, but with "anti"-colors, which have been associated to be negative according to a specific mood (e.g., red if the subject is already mad). Group C is the control group, which continues working without any influence from MAD-Coloring. This phase should be conducted over a larger time period (2-4 months or longer), as most likely some time is required to get used to the color changes. Especially at the beginning these changes could have a negative impact on the subjects.

By comparing the deltas of the three groups the essential effects of MAD-Coloring can be determined and whether the effect depends on specific colors or just generally on shifting these. Afterwards further evaluations can be planned targeted on the existing data.

VI. Related Research

While the idea of color psychology is not new, there is to our best knowledge no closely related research in the HCI context. However, some other research topics in the context can be viewed as relevant.

A. Blue Light Filtering

At the first sight blue light filtering software seems to differ quite significantly from our solution, but the fundamental ideas are quite similar. Both software solutions modify the color shade of the display to obtain effects on the human user. However, blue light filtering is based on different medical effects (cf. [10]) and in most cases it is implemented completely different than MAD-Coloring.

While MAD-Coloring is based on the psychological effect of colors and the emotions triggered by colors, the idea of blue light filtering, as described in [11] is based on physical and bio-chemical effects [12]. They determine that blue light emitted by screens contains more energy than any other color. Further, it is more exhaustive for the human eye than other colors. In addition to the physical aspects blue light suppresses the production of the sleeping hormone melatonin which can cause sleeplessness.

As aforementioned, blue filtering software is often implemented completely different than our solution. Its common among blue filters to adjustments the alpha channel to suppress parts of the blue light. The resource costs for this approach can be expected to be less than those for overlay based filters. This is due by the fact, that the graphics card is not required to compute a translucent overlay in. However, for our MAD-Coloring system an alpha shift approach does not fit the requirements since the software needs to display tints in various colors.

B. Colors and Trust in Userinterface Design

Hawlitschek et al. [13] thematize the influence of colors on the trustworthiness of user interfaces. They analyzed the moods and meanings associated to different colors via an experiment.

In this experiment, the probands had to pass a finance based trust experiment. The were provided with GUIs in different hues and small amount of money was handed to each proband. Then, by transfering money to other probands, they where able to increase the value of their sum by trading between each other. The experiment tried to determine if the color of their GUI had a impact on the trust they have in the other probands. However, they where not able to gain meaningful results from this experiment.

VII. CONCLUSION

In this paper, the novel MAD-Coloring framework was presented. Respecting the basics of color psychology a small footprint prototype was implemented, providing a transparent, color adjustable overlay for Linux X-desktop systems. Further, two clients were implemented, ready to be use with MAD-Coloring. A simple input client, allowing the manual change of the display color and an emotion recognition client, detecting the users current emotional state via a webcam and adjusting the display color accordingly. Also a Python-API was implemented, easing the creation and integration of new clients.

MAD-Coloring, in combination with this clients, is capable to display a decent, transparent overlay over multiple desktops according to the users current emotion. It can therefore be used by everyone, from people wanting to improve their experience on PCs to therapists working with color psychological approaches with their patients.

While fully functional, further work is required to refine and improve the system. On the one hand, medical studies are required to evaluate the psychological impact of the system and therefore confirming its usefulness. Following this further studies are required to find optimal color profiles to maximize the effect. On the other hand, some technical improvements can be conducted. The coloring service, heavily relying on Hudkit can be further slimed down, reduce the performance footprint to a minimum. Further, the support of more desktop environments could be realized. Finally more clients should be implemented, allowing more specific use cases and optimal support for more kinds if needs. These clients could also use smart devices like watches or fitness tracers, allowing the integration of blood pressure into the emotion recognition.

REFERENCES

[1] A. J. Elliot and M. A. Maier, "Color-in-context theory," in *Advances in Experimental Social Psychology*. Elsevier, 2012, pp. 61–125.

[2] R. M. Rider, "Color psychology and graphic design applications." Liberty University, 2010.

[3] C. Li and H. Shi, "Medical space oriented color psychology perception model," *Applied Mechanics and Materials*, vol. 587-589, pp. 461–467, 07 2014.

[4] M. A. Maier, A. J. Elliot, and R. A. Barton, "Color in achievement contexts in humans," in *Handbook of Color Psychology*, A. J. Elliot, M. D. Fairchild, and A. Franklin, Eds. Cambridge University Press, pp. 568–584.

[5] M. Rovai, "Real-time face recognition: An end-to-end project," 2018, last visited: 2021.06.14. [Online]. Available: https://towardsdatascience.com/real-time-face-recognition-an-end-to-end-project-b738bb0f7348

[6] D. Yang, A. Alsadoon, P. Prasad, A. Singh, and A. Elchouemi, "An emotion recognition model based on facial recognition in virtual learning environment," *Procedia Computer Science*, vol. 125, pp. 2 – 10, 2018, the 6th International Conference on Smart Computing and Communications.

[7] S. Ghosh, E. Laksana, L.-P. Morency, and S. Scherer, "Representation Learning for Speech Emotion Recognition," *Interspeech 2016*, pp. 3603–3607, Sep. 2016.

[8] M. Kido, "Bio-psychological effects of color," *Journal of International Society of Life Information Science*, vol. 18, pp. 254–268, 2000.

[9] (2021) The hudkit-projekt github page. Last visited: 2021.06.14. [Online]. Available: https://github.com/anko/hudkit

[10] (2020, jul) Harvard health letter - blue light has a dark side. Last visited: 2021.06.14. [Online]. Available: https://www.health.harvard.edu/staying-healthy/blue-light-has-a-dark-side

[11] S. Mitropoulos, V. Tsiantos, A. Americanos, I. Sianoudis, and A. Skouroliakou, "Blue light reducing software applications for mobile phone screens: measurement of spectral characteristics and biological parameters." in *RAP 2019 Conference Proceedings*. Sievert Association, 2020, pp. 220–224.

[12] R. Sutherland, "What is in a color? the unique human health effects of blue light," in *Envirionmental Healt Perspectives volume 118*. News Focus, 2010, pp. 23–27.

[13] F. Hawlitschek, L.-E. Jansen, E. Lux, T. Teubner, and C. Weinhardt, "Colors and trust: The influence of user interface design on trust and reciprocity," in *2016 49th Hawaii International Conference on System Sciences (HICSS)*. IEEE, jan 2016, pp. 590–599.

Do the Number of Creators and Their Conversations Affect Re-Evaluation of a Familiar Place in Making a Tourist Map?

Yoko Nishihara
Col. of Information Science and Engineering
Ritsumeikan University
Shiga, Japan
email: nisihara@fc.ritsumei.ac.jp

Xinran Lin
Col. of Information Science and Engineering
Ritsumeikan University
Shiga, Japan

Ryosuke Yamanishi
Faculty of Informatics
Kansai University
Osaka, Japan

***Abstract*—In this paper, we analyzed the effect of the number of creators and their conversations on making a tourist map as re-evaluating a familiar place. It means we try to study about collaborative decision making when mapping new places. We conducted experiments to make tourist maps where the participants described the tourist attractions as they actually walked in a familiar place. We compared three types of maps: (a) made by a single participant, (b) made by two participants without any conversations, and (c) with conversations. It was found that maps made by two participants with conversations had a higher proportion of unrevealed tourist attractions but a lower amount of tourist attractions than other maps. For these results, it seemed that conversations might bring introducing unrevealed tourist attractions to the conversation partner. Meanwhile, those also might waste the thinking-up time about the tourist attractions.**

Keywords-conversation analysis; tourist map; re-evaluation of a familiar place; discovery of a tourist attraction; collaborative decision making.

I. INTRODUCTION

People often refer to a tourist map that shows tourist attractions to see when they go sightseeing. A tourist map can be found in guide books, Web pages, and tourist information centers in tourist places. People check the tourist map to know the rough shape of a tourist place and find tourist attractions. Then, they plan a route to visit the tourist attractions they are interested in and enjoy visiting them. A tourist map is indispensable for sightseeing.

A well-known tourist place often has many tourist attractions or a few tourist attractions that cannot be missed. Therefore, it is easy to enumerate the tourist attractions necessary for creating a tourist map. On the other hand, a place where newly promotes itself as a tourist place must begin with discovering tourist attractions to be included in a tourist map. At this time, it is necessary to re-evaluate a place whether the place has spots valuable for a tourist map.

Even if a place is not currently a sightseeing place, the place may have valuable spots known only by people familiar with the place. **We call such a spot an unrevealed tourist attraction.** To discover unrevealed tourist attractions, the help of people who are familiar with the place is necessary. However, it may be difficult for them to spontaneously list spots that would be tourist attractions for others because they are familiar with the place. We assume that (1) each individual is influenced by his/her partner and can re-evaluate a place to list spots as tourist attractions if two people look for spots together instead of him/herself, and (2) the re-evaluation will be conducted efficiently if they have conversations when looking for such places. In this paper, we analyze the effects of the number of people and their conversations on the re-evaluation of a place in creating a tourist map. It means we try to study about collaborative decision making [1], [2] when mapping new places.

Many types of research are conducted to support tourism using the voice of people. For example, location information from microblogs is used to support tourism [3]. The previous studies focus on judging whether a spot is a tourist attraction. Our study focuses on analyzing the effects of the voice of people to discover tourist attractions.

Shirozu et al. designed a workshop to establish a mechanism that encourages people to deepen their awareness of their place and make discoveries by changing their perceptions of a familiar place and scene [4]. This study also asked participants to walk around a familiar place, acquire knowledge of the place, and create a tourist map. However, the present study differs in that it focuses on the effects of the number of people walking in a familiar place and the effects of the presence/absence of conversations when walking together.

II. HYPOTHESIS TESTING EXPERIMENT

The main hypothesis of this paper is: "if a tourist map is created by two people walking around a familiar place with conversations, the map will be different from a map created by a single person." We break down the main hypothesis into the four sub-hypotheses. (H1a): The number of tourist attractions will be larger if two people create a tourist map without any conversations than if a single person creates it. (H1b): The number of tourist attractions will be larger when two people create a tourist map with conversations than when without any conversations. (H2a): The proportion of unrevealed tourist attractions increases when two people create a tourist map without any conversations, rather than a single person creating it. (H2b): The proportion of unrevealed tourist attractions increases when two people create a tourist map with conversations than when without any conversations.

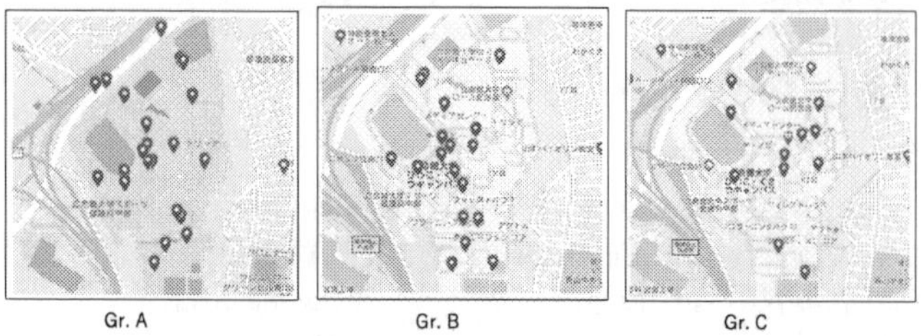

Figure 1. Examples of created tourist maps by Gr. A to C. We used Google map (https://www.google.com/maps) to make tourist maps.

Figure 2. Examples of tourist attractions obtained by Gr. C participants.

A. Experimental procedures

We conducted experiments to verify the hypotheses as follows. (P1) The experimenter instructs participants on how to make a tourist map. (P2) The participants walk around a place for 45 minutes and take photos of what they consider to be tourist attractions. (P3) The participants upload the photos to Google map, write the title and description of the photos, and complete to make the tourist map.

The participants created a tourist map of the Biwako Kusatsu Campus of Ritsumeikan University as a place that did not have many famous tourist attractions. The participants were 35 students who belonged to the campus for more than one year. All of them were familiar with the campus.

The participants were divided into three groups: a participant makes a tourist map alone (Gr. A, seven participants), two participants make a tourist map without any conversations (Gr. B, seven pairs, 14 participants), and two participants make a tourist map with conversations (Gr. C, seven pairs, 14 participants).

B. How to judge whether a place is unrevealed

On the campus, there are facilities used for lectures, research, administration offices, and so on. The participants might list these facilities as tourist attractions. (1) If a spot is a facility described on a campus map published by the university, the spot should be regarded as a famous tourist attraction that everyone knows well. (2) However, even a spot is that mentioned above, **if there is a description of personal memories or impressions, a new perspective of enjoying the spot will be added**. In this case, the spot on the campus map and the spot mentioned by a participant are considered to be different. Therefore, it should be regarded as *an unrevealed tourist attraction* is found in creating a map. (3) If a spot is not described on the campus map, the spot should be regarded as an *unrevealed* tourist attraction.

C. Experimental results

Figure 1 shows examples of created tourist maps by Gr. A through C. Balloons on the maps indicate the tourist attractions. Figure 2 illustrates examples of photos, titles, and descriptions of the tourist attractions obtained from the participants of Gr. C.

The averages of tourist attractions were 17.6 (Gr. A), 18.1 (Gr. B), and 10.3 (Gr. C). The average time for making a tourist map was 32.1 minutes (Gr. A), 28.6 minutes (Gr. B), and 22.1 minutes (Gr. C). The averages of the proportions of unrevealed tourist attractions were 68.3% (Gr. A), 73.7% (Gr. B), and 86.1% (Gr. C).

We found that the hypotheses H2a and H2b should be valid. Note that a significant difference was not obtained by statistical testings. It is necessary to increase the number of experiments in the future to conduct statistical analysis. We found that the hypotheses H1a and H1b were not valid. This is because that it took time to think about unrevealed tourist attractions, which reduced the number of tourist attractions on the maps.

III. CONCLUSIONS

In this paper, we analyzed the effects of the number of creators and their conversations on re-evaluating the familiar place in making a tourist map as a collaborative decision making study. We conducted experiments that participants walked a familiar place and made a tourist map. We found that when two participants made a tourist map with conversations, the tourist map has more unrevealed tourist attractions than that made by a single participant. However, the number of tourist attractions on the maps with that settings was the lowest among the three groups. For these results, it seemed that conversations might bring introducing unrevealed tourist attractions to the conversation partner. Meanwhile, the conversations also might waste the thinking-up time of participants about the tourist attractions. As a future work, we would conduct interviews to deepen the findings.

REFERENCES

[1] L. Westendorf, O. Shaer, P. Varsanyi, H. Meulen, and A. L. Kun, "Understanding Collaborative Decision Making Around a Large-scale Interactive Tabletop," Proc. of the ACM on Human-Computer Interaction, Nov. 2017, pp.1-21.

[2] N. Mahyar et al., "Consesnsus: Visualizing Points of Disagreement for Multi-criteria Collaborative Decision Making," Proc. of Companion of the 2017 ACM Conference on Computer Supported Cooperative Work and Social Computing, Feb. 2017, pp.17-20.

[3] B. Pat, Y. Kanza, and M. Naaman, "Geosocial Search: Finding Places based on Geotagged Social-media Posts," Proc. of the 24th International Conference on World Wide Web, May 2015, pp. 231-234.

[4] N. Shirozu, S. Sakaguchi, M. Matsushita, and C. Hanamura, "Paradise Scope: A Workshop for Stimulating a Student's Viewpoint - a Trial Practice of Shikakeology -," Proc. the 6th International Conference on Soft Computing and Intelligent Systems, and the 13th International Symposium on Advanced Intelligent Systems, Nov. 2012, pp. 691-694.

How AI is Enabling a Creativity Renaissance

Ben Falchuk
Systems, Cybersecurity and Machine Learning Dept.
Peraton Labs
Basking Ridge, NJ USA
e-mail: bfalchuk@peratonlabs.com

***Abstract*—Artificial Intelligence (AI) has infiltrated many aspects of our lives, in both recognizable and invisible ways. Deep learning and sophisticated new information technologies allow the deployment of AI at massive scales, and media giants like Facebook and Google have whole-heartedly adopted AI to exploit their massive data sets in the pursuit of their economic goals. Enterprise and consumer tools and apps are embracing these techniques too. But has this proliferation given users a breadth of creative aptitudes akin to – say - those of Leonardo da Vinci? In this article, we present a survey of impressive AI tools for creativity that provide users with profound new creative powers. We illustrate the sweeping breadth of potential for a human-AI creativity renaissance.**

Keywords-Artificial Intelligence (AI); User Interface (UI); creativity; Human-Machine Interface (HMI); web application.

I. Introduction

Artificial General Intelligence (AGI) refers to machine intelligence that achieves human-like or better cognitive abilities, and features planning, learning and reasoning. While AGI is considered a sort of moonshot, we already find ourselves amidst extremely impressive Artificial Narrow Intelligences (ANI) whose capabilities are superior to human capabilities in pre-defined realms, such as chess and mathematics. Surprisingly, many AI scientists believe that there is a greater than 50% chance that AGI will be achieved in the next 45 years or less [1]. The term artificial superintelligence refers to AI that is autonomous, self-improving, and vastly superior to humans in most every endeavor. Whether or not AGI will comprise a threat to humanity or exhibit consciousness are hotly debated topics among philosophers and computer scientists [2].

Deep learning is a computational AI technique in which so-called Artificial Neural Networks (ANN) – many layers deep – form a basis for predicting results from inputs [3][4]. Deep ANN's are essentially processing engines based loosely upon the mammalian cerebral cortex (synapses, potential functions, etc.) in which an input layer feeds into intermediate layers and finally into an output layer. Each layer has many "neurons" at which mathematical adjustment continually takes place during training. A principle goal is to train the ANN sufficiently so that it can make useful predictions about data it has never seen before. In so-called supervised learning, an ANN learns to produce ideal outputs from labeled data (e.g., artworks, voices, etc.). In unsupervised learning, the data is unlabeled and the goal is to uncover latent patterns and clusters. Classification and prediction are critically important in realms such as meteorology, navigation, and medicine, and it is clear that even narrow AI technologies are changing our lives profoundly. The impact of narrow AI is seen in the data sciences, social sciences, and engineering, and is an underpinning of social network feeds, self-driving vehicle navigation systems, and Natural Language Processing (NLP) to name just a few. The application of AI in traditional creative fields, such as painting and writing, is relatively nascent, but growing rapidly in both theory and practice [5]. A technique called Generative Adversarial Networks (GAN) is often used to generate things that "look authentic". It does so by pitting two ANN's against each other in a sort of zero-sum game of generation and recognition [3].

In this article, we do not attempt to answer the question, "what is art?" nor distinguish between amateur and professional human artists. Instead, we focus on how the creative class (as defined in [6]) can now collaborate with AI's in new ways. The works included herein are organized by category and are either recent advances, or representative of the field; we have favored accessible systems that readers can try themselves. Older technologies are mentioned when they serve to illustrate the field's vector of progress. The remainder of this article is structured as follows. Section II provides our survey. Acknowledgements and conclusions close the article.

II. AI Creativity Technologies

We will never know what da Vinci – the quintessential *Renaissance man* - might have created had he been armed with 21st century tools, such as Photoshop, Internet, and AutoCAD. This section surveys how applications of AI and human-AI collaborations can help to turn merely creative people into latent da Vinci's. The quest to understand approaches for instilling creativity in computer AI is not new (e.g., [63][64]); this article assembles recent, noteworthy and accessible systems across several domains of creativity.

A. Painting, Drawing and Sculpture

Artistic painting and drawing techniques are thousands of years old but today we find deep learning and AI technologies are breaking new ground. In 2018, an artwork called La Famille de Belamy sold for over $400,000 in auction [7]. It was created by a GAN trained on 15,000 painted portraits spanning several periods (see Figure 1, left). The dramatic sale marked an early and significant moment, and illustrated the commercial potential of AI art. More recently, an AI artwork by a robot called Sofia sold for $688,888 [62]. Meanwhile, Google DeepDream is a means for visualizing the internal state of a convolutional neural network (CNN) as it learns to classify images [8]. DeepDream is used by artists as a means to create surreal animated journeys "through the layers of a neural network" by recursively processing images, zooming in, and creating new variants (see Figure 1, right). Each variant attempts to re-create particular types of elements, such as trees or dogs (as directed by the artist), giving the resulting animations a meandering creative feel.

Figure 1. La Famille de Belamy (left); DeepDream image (right) [7,8]

DeepArt.io is an algorithmic artistic style transfer algorithm that outputs new works of art in the style of other artworks (on which it has been trained), and gained notoriety for its ability to rapidly transfer the style of the painter Van Gogh to arbitrary images [9]. DeepArt.io and other style transfer techniques are leveraged by artists in unique and beautiful ways (e.g., dinosaurs made of flowers [10]) and are embedded in scores of popular iOS and Android mobile apps, such as the popular PicsArt editor.

Figure 2. GauGAN: human user's broad strokes (left), corresponding AI-generated scene (right) [9]

Research in GAN's and techniques for converting segmentation maps into lifelike imagery has resulted in a tool named GauGAN [11]. Human artists working with this tool need merely to sketch a broadly-stroked image and ask GauGAN to fill in the details, texture, reflection, and colors, which it does by referencing its vast training set of images. In such a human-AI collaboration, then, the human steers the broad strokes while the AI creates details (see Figure 2).

In a similar vein, the Art42 webapp leverages GAN's trained on Cubist period art to provide a continuous stream of convincing new AI-generated artworks on each access [12]. Each output is a sort of Cubist daydream, vaguely familiar yet swirly and free in a way that belies its AI origins. Elsewhere, AI's are infiltrating the sculptural arts and seem poised to jump into the 3rd dimension. For example, *RobotSculptor* explores how humans can teach robotic arms and hands to sculpt clay in an optimal repeatable fashion by finding the robotic motions to optimally satisfy human objectives for the surface [13]. AI is also dramatically improving aspects of 3d printing through fault diagnosis and property predictions [14].

B. Writing, Poetry and Illustrated stories

The expression of human thought as written stories is transcendent, and yet even here, AI is encroaching. The OpenAI Generative Pre-trained Transformer (GPT) technologies are language prediction models capable of producing human-like text, with massive billion-parameter neural networks [15]. Write with Transformer is an online demo illustrating the breadth of GPT-2 by autocompleting lines of human-written text with phrasings that mostly make sense [16]. This is possible, in part, because it has sampled and learned from 8 million Internet web pages. Figure 3 shows exemplary results in which human inputted text is plain and GPT-2 contributions are highlighted in color.

The flowers in the garden are very special. Their scent is so different from anything I have ever smelled before. But when I approached the
- plant, I could sense a familiar fragrance.
- garden a couple of weeks ago and placed a single rose..
- flowers with the glass lid in I was surprised to find out..

Figure 3. Write with Transformer sample [15].

Human writers can use GPT-like AI to help them produce new kinds of creative output – never before possible - involving textual phrases. In one light-hearted experiment an ANN generated new Candy Heart messages ("Love bun", "Call me", etc.) by leveraging its training on existing candies [17]. Remixing language on custom source materials and then applying language models can yield new results in the style of the source. An Amazon-funded company trained Alexa's NLP on the full Harry Potter corpus and then used the resulting ANN to generate an entirely new chapter. The text sounded quite a bit like J. K. Rowling's voicing but lacked a singular train-of-thought [18]. Fascinating advances in ANN encodings allow AI to generate coherent novel sentences that interpolate between two given sentences [19]. Such a capability could be imagined as part of a collaborative human-AI poem-writing process in which the human user bounds the prose and the AI fills in the middle parts. When a different ANN was trained on the corpus of Shakespeare sonnets and asked to generate new ones it adequately captured the aspects of both rhyme and meter [20]. On the other hand, expert human evaluators were able to distinguish the sonnets as fakes largely due to degraded readability and emotional pull. A system called Hafez combines finite state machinery with deep learning, yielding an ability to create a rhyming poem about an arbitrary word, such as *tree* [21]. A short story called *The Day a Computer Writes a Novel* – the result of a human-AI collaboration - made it through the first round of a Japanese literary contest in the mid 2010's. In other work, when researchers got both GPT-3 and humans to write college essays and had the results graded by experts, GPT-3 got passing marks, and even more praise than human essays in some respects. On the other hand, the AI failed to create strong narratives "incorporating the 5 senses", and was at times vague or awkward [22].

The AI that underpins the Verse by Verse application was trained on full-text poetry of more than 12 classical era poets and is very effective at generating a line of poetry to follow any line written by a human (given a preference for a particular poet). In this way, human and AI may forge a new poem, line by line, that has the voice of both the human and a historical poet, such as Dickenson or Whitman [23]. A Google Arts and Culture experiment called Poem Portraits fuses visual art with poetry creation [24]. It not only creates a long-running poem in 19th century style around user-inputted words, but it creates a visual portrait of each contributor's face. Its ANN is trained on over 25 million words of poetry using a long short-term memory recurrent neural network. A related project named Please Feed the Lions employed AI to create a novel poem based on viewer inputs, and projected the poem onto a huge lion sculpture in London's Trafalgar Square. These are good ways to introduce people to the potential of AI poetry.

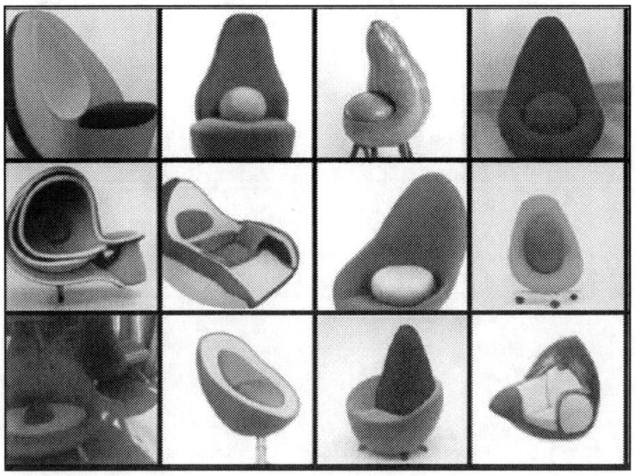

Figure 4. Images created by DALL-E in response to the prompt, "an armchair in the shape of an avocado" [26]

OpenAI's DALL-E tool can generate images from almost any text descriptions by leveraging GPT-3 and Image GPT [25]. The resulting images are impressive. In particular, many results seem to exhibit a styling that is somehow clever, belying the computational nature of their inception. For example, the text, "an armchair in the shape of an avocado" produces numerous images of exactly that but the images seem more like the result of human brainstorming than those of a computer algorithm (see Figure 4). Indeed, almost anything that one types to DALL-E is similarly visualized. It is easy to imagine human-AI collaborative loops in which a human author's poem is illustrated in near real-time (as it is typed) by an AI partner. The images, in turn, spark new textual ideas for the human.

C. *Culinary Arts*

This section highlights advances in AI related to the culinary arts. Unscientific experiments with GPT-3 have shown that it can output textual recipes, but its lack of knowledge of procedure or chemistry make the results more silly than useful. For example, one might get a recipe for "watermelon cookies" that makes very little practical sense [27]. On the other hand, food scientists have trained an ANN on vineyard weather and irrigation parameters to predict wine aroma profiles, a practical tool that could give growers and winemakers powerful insights for business operations and new product design [28]. Meanwhile, researchers found over 300 unique ingredients by training an ANN on millions of recipes from Recipe1M. They then recovered a scored set of over 300,000 food pairings from these ingredients [29]. In principle, this kind of AI could be effective as an assistant to a human chef in a food preparation use case.

Figure 5. The AI-generated recipe "Caymanian Plantain Dessert", as cooked by Engadget's T.O'Brien [60]

Elsewhere, a different platform for creativity in support of culinary recipes employs machine learning, Bayesian probability, chemoinformatics, traditions, and crowdsourced seedling recipes, and leverages IBM Watson. The resulting recipes show apparent novelty and are rated as "very creative" by domain experts (e.g., "Caymanian Plantain Dessert", created with ~17 ingredients, is depicted in Figure 5) [30]. IBM published a full book of these AI recipes in 2015 and it has mostly 4 and 5 star reviews on Amazon. Google and Sony have also pointed their AI prowess at the culinary arts and, in 2021, helped human bakers innovate a new dessert type [61].

Alternatively, ANN's trained on recipes, food imagery, and topic networks can perform so-called image-to-recipe in which AI predicts the ingredients of photographed foods [31]. Such a technology could be the basis for an AI sous-chef that watches food preparation, infers ingredients, finds food pairings, and interacts with the chef using natural language.

D. Photography, Portraiture, and Beyond

This section describes the promise of AI to not only enhance photography and portraits but also enable new forms of visual portraiture, not even remotely possible in da Vinci's time. Super Resolution (SR) is a pragmatic technique (offered by Adobe and others) in which ANN's trained in narrow image categories (e.g., cars, animals) can upscale small images to much larger resolution ones by "hallucinating" - and filling in - convincing details [32][33]. To some extent, SR frees the human artist from practical scale constraints.

GANPaint employs ANN GAN's to improve the manner and consistency in which synthetic elements can be added to photographs [34][35]. Artists can now augment imagery with convincing new semantic elements, such as adding a convincing new window into a photo of a window-less kitchen. Figure 6 illustrates a GANPaint use case in which the human artist broadly strokes a tree into the image in order to replace the tower; the AI then performs a seamless replacement. In principle, this technique also works with facial features and portraits.

Figure 6. GANPaint – original urban photo with CN Tower (left); image after "painting a tree" atop the tower (right) [35]

The StyleGAN (and StyleGAN2) generator is an efficient way to generate unique high quality facial images while controlling aspects of style, such as hair or facial features [36]. The best of these results have proven to be stunningly detailed and extremely convincing. The webapp This Person Does Not Exist displays a stream of StyleGAN-generated faces, each evoking an eerie humanity [37]. Exemplary images from this new kind of portraiture are illustrated in Figure 7.

Artbreeder - a GAN that "breeds" new images from chosen ones – enables a new form of human-AI portraiture process [38]. For example, a human artist who has created a portrait image can breed it towards the features of a mountain lion. To do this, she chooses mountain lion images as parent images for the portrait and asks artbreeder to evolve her original portrait [39]. Artbreeder (see also *picbreeder*) encourages a human-AI collaboration during which the artist and an AI hone new images in a series of interactive steps. The results are often visually stunning AI-generated portraits [40].

Figure 7. Two non-existent people from This Person does not Exist [37]

So-called style-transfer GAN's can leverage large homogeneous training sets to amazing effect. In 2019 a webapp called Toonify used GAN's and trained on characters from animated films [41]. It could then use this network to apply Disney-esque facial features to real photographs, essentially "finding and assembling" features in cartoon images to correspond to features of the photograph. The resulting images (Figure 8) were largely perceived as cheerful and surreal and were so popular and interesting that the developer's demo website was quickly out of bandwidth.

The notion of portraiture is changing to include dynamic visual effects. Artists can now animate the mouths and faces of static portraits to match a target audio (e.g., using temporal annotated GAN) to very dramatic – and potentially politically dangerous - effect [42][43]. These animations are sometimes called deepfakes (i.e., they use "deep" learning).

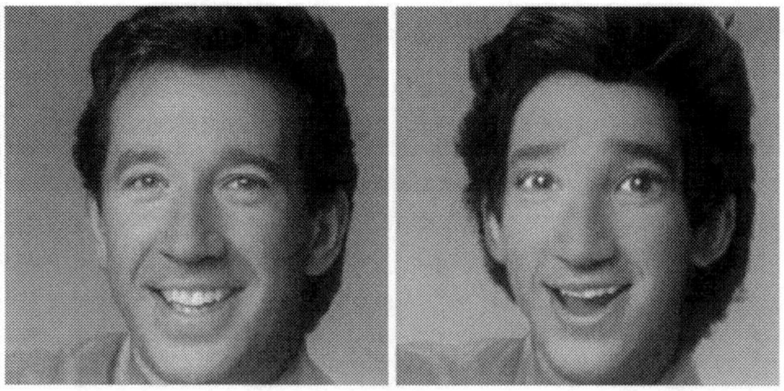

Figure 8. Exemplary Toonify output (right) from photo input (left) [36].

In a related vein, a brilliant AI-driven augmented reality prototype finds a body in any photo or artwork and then animates it to walk right off the page before your eyes [44] (Figure 9, shown from third person). This new form of art allows creators to think in multiple modalities beyond 2d (and would almost certainly be considered sorcery by da Vinci).

Figure 9. AI turns a 2d image into an animated 3d scene on an augmented reality platform [44].

E. *Music*

Music is a vital part of all cultures. Da Vinci himself invented various musical technologies and was a good musician. Today, deep learning is encroaching on - and contributing to - musical culture. OpenAI has demonstrated a Jukebox capability comprised of an ANN trained on 1.2 million songs, lyrics, and genres. The ANN can predict compressed audio tokens [45] and JukeBox has created convincing new songs with good coherence, although lacking a certain degree of musical structure. Meanwhile, an app named DeepSinger – trained on 92 hours of singing data – can synthesize singing voices in multiple languages using a feed-forward transformer [46].

The classic rock singer Freddie Mercury is immortalized in the AI webapp called FreddieMeter in which an AI judges precisely how much a viewer sounds like Freddie when she is prompted to sing his songs. The convolutional encoder underpinnings of FreddieMeter represent a novel approach to voice processing [47].

DrumBot demonstrates the nascent promise of AI-based musical accompaniment; in this webapp prototype, an AI derives a drum track to accompany any simple melodic sequence made by a human artist [48]. Figure 10 illustrates the simple user interface of DrumBot.

The webcam webapp called Air Guitar creates guitar music driven by the position of the musician's hands in the webcam [49]. In fact, there is a plentiful variety of similar such demonstrators spanning many body parts, gestures, and musical instruments.

Deep Music Visualizer employs a GAN to visualize music with imagery from trained datasets; the ever-changing AI-generated imagery is responsive to parameters of the music, such as tempo and timbre [50]. In this way, the AI is contributing a lucid visual accompaniment that is sensitive to the context of the music. Lucid Sonic Dreams is a similar music visualizer [51].

By leveraging the Google Magenta technology (in which a deep learning system has made advances in the length of musical compositions that it can generate [65]) a team has trained an AI to compose new songs in the style of existing rock artists such as the Beatles. A recent initiative resulted in a convincing new Nirvana song whose words and music were AI-generated [66].

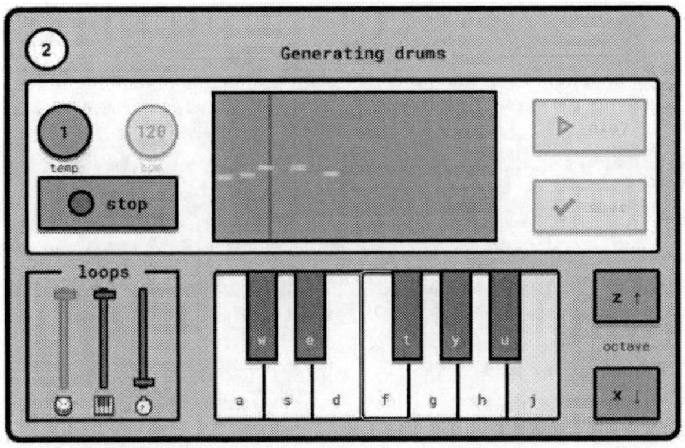

Figure 10. DrumBot web application creates a drum track to the melody track inputted by the user (shown in yellow dashes) [48].

Figure 11. A user interface of Lobe, image classification use case, uses familiar widgets like gauges to convey feature detection [56].

F. *Frameworks*

Where Da Vinci would have employed easels and art supply bags, today's artists are now beginning to employ AI-based frameworks. These software tools serve as scaffolding for creative computation and abstract away unnecessary technical concepts. Their emergence is a sign that human-AI creativity is gaining importance, and that a purely coding-centric view of AI is yielding to a higher-level view more amenable to creative non-coders. Both SageMaker and AutoML are frameworks allowing users to train ANN's, use existing models (e.g., vision, NLP), and deploy them, using a simple UI [52][53].

MediaPipe promises cross-platform tools for creative visual apps, such as those leveraging pose, face detection, and object tracking [54], and deployments that work on web and mobile platforms alike. Figure 12 illustrates MediaPipe body and face tracking. Runway is a framework tailored to creative pros and their workflows, such as animation and green screen video-editing [55]. Lobe is a code-free AI model maker by Microsoft. It currently supports only image classification but the Lobe UI (see Figure 11) is notable for how well it abstracts away complexity and makes ANN training into something simple, elegant and fun [56].

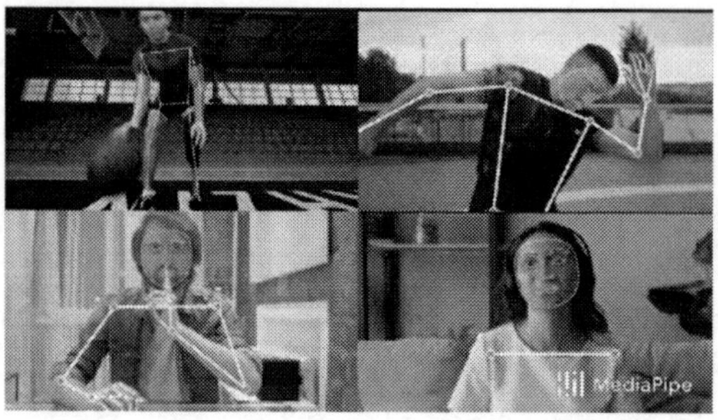

Figure 12. MediaPipe body and face tracking (body pose estimators shown as white skeletal lines, facial features as blue) [54]

TensorFlow is a machine learning underpinning for an ever-changing landscape of creative projects. Its capabilities include pose, hand, and body tracking, and deep learning, and all of these can run directly in most desktop web browsers [57][58][59].

III. CONCLUSION

The barriers to human-AI collaborations are rapidly lowering thanks in part to ever-advancing UI designs, hardware and GPU's, and Internet and web accessibility and protocols. This article has highlighted only a small subset of tools that illustrate the vast potential of human-AI creativity. Our future work may include further detailed analysis of particular creative domains and the AI techniques that support them, particularly on web platforms. Even in their present (sometimes) nascent states, these technologies have already enabled new forms of art - ranging from painting to poetry, cooking, and music - that both inspire and boggle the mind. We observe the following trends:

- Increasing potential for human-AI collaborative flows in which each actor contributes unique value
- Improved accessibility to human-AI tools thanks user interface and web technologies
- Single-domain tools currently dominate the scene, while tools with domain-crossing skills are more rare

On the other hand, daunting research challenges remain, such as training set bias, fairness, accessibility, and sustainability. Furthermore, it is unclear how the notions of consciousness, ethics, language, empathy, personality, and experience relate to a machine's ability to perform as a creative partner. The nascent field of human-AI creativity will continue to be driven by the combined advances from the sciences, philosophy, and the digital arts. We are not all da Vinci's just yet but we may be inching closer. Yet even more likely, AI will move us in altogether unpredictable creative directions.

ACKNOWLEDGMENT

We thank the reviewers for their valuable comments.

REFERENCES

[1] K. Grace, J. Salvatier, A. Dafoe, B. Zhang and O. Evans, "Viewpoint: When Will AI Exceed Human Performance? Evidence from AI Experts" , Journal of AI Research, Vol.62, 2018

[2] N. Bostrom, Superintelligence: Paths, Dangers, Strategies. Oxford University Press, Oxford, UK, 2014.

[3] A. Burkov, The Hundred Page Machine Learning Book, self-published, 2019.

[4] J. Schmidhuber, Deep Learning in Neural Networks: An Overview, TR IDSIA-03-14 / arXiv: 1404.7828 v4, 2014.

[5] A. Miller, The artist in the machine: the world of AI-powered creativity, MIT Press, Cambridge, 2019.

[6] R. Florida, Rise of the Creative Class, Basic Books, New York, 2012.

[7] BBC News, *Portrait by AI program sells for $432,000*, Oct. 2018. [Online]. Available from: https://www.bbc.com/news/technology-45980863 [retrieved: June 2021]

[8] A. Mordvintsev, C. Olah and M. Tyka, *DeepDream - a code example for visualizing Neural Networks*, 2015 [Online]. Available from: https://ai.googleblog.com/2015/07/ [retrieved: June 2021]

[9] L. Gatys, A. Ecker and M. Bethge, A neural algorithm of artistic style, arXiv:1508.06576v2, 2015.

[10] A. Liszewski, *A Neural Network Turned a Book of Flowers Into Shockingly Lovely Dinosaur Art*, June 2017. [Online]. Available from: https://gizmodo.com/a-neural-network-turned-a-book-of-flowers-into-shocking-1796221045 [retrieved: June 2021]

[11] NVIDIA Inc., *GauGAN Beta*. [Online]. Available from: http://nvidia-research-mingyuliu.com/gaugan [retrieved: June 2021]

[12] V. Vieriu, *Art42 - Infinite cubist art*. [Online]. Available from: https://art42.net/ [retrieved: June 2021]

[13] Z. Ma, S. Duenser, C. Schumacher, R. Rust, M. Bacher, F. Gramazio, M. Kohler and S. Coros, "RobotSculptor: Artist-directed robotic sculpting of clay", Symp. On Computational Fabrication, 2020.

[14] G. D.Goh, S. Sing and W. Yeong, "A reivew on machine learning in 3d printing", AI Review, Vol.54, 2021.

[15] M. Hutson, "Robo-writers: the rise and risks of language-generating AI", Nature, V.591. [Online]. Available from: https://nature.com/articla/d41586-021-00530-0 [retrieved: June 2021]

[16] Write with Transformer, https://transformer.huggingface.co .

[17] J. Shane, *Okay GPT-3: Candy hearts!*, Feb., 2021. [Online]. Available from: https://janellecshane.substack.com/ p/okay-gpt-3-candy-hearts [retrieved: June 2021]

[18] Botnik Inc., *Harry Potter*. [Online]. Available from: https://botnik.org/content/harry-potter.html [retrieved: June 2021]

[19] R. Bowman, L. Vilnis, O. Vinyals, A. Dai, R. Jozefowicz and S. Bengio, Generating Sentences from a Continuous Space, arXiv:1511.06349v4, 2016.

[20] J. Lau, T. Cohn, T. Baldwin, J. Brooke and A. Hammond, "Deep-speare: A joint neural model of poetic language, meter and rhyme", Proc. 56th Annual Meeting of the ACM Linguistics, Melbourne, 2018.

[21] M. Ghazvininejad, X. Shi, Y. Choi and K. Knight, "Generating Topical Poetry", Proc. Empirical Methods in NLP, Austin, 2017.

[22] EduRef, *What Grades can AI get in College?*, [Online]. Available from: https://www.eduref.net/features/what-grades-can-ai-get-in-college/ [retrieved: June 2021]

[23] Google Research, *Verse by Verse*. [Online]. Available from: https://sites.research.google/versebyverse/ [retrieved: June 2021]

[24] S. Devlin and R. Goodwin, *Poemportraits*. Available from: https://experiments.withgoogle.com/poemportraits [retrieved: June 2021]

[25] A. Ramesh, M. Pavlov, G. Goh, S. Gray, C. Voss, A. Radford, M. Chen and I. Sutskever, Zero-shot text-to-image generation, arXiv:2021.12092, 2021.

[26] OpenAI, *DALL-E:creating images from text*, [Online]. Available from: https://openai.com/blog/dall-e/ [retrieved: June 2021]

[27] J. Schachter, Twitter feed, [Online]. Available from: https://twitter.com/joshu/status/1286009425220706305 [retrieved: June 2021]

[28] S. Fuentes, E. Tongson, D. Torrico and C. Gonzalez Viejo, "Modeling Pinot Noir Aroma Profiles Based on Weather and Water Management Information Using Machine Learning Algorithms", Foods 9(1), 2021.

[29] D. Park, K. Kim, Y. Park, J. Shin and J. Kang, "KitcheNette: Predicting and Ranking Food Ingredient Pairings using Siamese Neural Networks", Proc. Int'l. Joint Conf. on AI (IJCAI-19), Macao, 2019.

[30] L. Varshney, F. Pinel, K.R. Varsheny, D. Bhattacharjya, A. Schorgendorder and Y-M..Chee, "A big data approach to the computational creativity: The curious case of Chef Watson", IBM Journal of Research and Development, 63(1), 2019

[31] M. Serifovic, *Image-to-recipe translation with Deep Convolutional Neural Networks*, 2018. [Online]. Available from: https://towardsdatascience.com/this-ai-is-hungry-b2a8655528be [retrieved: June 2021]

[32] C. Ledig et al, Photo-realistic image super-resolution using a generative adversarial network, arXiv:1609.04802v5, 2017.

[33] DeepAI, *Super Resolution API*. [Online]. Available from: https://deepai.org/machine-learning-model/torch-srgan [retrieved: June 2021]

[34] D. Bau, H. Strobelt, W. Peebles, J. Wulff, B. Zhou, J-Y Zhu and A. Torralba, "Semantic Photo Manipulation with a Generative Image Prior", Proc. ACM SIGGRAPH, Los Angeles, 2019.

[35] MIT and IBM, *GANPaint Studio*, [Online]. Available from: https://ganpaint.io [retrieved: June 2021]

[36] T. Karras, S. Laine, M. Aittala, J. Hellsten, J. Lehtinen and T. Aila, Analyzing and improving the image quality of StyleGAN, arXiv: 1912.04958v2, 2019.

[37] NVIDIA Research, *This person does not exist*. [Online]. Available from: https://thispersondoesnotexist.com [retrieved: June 2021]

[38] B. Uterwijk, *A.I. generated portraits*. [Online]. Available from: https://www.basuterwijk.com/portfolio [retrieved: June 2021]

[39] Artbreeder (formerly Ganbreeder). [Online]. Available from: https://www.artbreeder.com [retrieved: June 2021]

[40] picbreeder, [Online]. Available from: http://picbreeder.org/intro.php [retrieved: June 2021]

[41] J. Pinkney, *Making Toonify Yourself*. [Online]. Available from: https://www.justinpinkney.com/making-toonify [retrieved: June 2021]

[42] K. Vougioukas, S. Petridis and M. Pantic, Realistic speech-driven facial animation with GAN's, arXiv:1906.06337v1, 2019.

[43] D. Coldewey, "Mona Lisa frown: machine learning brings old paintings and photos to life", Techcrunch, May 22, 2019.

[44] C-Y. Weng, B. Curless and I.K. Shlizerman, *Photo wake-up: 3d character animation from a single photo*. [Online]. Available via: https://grail.cs.washington.edu/projects/wakeup [retrieved: June 2021]

[45] OpenAI, *Juebox*. [Online]. Available from: https://openai.com/blog/jukebox/ [retrieved: June 2021]

[46] Y. Ren et al, *DeepSinger: Singing voice synthesis with data mined from the web*. [Online]. Available from: https://speechresearch.github.io/deepsinger/ [retrieved: June 2021]

[47] Google, *Freddie Meter A.I. Experiment*. [Online]. Available from: https://freddiemeter.withyoutube.com/ [retrieved: June 2021]

[48] Drumbot, [Online]. Available from: https://drumbot.glitch.me/ [retrieved: June 2021]

[49] K. Newcombe, *Webcam Air Guitar*. [Online]. Available from: https://codepen.io/kevinnewcombe/pen/QRZdYP [retrieved: June 2021]

[50] M. Siegelman, *Deep Music visualizer*. [Online]. Available from: https://github.com/msieg/deep-music-visualizer [retrieved: June 2021]

[51] M. Alafriz, *Introducing "Lucid Sonic Dreams": Sync GAN Art to Music with a Few Lines of Python Code*. [Online]. Available from: https://towardsdatascience.com/introducing-lucid-sonic-dreams-sync-gan-art-to-music-with-a-few-lines-of-python-code-b04f88722de1 [retrieved: June 2021]

[52] Google Cloud, *AutoML*. [Online]. Available from: https://cloud.google.com/automl [retrieved: June 2021]

[53] Amazon, *SageMaker*. [Online]. Available from: https://aws.amazon.com/sagemaker/ [retrieved: June 2021]

[54] Google, *MediaPipe on Github*. [Online]. Available from: https://github.com/google/mediapipe [retrieved: June 2021]

[55] Runway | Make the impossible, [Online]. Available from:: https://runwayml.com/ [retrieved: June 2021]

[56] Microsoft, *Lobe desktop application*. [Online]. Available from: https://lobe.ai/ [retrieved: June 2021]

[57] V. Dibia, *Handtrack.js*, TensorFlow Blog [Online]. Available from: https://blog.tensorflow.org/2019/11/handtrackjs-tracking-hand-interactions.html [retrieved: June 2021]

[58] TensorFlow, *Pose estimation with TensorFlow*. [Online]: https://www.tensorflow.org/lite/examples [retrieved: June 2021]

[59] deeplearn.js, cghawthorne GitHub. [Online]. Available from: https://github.com/cghawthorne/deeplearnjs [retrieved: June 2021]

[60] T. O'Brien, *Cooking with Watson: Caymanian Plantain Dessert*, Engadget, June 2015.

[61] S. Robinson and A. Behbi, *How Sweet it is: using Cloud AI to whip up new treats with Mars Maltesers*, [Online]. Available from: https://cloud.google.com/blog, 2021 [retrieved: June 2021]

[62] M. Ives, "The Latest Artist Selling NFTs? It's a Robot", New York Times, March 25, 2021.

[63] M. A. Boden, Creativity and artificial intelligence, Artificial Intelligence, 102(1-2), pp. 347-356, 1998.

[64] J. Rowe, D. Partridge, "Creativity: a survey of AI approaches", Artifical Intelligence Review, 7(1), 2009.

[65] C-Z. A.Huang, A. Vaswani, J. Uszkoreit, N. Shazeer, I. Simon, C. Hawthorne, A. Dai, M. Hoffman, M. Dinculescu and D. Eck, Music Transformer, arXiv: 1809.04281v3

[66] K. Grow, *In Computero: Hear How AI Software Wrote a New Nirvana Song*, [Online]. Available from: https://www.rollingstone.com/music/music-features/nirvana-kurt-cobain-ai-song-1146444/ [retrieved: June 2021]

Interpretation Support System for Classification Patterns Using HMM in Deep Learning with Texts

Masayuki Ando
Graduate School of Engineering,
The University of Shiga Prefecture
Hikone, Japan
email: oh23mandou@ec.usp.ac.jp

Yoshinobu Kawahara
Institute of Mathematics for Industry, Kyushu University, and
RIKEN Center for Advanced Intelligence Project
Fukuoka, Japan
email: yoshinobu.kawahara@riken.jp

Wataru Sunayama
School of Engineering, The University of Shiga Prefecture
Hikone, Japan
email: sunayama.w@e.usp.ac.jp

Yuji Hatanaka
Faculty of Science and Technology, Oita University
Oita, Japan
email: hatanaka-yuji@oita-u.ac.jp

***Abstract*—This paper describes an interpretation support system for classification patterns extracted from deep learning with texts using a Hidden Markov Model (HMM), and verified its effectiveness. It is well known that classification patterns by deep learning models are often difficult to interpret the reasons derived. Therefore, an interpretation support system for deep learning classification patterns using HMMs is proposed as a tool for extracting and interpreting the learning content of deep learning. The proposed system uses an HMM to extract the contents of the learning results in deep learning with texts and provide an interface to assist in the interpretation of learned patterns. The proposed system is expected to enable system users to easily understand the complexity of deep learning, acquire new skills, and create knowledge. Verification experiments were conducted to confirm the effectiveness of the system on the basis of the learning result of deep learning classifying sentences. In the experiment, test subjects were divided into two groups. One group used the proposed system and the other used a system that displays words with high Term Frequency-Inverse Document Frequency (TFIDF) values. Both groups were instructed to provide meanings to classification patterns unusual to each output. The results show that the test subjects who used the proposed system were able to understand the meanings of the classification patterns of deep learning with texts more deeply than those who used the comparison system.**

***Index Terms*—interpretation support; deep learning, text mining; text classification; data visualization**

I. Introduction

Artificial intelligence (AI) systems based on deep learning have been rapidly increasing their number of applications. These systems have been used in a variety of fields, including image recognition, automatic driving of automobiles, automatic delivery of packages using drones, and assistance in diagnosis by doctors, with the advent of easy AI systems such as cloud AI [1] .

However, there is a black box problem in deep learning. Deep learning learns information through a very complex process and can make predictions and classifications with high accuracy. However, due to the complexity of this process, it is very difficult for humans to explain the decision criteria of deep learning.

Explainable AI (XAI) [2] has been attracting attention as a research field that focuses on explaining the reliability and fairness of deep learning models and understanding the decision criteria. The necessity of explaining what has been learned has been proposed to understand and trust the behavior of deep learning models [3] [4]. In addition, research has been conducted to try to explain the behavior of the model itself, such the model's data and correlations between variables [5], and models using counterfactual conditional statements [6]. Alternatively, there are studies that focus not only on the interpretation of model behavior but also on its stability and reliability, such as [7] [8], which evaluate model behavior by applying it to logic circuits and decision trees.

Here, if we focus on informational systems [9] [10], in which additional information is added to the output of the model where a user infers the validity or correctness of the AI's answer. In the field of image processing, for example, a method to emphasize parts of an input image that contribute to the output [11] [12] has been proposed. However, in the field of natural language processing, it is difficult to directly apply the methods used in the image processing field. In addition, just highlighting a part of the input text, known as the attention method [13], does not tell us what kind of learning is going on inside the deep learning process. In other words, the classification criteria is considered to be insufficiently explained.

Therefore, in this study, we propose a system that extracts the most likely classification patterns and assists in the interpretation of classification criteria by considering a weighted network of a trained deep learning as a single hidden Markov model (HMM), as the subject of a text classification problem. In particular, we believe that by constructing a system that enables even novice data analysts to interpret classification patterns, we can create an environment in which users of

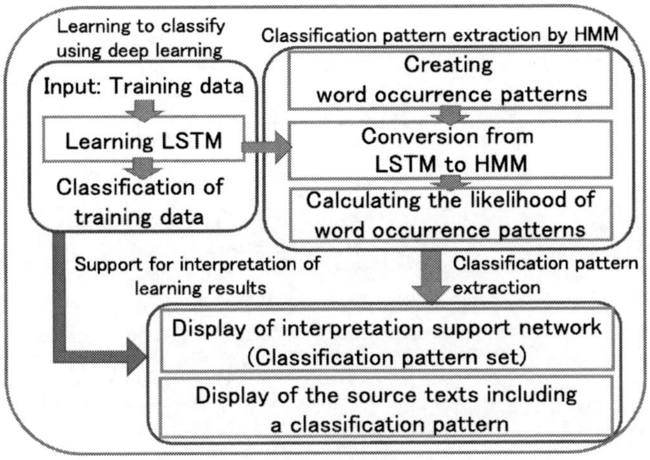

Fig. 1: System configuration

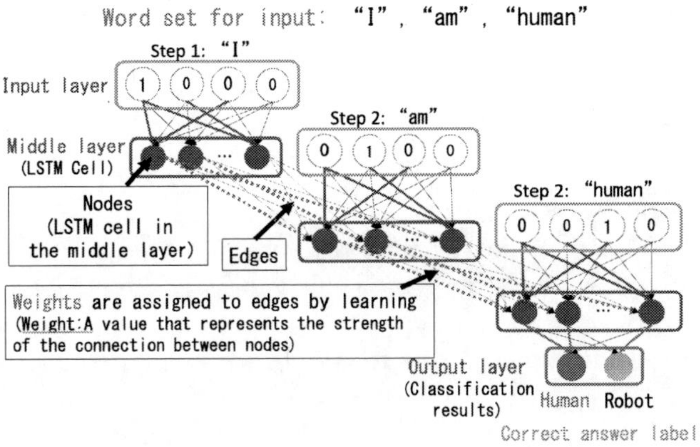

Fig. 2: Example of weighting by LSTM

cloud-based machine learning APIs and individuals who wish to perform simple text mining can easily interpret the learning results.

The following is the structure of this paper. In Section II, the structure and details of the classification pattern interpretation support system from deep learning network using HMM are described. In Section III, evaluation experiments of the proposed system are described. In Section IV, this paper is concluded.

II. Support System for Interpreting Classification Patterns Using HMM

In this section, we describe the configuration and details of our system for supporting the interpretation of classification patterns using HMMs in deep learning networks for text-based classification tasks.

A. System Configuration

The structure of the proposed system is shown in Figure 1. In the proposed system, a set of texts with correct labels is first used as training data, and classification is performed by Long Short-Term Memory (LSTM). Then, the trained weighted network is transformed into an HMM, and the likelihood of word occurrence patterns in the training text set (source text) is calculated. Finally, the word occurrence patterns with high likelihood are displayed in the interface as classification patterns, which the user can interpret.

B. Learning LSTM

In this study, we consider a deep learning model called LSTM, which is generally used to learn order patterns of time-series data, and a situation where it is applied to the problem of classifying a set of texts (Figure 2). The reason for using LSTMs is that we consider the time-series relationship of word occurrences in a text to be an important factor in this research. In addition, we do not aim to obtain high classification accuracy, but rather to build a system that encourages the interpretation of deep learning networks, which are generally difficult to interpret.

The LSTM takes as input a word vector (nouns, verbs, and adjectives in the text, with 0 and 1 representing their occurrence and non-occurrence, respectively) for each text on the basis of the set of texts given the correct answer labels. The edge weights in the LSTM with one intermediate layer are then learned so that its classification accuracy is high.

Here, to interpret the learned classification patterns, it is assumed that proper training has been performed. Therefore, we assume that the classification accuracy of the test data in the 10-fold cross-validation during training or the test data different from the training dataset is 90% or higher, and that the network does not contain substantial errors.

C. Creating Word Occurrence Patterns

To improve the interpretability of the classification patterns by making them closer to the actual text, the system uses the word occurrence patterns used in the source text for training the LSTM as input to the HMM. In this case, the word occurrence patterns to be used are all patterns that satisfy the following conditions.

- The words in a word occurrence pattern are nouns, verbs, and adjectives in the source text (adjectives may be omitted in the experiment).
- The words in a word occurrence pattern are only those in which the number of sentences where the word appears (sentence frequency) is 1% or more.
- The order of words in a word pattern should be based on the actual order in the source text.

D. Conversion of LSTM to HMM

An HMM is a non-deterministic finite state automaton model with two processes: a state and an observation symbol (output), which are a stochastic transition and output, respectively. HMMs can calculate the value (likelihood) of how plausible an observation symbol is for a given change in the state. Therefore, by applying the LSTM to the HMM, we can express the contribution of a certain word occurrence pattern to the output of the LSTM in terms of likelihood.

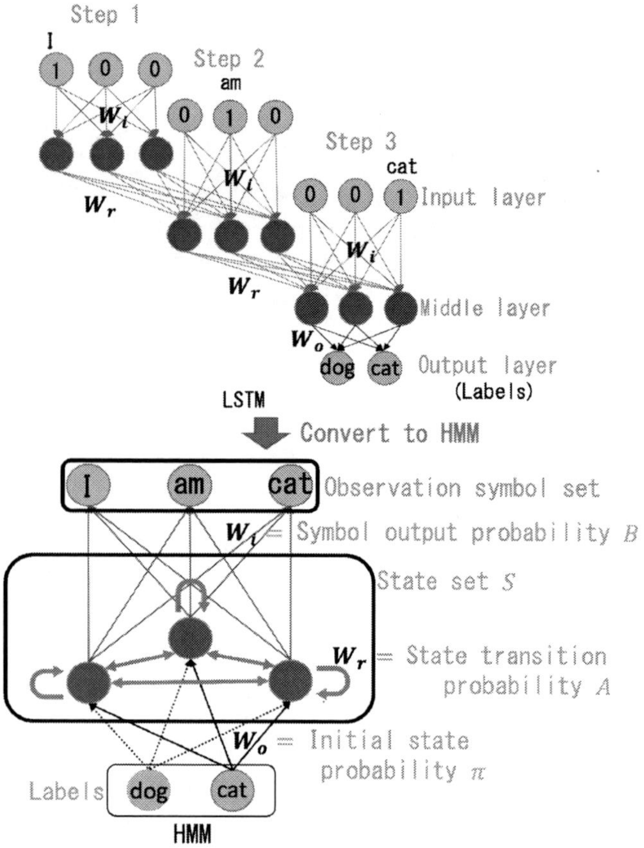

Fig. 3: Interrelationship between LSTM and HMM

In the proposed system, the weighted network obtained from the LSTM training is transformed into an HMM to estimate the likelihood of a word occurrence pattern (Figure 3). First, the input layer node of the LSTM is the observation symbol set of the HMM, and the intermediate layer node (LSTM unit) is the state set $\boldsymbol{S}$. Next, let the weight set $\boldsymbol{W_r}$ between the time series in the intermediate layer (by recursive processing) be the state transition probability $\boldsymbol{A}$, and the weight set $\boldsymbol{W_i}$ between the input layer intermediate layers be the symbol output probability $\boldsymbol{B}$. Finally, the set of weights between the output layers of the middle layer $\boldsymbol{W_o}$ is set to the initial state probability $\boldsymbol{\pi}$ (where $\boldsymbol{\pi}$ depends on the destination to be selected at that time).

E. Likelihood Estimation of Word Occurrence Patterns Using HMM

This section describes how to calculate the likelihood for the set of word occurrence patterns created in Section II-C. For the weighted network of the LSTM converted to an HMM in Section II-D, the observation series of observation symbols (the aforementioned word appearance patterns) is input to $\boldsymbol{O} = \{o_1, o_2, ...O_T\}$ (T is the length of the observation series, i.e., the length of the word appearance pattern). The number of states (number of intermediate layer nodes) is N (state number is i, j). From the aforementioned information, we can express

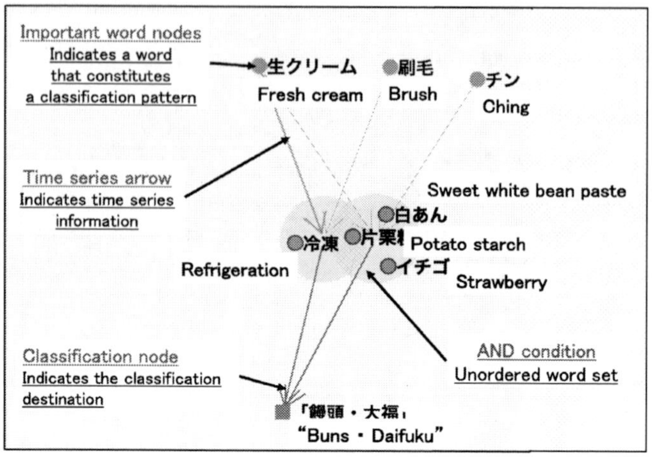

Fig. 4: Example of the system screen

the state transition probability $\boldsymbol{A}$ as (1), the symbol output probability $\boldsymbol{B}$ as (2), and the initial state probability $\boldsymbol{\pi}$ as (3).

$$\boldsymbol{A} = \{a_{ij} | a_{ij} = P(s_{t+1} = j | s_t = i)\} (1 \leq i, j \leq N) \quad (1)$$

$$\boldsymbol{B} = \{b_{ij}(o_t) | b_{ij}(o_t) = P(o_t | s_{t-1} = i, s_t = j)\} \\ (1 \leq i, j \leq N, 1 \leq t \leq T) \quad (2)$$

$$\boldsymbol{\pi} = \{\pi_i | \pi_i = P(s_0 = i)\} (1 \leq i \leq N) \quad (3)$$

Suppose that there exists a word occurrence pattern $\boldsymbol{O}$ for a classifier x. If we denote the initial state probability as $\boldsymbol{\pi}_x$, the likelihood $P(O|\boldsymbol{\pi}_x, \boldsymbol{A}, \boldsymbol{B})$ is calculated by (4).

$$\begin{aligned} P(\boldsymbol{O}|\boldsymbol{\pi}_x, \boldsymbol{A}, \boldsymbol{B}) &= \sum_{all \boldsymbol{S}} P(\boldsymbol{S}|\boldsymbol{\pi}_x, \boldsymbol{A}, \boldsymbol{B}) P(\boldsymbol{O}|\boldsymbol{S}, \boldsymbol{\pi}_x, \boldsymbol{A}, \boldsymbol{B}) \\ &= \sum_{all s_0 \dots s_T} \pi_{x s_0} a_{s_0 s_1} b_{s_0 s_1}(o_1) \cdot a_{s_1 s_2} b_{s_1 s_2}(o_2) \cdot \\ &\quad \dots \cdot a_{s_{T-1} s_T} b_{s_{T-1} s_T}(o_T) \end{aligned} \quad (4)$$

Finally, the likelihood for all word occurrence patterns are calculated by using (4), and, in the order of increasing likelihood, the word occurrence patterns are extracted as classification patterns that contribute to the classification.

F. Interpretation Support Network Display

In the interpretation support function, the set of classification patterns extracted in the previous section, which are strongly connected to the destination, is displayed as an interpretation support network. In this network, words are displayed as nodes and time-series relationship of words as arrows to make it easier to understand the words and time-series relations between words in the classification pattern. Furthermore, nodes that have arrows in both directions are

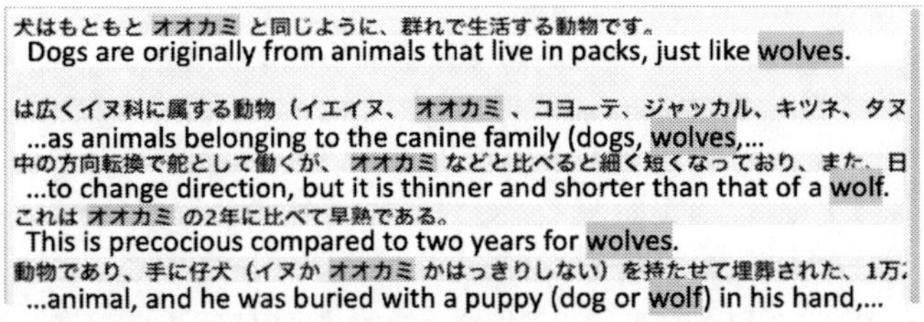

Fig. 5: Example of source text (select the word "wolf" for text about wolves)

displayed as a group. In addition, to indicate which classification pattern belongs to which destination, a red arrow connecting the destination name node and the last word node of the classification pattern is displayed.

As an example, Figure 4 shows an interpretation support network displayed from a set of texts on how to make five types of Japanese sweets [14]. The user selects a node at the bottom of the interface where the name of the classifier (in this case, "buns and daifuku") to be interpreted is displayed. At this time, the system extracts the user's any number of the classification patterns (in this case, five classification patterns) for the selected destination name in the order of likelihood. The extracted classification patterns are "Fresh cream $\rightarrow$ Refrigeration $\rightarrow$ Potato starch", "Fresh cream $\rightarrow$ Potato starch $\rightarrow$ Refrigeration", "Strawberry $\rightarrow$ Sweet white bean paste $\rightarrow$ Potato starch", "Brush $\rightarrow$ Potato starch $\rightarrow$ Refrigeration", and "Ching $\rightarrow$ Sweet white bean paste $\rightarrow$ Strawberry". Then, an interpretation support network is displayed, with the words of the extracted classification patterns as nodes and the time-series relations between words as arrows. However, if there are nodes that have the same word, they will be displayed overlapping. And, if they are pointing arrows at each other, they will be displayed together as a group with no ordering relationship. Finally, by looking at the interpretation support network, the user finds patterns of what words and time-series relations between words contribute to the selected classification destination and interprets them.

G. Function for Displaying the source text of Classification Patterns

When interpreting classification patterns, it is difficult to understand the actual context in which the words were used from the word information alone. For this reason, the source text display function shows how the words in the classification pattern are actually used in the text used for training.

By selecting the user's any words (the max is two words) on the interpretation support network, the user can see the sentence that contains the word in the source text. However, for ease of viewing, we limited the number of words displayed to ten before and after the selected word per sentence. In addition, up to two types of words can be selected, in which case, all sentences between the words are displayed. Figure 5 shows an example of the source text display of the classification pattern when the word "wolf" is selected using the text about wolves [15].

III. Verify the Effectiveness of a Text Classification Pattern Interpretation Support System Applying HMM

In this section, we describe an experiment to verify whether test subjects without deep knowledge of deep learning can interpret the classification patterns on the basis of the word occurrence patterns output by the proposed system.

A. Experimental Procedure

In the experiment, the test subjects were asked to interpret the classification patterns of the sentences classified into the "output labels" of each task for the three tasks shown in Table I. In addition, the details of the data used in each task are as follows.

- Task 1 "Character dialogue": We used 500 "tsundere," "deredere," and "normal" character dialogues of each from "tsundere bot," "deredere bot," and "character dialogue bot" on Twitter [16].
- Task 2 "Consumer electronics reviews:" From the top 50 most popular consumer electronics products on Amazon [17]. We used 1036 "useful" (highly rated with over four stars and over ten people who said this review was helpful), "useless" (High rating, but people said this review was helpful is zero), and "low-rated" (less than two stars) reviews of each.
- Task 3 "Game review," From the top 100 most popular game software on Amazon [17]. We used 1,473 "useful," "useless," and "low-rated" reviews of each.

To make the interpretation easier for the test subjects and to facilitate the analysis of the interpretation results, we set an interpretation objective for each task. The experiment was conducted with 16 undergraduate and graduate students who had no deep knowledge of deep learning. They were divided into two groups: one using the proposed system and the other using the comparison system. In the group using the proposed system, the test subjects were asked to find words (one word, combinations, and time series) that contribute to classification using the proposed system. We prepared a comparison system that extracts words specific to a specified output label by the TFIDF value of (5) and presents them in a list form. The comparison system is also able to use the source text display function of the proposed system.

$$\text{TFIDF}_i \text{ of a word } i = \text{Sentence frequency of word } i \times (\log(\frac{\text{Number of output labels}}{\text{DF value of word } i}) + 1) \quad (5)$$

The experimental procedure was interpreted by the test subjects of both groups using the following procedure. The number of classification patterns displayed by the proposed system was set to five, consisting of three words in order of increasing likelihood. The number of words displayed by the

TABLE I: EXPERIMENTAL TASKS GIVEN TO TEST SUBJECTS AND INTERPRETIVE OBJECTIVES

test subject name	Contents	Interpretive objectives
Task 1 "Character dialogue:" Output label "tsundere"	Categorization of lines of characters with specific characteristics in anime and manga: Ask test subjects to interpret the characteristics of lines of characters with "tsundere" characteristics.	Assuming you are a novelist, find a pattern of word usage specific to a "tsundere" character for your novel and give an interpretation of it.
Task 2 "Consumer electronics review:" Output label "Useful"	Categorization of reviews about popular consumer electronics on Amazon: Ask test subjects to interpret the characteristics of reviews with a large number of "this review was helpful."	Assuming you are a reporter introducing consumer electronics, find a pattern of word usage specific to "helpful reviews" of popular consumer electronics products and give your interpretation of it.
Task 3 "Game review:" Output label "Useful"	Categorization of reviews about popular game software on Amazon: Ask test subjects to interpret the characteristics of reviews with a large number of "this review was helpful."	Assuming that you are a reporter introducing game software, find a pattern of word usage specific to "helpful reviews" of game software and give your interpretation of it.

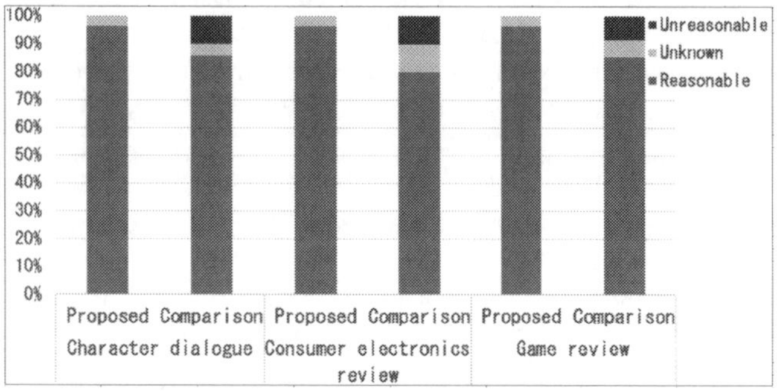

Fig. 6: Breakdown of validity of test subject's interpretation (test subject average)

comparison system was also set to 15 in accordance with the proposed system.

Step 1 Select output labels to be interpreted: For the "Character dialogue" task, we targeted lines of characters classified as "tsundere." For the "Consumer electronics review" and "Game review" tasks, we included reviews with a rating of four or more and a "usefulness" rating of ten or more.

Step 2 Read the "interpretation objectives" corresponding to each selected output label to understand its content.

Step 3 For the selected output, display the "interpretation support network" and find ten features (one word, combinations, chronological order, etc.) that may contribute to the output.

Step 4 Devise your own interpretations of the highlighted features in accordance with the "interpretive objectives," using the source text display function.

B. Experimental Results and Discussion

First, the breakdown of the validity of the interpretations described by the test subjects (test subject average) is shown in Figure 6. However, the breakdown of interpretive validity was classified by one of the authors on the basis of the following definitions.

- Reasonable interpretation (reasonable): The correctness of the content can be confirmed from the source text, and it meets the "purpose of interpretation."
- Interpretation that cannot be judged as reasonable (unknown): The intent of the content is not clear, and it cannot be judged as reasonable or not reasonable.
- Unreasonable interpretation (unreasonable): The content of the interpretation was found to be incorrect or not in line with the "purpose of the interpretation."

Regarding the judgment of whether the subjects' interpretations are valid or not, the author have classified them by paying attention to whether all the following criteria are met. In addition, this process was repeated at least ten times to check for errors, and the percentage of validity classified is considered to be sufficiently objective. moreover, the purpose of this experiment is only to confirm how much better the subjects can interpret the data by using the proposed system compared to the comparison system, and the comparison of the output of the systems will not be considered in this experiment.

- Checking that the features found by the subjects are included in the source text.
- Compare the subject's interpretation with the source text, and confirm that there is at least one description that matches the claimed content.

Figure 6 shows that more than 97% of the interpretations in the proposed system were classified as reasonable interpretations, confirming their correctness. In particular, there were no interpretations that were not valid, which accounted for nearly 10% in the comparison system. In addition, the results of the proposed system showed that less than 3% of the interpretations were reasonable or unreasonable, while those of the comparison system were 5% to 10%. Therefore, we can say that the proposed system has clearer intentions and more reasonable interpretations.

Next, the percentages of source sentences that fit the interpretation (test subject average), as given by the test subjects, are shown in Figure 7. The number of source texts that match these interpretations is calculated by dividing the number of source texts for each task (500 for the "Character dialogue" task, 1036 for the "Consumer electronics review" task, and 1473 for the "Game review" task) by the percentage of source texts that match the interpretation. Regarding the number of source texts that fit the subject's interpretation, the author counted the number of source texts that were confirmed to meet all of the following criteria. In addition, this process was

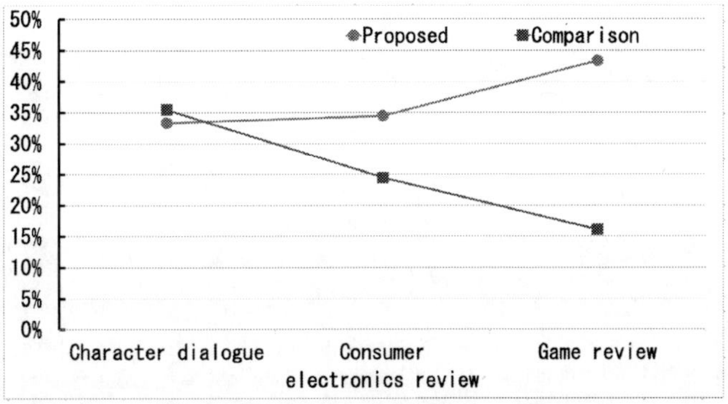

Fig. 7: Percentage of source texts to which the test subject's interpretation applies (test subject average)

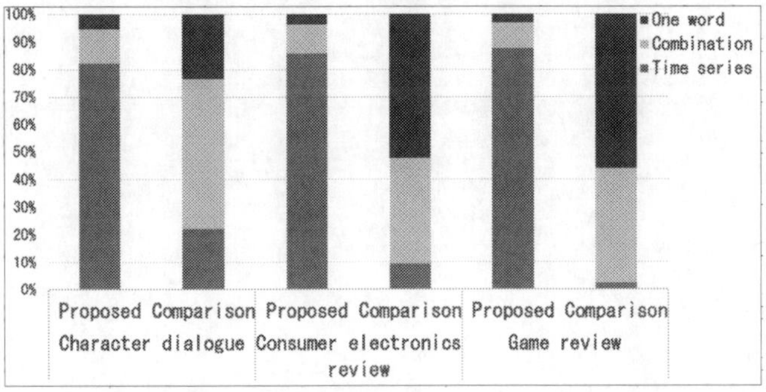

Fig. 8: Breakdown of features focused on by test subjects (test subject average)

also repeated more than 10 times to check for errors, and the number of source texts that fit the subject's interpretation is considered sufficiently objective.

- Checking that the features found by the subjects are included in the source text.
- Compare the subject's interpretation with the source text, and confirm that there is at least one description that matches the claimed content.

The results for the "Character dialogue" task were almost the same. However, those of the "Consumer electronics review" and "Game review" tasks showed that the proposed system was able to derive more interpretations that applied to the source text. In particular, for the "Game Review" task, the proposed system outperformed the results of the comparison system by nearly 30%. Therefore, we can say that the interpretation support network displayed by the proposed system was able to derive more typical interpretations that applied to a wider range of source texts.

Figure 8 shows the breakdown (test subject average) of the features (one word, combinations, time series, etc.) the test subjects focused on for interpretation. However, this breakdown was classified by one of the authors on the basis of the following definitions.

- One word: One interpretation is made from one word.
- Combination: One interpretation is made from multiple words, without any particular consideration of time-series relationships.
- Time series: One interpretation is made from multiple words, taking into account the time-series relationship.

The results in Figure 8 show that more than 80% of the interpretations in the proposed system focused on the time-series relationship of words, compared with the about 10% in the comparison system. The rest of the interpretations were based on individual words and combinations of words in the same proportion. This may be because the interpretation support network of the proposed system made the time-series relationship of the words easy to understand, and thus the test subjects paid more attention to the time-series relationship of the words and made more interpretations. However, in the comparison system, although the characteristic words of the top TFIDF were displayed, it was difficult to understand the connection between the words. Therefore, it is likely that the system was often interpreted from a single word or a combination of words with similar meanings. Therefore, we can say that the proposed system performed a typical interpretation considering the time-series relationship of words.

In summary, we confirmed that the proposed system is able to derive typical and reasonable interpretations that are applicable to a wide range of source texts with a higher rate of correct answers than the comparison system. This can be attributed to the fact that the proposed system focuses on the chronological relationship between multiple words. Furthermore, even for short texts, such as the "character dialogue" task, the proposed system is able to derive typical interpretations at the same level as referring to words with high TFIDF values.

IV. CONCLUSION AND FUTURE WORK

In this study, we proposed a classification pattern interpretation support system to classify multiple text data with an LSTM that can learn the time-series relationship of words and interpret the trained network. One of the features of this research is that it applies the network structure of the learned recursive deep learning to an HMM for processing. Therefore, the system can easily extract the time-series information of the learned features without changing the structure of the model. In the verification experiment to confirm the effectiveness of the proposed system, we confirmed that the proposed environment can result in a reasonable interpretation that covers a wide range of the original content from the classification patterns, including time-series information, even for users who are not familiar with deep learning.

In the future, we plan to investigate the effectiveness of the proposed system more objectively by statistically examining the subjects' interpretations, such as the length of their interpretations and the types of words in the sentences. In addition, we will change the input of the LSTM to a distributed representation that includes information on the relationship between words, so that the interpretation can be more focused on the meaning of the words, and also build an interpretation environment for more complex deep learning networks, such as the Bidirectional Encoder Representations from Transformers (BERT). In addition, we would like to build a framework that can validate the knowledge obtained as a hypothesis by obtaining data from inside and outside the training data to support the validity of the interpretation given by the user and presenting it to the user.

REFERENCES

[1] H. Wang, et al., "Attack of the Tails: Yes, You Really Can Backdoor Federated Learning", Advances in Neural Information Processing Systems 33 (NeurIPS 2020), pp. 16070-16084, 2020.

[2] D. Gunning and D. Aha, "DARPA' s Explainable Artificial Intelligence (XAI) Program", AI Magazine, Vol. 40(2), pp. 44-58, 2019.

[3] A. Fernandez, F. Herrera, O. Cordon, M. Jose del Jesus, and F. Marcelloni, "Evolutionary fuzzy systems for explainable artificial intelligence: Why, when, what for, and where to?," IEEE Computational Intelligence Magazine 14 (1), pp. 69-81, 2019.

[4] J. Haspiel, et al., "Explanations and expectations: Trust building in automated vehicles," Companion of the ACM/IEEE International Conference on Human-Robot Interaction, ACM, pp. 119-120, 2018.

[5] O. Goudet, D. Kalainathan, P. Caillou, I. Guyon, D. Lopez-Paz, and M. Sebag, "Learning functional causal models with generative neural networks," Explainable and Interpretable Models in Computer Vision and Machine Learning, Springer, pp. 39-80, 2018.

[6] R. M. J. Byrne, "Counterfactuals in explainable artificial intelligence (XAI): Evidence from human reasoning," Proceedings of the Twenty-Eighth International Joint Conference on Artificial Intelligence, IJCAI-19, pp. 6276-6282, 2019.

[7] G. Audemard, F. Koriche, and P. Marquis, "On Tractable XAI Queries based on Compiled Representations," KR Proceedings 2020 Special Session on KR and Machine Learning, pp. 838-849, 2020.

[8] Q. Zhang, Y. Yang, H. Ma, and Y. N. Wu, "Interpreting CNNs via decision trees," IEEE Conference on Computer Vision and Pattern Recognition, pp. 6261-6270, 2019.

[9] A. Barredo Arrieta, et al., "Explainable Artificial Intelligence (XAI): Concepts, taxonomies, opportunities and challenges toward responsible AI," Information Fusion, vol. 58, pp. 82-115, 2020.

[10] E. Tjoa and C. Guan, "A Survey on Explainable Artificial Intelligence (XAI): Toward Medical XAI," IEEE Transactions on Neural Networks and Learning Systems 20 Oct 2020, pp. 1-21, 2020.

[11] J. Wagner, J. M. Kohler, T. Gindele, L. Hetzel, J. T. Wiedemer, and S. Behnke, "Interpretable and fine-grained visual explanations for convolutional neural networks," Proceedings of the IEEE Conference on Computer Vision and Pattern Recognition, pp. 9097-9107, 2019.

[12] C. Panigutti, A. Perotti, and D. Pedreschi, "Doctor XAI: an ontology-based approach to black-box sequential data classification explanations," Proceedings of the 2020 Conference on Fairness Accountability and Transparency, pp. 629-639, 2020.

[13] M Daniluk, T Rocktaschel, J Welbl, and S Riedel, "Frustratingly Short Attention Spans in Neural Language", In Proceedings of ICLR 2017, 2017.

[14] Cookpad Inc., "cookpad", http://cookpad.com, <link> 2021.06.15.

[15] Wikimedia Foundation, Inc., "Wikimedia", https://ja.wikipedia.org, <link> 2021.06.15.

[16] Twitter, Inc., "Twitter", http://twitter.com, <link> 2021.06.15.

[17] Amazon.com, Inc., "Amazon.co.jp", https://www.amazon.co.jp, <link> 2021.06.15.

Personality Traits in the Relationship of Emotion and Performance in Command-and-Control Environments

Alina Schmitz-Hübsch, Sophie-Marie Stasch, Ron Becker, Sven Fuchs
Fraunhofer Institute for Communication, Information Processing and Ergonomics FKIE
53343 Wachtberg, Germany
e-mail: {alina.schmitz-huebsch, sophie-marie.stasch, ron.becker, sven.fuchs}@fkie.fraunhofer.de

Abstract—**Affect-adaptive systems are capable of adapting human-machine interaction with respect to the current emotional user state and situational needs. To set the ground for a future affect-adaptive system, we examined interindividual differences in the relationship between emotional user states – composed of emotional valence and arousal - and performance in a command-and-control environment in a lab experiment (*N* = 51, 19-57 years, *M* = 32.75 *SD* = 9.8). We suspect that observed interindividual differences are caused by two personality traits: neuroticism and conscientiousness. We used personality, valence, and arousal to model task performance in a linear mixed-model and found significant effects for valence as a random effect and arousal as a fixed effect. Furthermore, we found interaction effects with neuroticism and conscientiousness. Our results suggest that future affect-adaptive systems may benefit from considering personality traits to address interindividual differences in the relationship of emotional user state and performance.**

Keywords–Affective computing; Affect-adaptive systems; Affective user state; Command-and-control; Personality traits.

I. INTRODUCTION

In human-machine interaction, critical user states, such as fatigue [1] or an incorrect focus of attention [2], may impair the performance of the human-machine system. Some adaptive systems permanently observe the user state and adapt their interaction mechanisms when critical or undesired states are detected to mitigate performance decrements [3]. This investigation focuses on the emotional user state as one of the dimensions in a multidimensional model of user state [4]. [5], such as command-and-control (C2) environments. Considering that emotion and performance are closely linked [6][7], a deeper understanding of the emotional user state and its correlation with performance is necessary for our goal of developing an affect-adaptive C2 system. In a simulated C2 task, we examined the influence of personality traits on this correlation. In accordance with [8], both the valence component and the arousal component of the emotional state were analyzed.

Following this introduction, we provide theoretical background regarding the correlation of emotional user state and performance and the role of personality (Section 2). Section 3 describes the method we used to investigate the research question. Section 4 presents the results of the statistical analyses that are then discussed in Section 5. The paper closes with our conclusions drawn from this investigation (Section 6).

II. BACKGROUND

In previous investigations [9][10], we observed remarkable interindividual differences in the correlation of the emotional user state and performance. While a state of low arousal and neutral valence was beneficial for many subjects, some benefitted from states of positive or negative valence. About 50% of the subjects did not show any association between emotional user state and performance. These results pose a challenge for affect-adaptive mechanisms as there may be a group of users that performs best in a state of neutral valence, while others thrive in a positive or negative emotional state. An affect-adaptive system that does not consider these individual differences in its adaptation mechanisms could actually hinder performance, for example by promoting neutral valence in a subject that performs best in a positive state of valence. We therefore aim at testing the feasibility of developing distinct *Affective Response Categories* of users that benefit from different emotional user states. An effective affect-adaptive system should be able to distinguish these categories, assign users to them, and adapt interaction accordingly.

Our approach to assign users to these categories is based on the Appraisal Theory of Emotion [11]. According to this theory, emotions are caused by the appraisal of a stimulus and matching it with individual goals and expectations. Multiple processes like bodily sensations and situational factors contribute to the emotional experience [12]. We suspect that the individual differences observed in our previous investigations emerge at the stage of appraisal. For example, if an individual tends to an anger-prone appraisal style, events are often appraised in a way that leads to an anger experience [13]. Previous research indicates that personality traits have a key role in this process [14][15]. Personality traits are associated with certain coping strategies for emotional states. Neuroticism, for example, has been associated with low perceived coping ability, experience of negative emotions such as anxiety, and emotion-focused coping strategies. Conscientiousness, on the other hand, appears to be correlated with problem-focused coping and high perceived coping ability [16]. These findings indicate that the personality-appraisal relationship differs between individuals and could offer an explanation for the interindividual differences in the correlation of the emotional user state and performance we found in earlier investigations [9][10].

Supporting evidence for the moderating effect of personality on emotional reactions is also provided by Brouwer, Van Schaik, Korteling, van Erp and Toet [17], who investigated the relationship between conscientiousness, stress sensitivity, and arousal. Subjects with a low conscientiousness score showed a higher increase in heart rate than subjects with a high conscientiousness score during a stressful situation. Additionally, Roslan et al. [18] found an increase in emotional arousal, measured by physiological correlates, for subjects scoring high on neuroticism. During a speaking task, subjects with high neuroticism scores showed a higher increase in skin conductance and heart rate than subjects with a low neuroticism score.

We therefore suspect that personality traits, particularly neuroticism and conscientiousness, moderate the interindividual differences and would like to test the feasibility of determining a user's Affective Response Category by his or her personality characteristics.

1) Hypothesis 1: The emotional user state is associated with task performance.

a) Higher pupil width is significantly associated with low performance for all subjects.

b) The relationship between emotional valence (positive, neutral, negative) and performance varies across subjects.

2) Hypothesis 2: Personality traits have a moderating effect on the emotion-performance relationship.

a) There are significant interaction effects of neuroticism with valence (I) and arousal (II).

b) There are significant interaction effects of conscientiousness with valence (I) and arousal (II).

c) There are significant interaction effects of neuroticism and conscientiousness with valence (I) and arousal (II).

The present investigation aims to test these hypotheses in a simulated C2 task as a step towards an affect-adaptive C2 environment that considers individual differences in the affective response.

III. Method

A laboratory experiment was conducted to test the hypotheses.

A. *Sample Description*

Fifty-one ($N = 51$) subjects aged 18 to 57 years ($M = 32.75$, $SD = 9.8$) participated in the experiment. All participants were employees of the Fraunhofer Institute for Communication, Information Processing and Ergonomics (FKIE) who were invited via e-mail. Thirty-three percent of the participants were female. Participation was not generally compensated, but the three best-performing subjects earned a voucher for motivational purposes.

B. *Experimental Task*

To simulate a C2 task, we used the Rich and Adaptable Test Environment for C2 (RATE) [19], a modular and scalable task environment that allows for flexible design of experimental tasks and customized performance scoring. Inspired by the Warship Commander Task [20], we developed an air defense task using a simulated radar display (Figure 1). In order to protect their own ship, participants had to perform three subtasks.

1) Identify: All unknown tracks need to be assigned an identification (hostile, neutral or friendly) according to certain parameters and rules.

2) Warn: Hostile tracks approaching the ship must be warned upon entering the outer safety zone.

3) Engage: Hostile tracks entering the inner safety zone despite prior warning must be engaged.

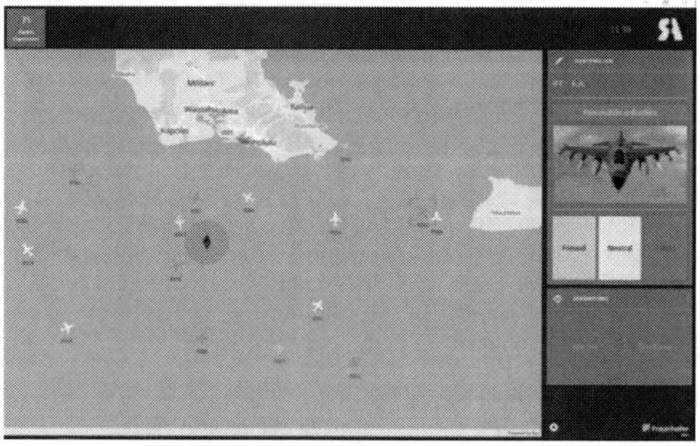

Figure 1. Rich and Adaptable Test Environment (RATE) for C2 [19].

All participants went through a training session followed by twelve scenarios of varying difficulty. Each scenario lasted 3:30 minutes. Based on the cognitive task load model validated in a C2 task by de Greef and Arciszewski [21], difficulty levels were determined by the total number of tracks and the relative proportion of enemy tracks. The number of tracks in each scenario was 6, 12, 18, or 24. The relative percentage of enemy tracks was 17%, 33%, or 47%. To avoid sequence effects, difficulty levels were randomized between subjects.

C. *Variables*

1) Independent Variables:

a) Big Five Personality Factors were assessed by the German version of the NEO-FFI [22]. In the present investigation, we focused on conscientiousness and neuroticism only.

b) Scenario difficulty varied across all twelve scenarios to cover a broad spectrum of difficulty levels.

c) Emotional valence was derived from facial expressions using Emotient FACET, an emotion detection tool that analyzes facial expressions in real time using a regular webcam.

d) Emotional arousal was indicated by pupil width, measured with a Tobii Pro Spectrum 300 Hz eye tracker.

2) Dependent Variables:

Performance was assessed via a performance score that considered priority of the tasks, accuracy, and response time [17]. The score was visible in the upper left corner of the screen (see Figure 1), so that participants were able to assess their own performance at all times.

D. *Statistical Analysis*

A linear mixed-model was calculated using the *lme4* package [23] in R (Version 4.0.5) [24]. Performance was included as the dependent variable. The median of a time window of 10 seconds was calculated for the performance score, emotional valence values, and pupil width, respectively. To control for confounding variables we included difficulty level, gaming experience and age as fixed effects before adding the emotional state. Pupil width was included as fixed effect as we expected that higher pupil width is associated with low performance across all subjects.

As fixed effects, we added difficulty level, gaming experience, age, and pupil width. Since previous investigations showed individual differences in emotional valence, classification outcome for neutral, positive, and negative valence was included as random effects. Moreover, conscientiousness and neuroticism were included as fixed effects to test the moderating effect of personality on the emotion-performance relationship.

The *lmerTest* package [25] was used to test for the significance of fixed effects. The Akaike information criterion (AIC) was used to compare models. All independent variables were centered within subjects to perform group-mean centering before running the statistical analysis. All models were fitted with the maximum-likelihood estimation.

IV. RESULTS

In this section, we describe the results of our analyses.

A. *The fixed effect model:*

The Intraclass-Correlation-Coefficient (ICC) of the random-intercept-only-model was 0.21, showing that 21% of the observed variance in performance can be attributed to between-subject factors. The AIC of the first model was 86092.62. The estimate of the significant intercept was 72.87, representing the average performance value of all subjects across all levels of difficulty. The second model included difficulty level as a fixed effect. The AIC of the second model decreased to 75851.911, ANOVA comparison between the random-intercept-only-model and the second model showed a significant increase in model fit on a $p < 0.001$ level. Gaming experience was added as the second fixed effect to the third model. The AIC decreased significantly ($p < 0.01$) from 75651.911 to 75646.272. The fourth model included age as a fixed effect. The AIC of the fourth model decreased significantly ($p < 0.001$) from 75646.272 to 75631.464. The fifth model included pupil width as a fixed effect. The AIC decreased from 75646.272 to 74162.670 and was a significant improvement in model performance ($p < 0.001$), confirming H1a.

B. *The random effect model*

The addition of positive valence as a random effect decreased the AIC to 73765.647, the addition of neutral valence decreased the AIC to 73532.586, and the addition of negative valence decreased the AIC to 73449.612. ANOVA comparison showed a significant improvement ($p < 0.001$) of each model, respectively, confirming H1b.

C. *The interaction model*

The interaction models tested the moderating effects of the personality traits conscientiousness and neuroticism on the relationship between emotions and performance. We tested for model improvement using ANOVA comparisons between the random effects model and interaction model of interest.

*1) Neuroticism * emotional valence*

The addition of an interaction term between positive valence and neuroticism to the model increased the AIC to 73452.544. The interaction between neutral valence and neuroticism increased the AIC to 73455.242. The interaction between negative valence and neuroticism showed an AIC of 73455.387. None of the interactions models showed a significant improvement in model fit compared to the random effects model that included valence as a random effect. Therefore, the moderating influence of neuroticism on the relationship between valence and performance stated in H2a (I) was not confirmed in the current experiment.

*2) Conscientiousness * emotional valence*

The addition of an interaction term between positive valence and conscientiousness to the model increased the AIC to 73450.694. The interaction between neutral valence and conscientiousness increased the AIC to 73452.165. The interaction between negative valence and conscientiousness showed an AIC of 73452.277. Similar to the interaction between neuroticism and valence, none of the interactions models showed a significant improvement in model fit to the random effects model. The moderating effect of conscientiousness on emotional valence stated in H2b (I) was not confirmed in the current experiment. As neither of the personality traits interacted with valence, H2c (I) was rejected.

*3) Neuroticism * arousal*

Although neuroticism had no direct influence on performance as a fixed effect, it significantly influenced pupil width. The model including an interaction between neuroticism and pupil width demonstrated an AIC of 73439.335, representing a significant increase in model fit on a $p < 0.001$ level compared to the random effects model, confirming H2a (II). In low-arousal conditions, as indicated by smaller pupil size, participants with a low neuroticism score performed better than subjects with a high neuroticism score (see Figure 2).

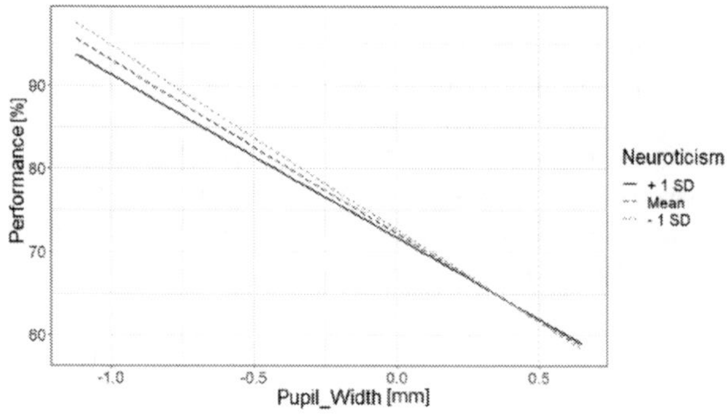

Figure 2. The Interaction between Pupil Width and the Personality Factor Neuroticism.

*4) Conscientiousness * arousal*

Similar to neuroticism, conscientiousness had no direct influence as a fixed effect on performance. However, the addition of the interaction term between conscientiousness and pupil width also gained a significant increase in model performance. The AIC decreased significantly from 73439.335 to 73436.082 ($p < 0.05$), supporting H2b (II). In high arousal conditions, as indicated by higher pupil size, low conscientiousness is associated with low performance.

*5) Neuroticism * conscientiousness * pupil width*

Given that both personality traits interacted with pupil width in the current experiment, a three-way interaction between neuroticism, conscientiousness, and pupil width was investigated as well. Compared to the model including both two-way interactions terms, the current model showed an AIC of 73433.829. This increase in model fit of the three-way interaction model compared to the model including both two-way interactions was significant ($p < 0.05$), supporting H2c (II). Subjects scoring high on neuroticism and low on conscientiousness demonstrate in highly arousing states, as indicated by a higher pupil size, an association with low performance.

D. *The final model*

The final model (see Table 1) includes the fixed effects of difficulty level, gaming experience, pupil width, and age, the random effects of emotional valence and the three-way interaction between neuroticism, conscientiousness, and pupil width. While difficulty level is a negative predictor of performance with an estimate of -2.58, gaming experience shows a positive influence on performance with an estimate of 2.89. Furthermore, pupil width and age are negative predictors of performance with an estimate of -34.42 and -0.41, respectively. While the interaction between neuroticism and pupil width is still significant on a $p < 0.01$ level, the interaction between conscientiousness and pupil width was no longer significant. However, the higher order interaction between neuroticism, conscientiousness, and pupil width explains that finding. We therefore limit the interpretation to the higher-order interaction. Figure 3 visualizes this three-way interaction effect. The influence of neuroticism on pupil width in the two-way interaction was positive with an estimate of 11.66. The inclusion of conscientiousness within the three-way interaction moderates this relationship by shifting the estimate to -3.35.

In instances of low performance, participants with a high neuroticism score and a low conscientiousness score demonstrate a higher pupil width than subjects with a high neuroticism score and a high conscientiousness score (see Table 1 and Figure 3).

TABLE I. RESULTS OF FIXED EFFCTS, RANDOM EFFECTS, AND THE INTERACTION BETWEEN PUPIL WIDTH AND PERSONALITY

Final Model

	Performance		
Predictors	*Estimates*	*CI*	*p*
(Intercept)	103.45	75.11 – 131.78	**<0.001**
Difficulty_Level	-2.58	-2.61 – -2.54	**<0.001**
Gaming_Experience	2.89	1.06 – 4.71	**0.002**
Age	-0.41	-0.59 – -0.24	**<0.001**
Pupil_Width	-34.42	-49.17 – -19.66	**<0.001**
Conscientiousness	-0.42	-9.19 – 8.34	0.925
Neuroticism	3.07	-11.55 – 17.68	0.681
Pupil_Width * Conscientiousness	3.61	-1.31 – 8.52	0.150
Pupil_Width * Neuroticism	11.66	4.02 – 19.30	**0.003**
Conscientiousness * Neuroticism	-1.34	-6.30 – 3.62	0.597
(Pupil_Width * Conscientiousness) * Neuroticism	-3.35	-6.03 – -0.67	**0.014**
Random Effects			
σ^2	68.88		
$\tau_{00\ Subject}$	39.34		
$\tau_{11\ Subject.Positive\_Valence}$	14.54		
$\tau_{11\ Subject.Neutral\_Valence}$	56.68		
$\tau_{11\ Subject.Negative\_Valence}$	67.33		
ρ_{01}	-0.05		
	-0.04		
	0.20		
ICC	0.36		
$N_{Subject}$	51		
Marginal R^2 / Conditional R^2	0.636 / 0.769		
AIC	73433.829		

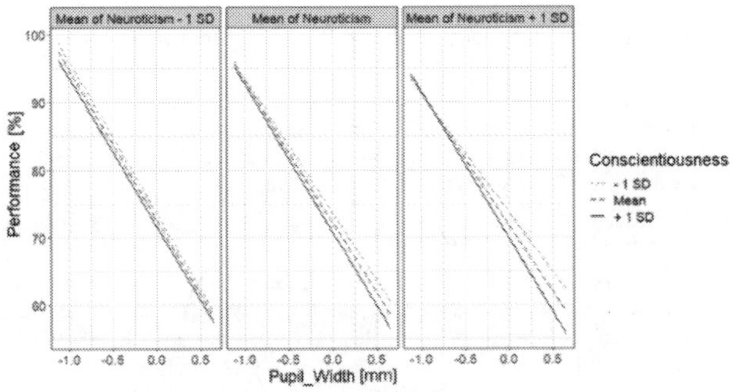

Figure 3. The Interaction between Pupil Width and the Personality Factors Neuroticism and Conscientiousness.

V. DISCUSSION

We investigated the correlation of the emotional user state and performance in a C2 environment, as well as the influence of personality traits on this correlation. All three classifiers of emotional valence were associated with performance and contributed significantly to the performance model as random effects. This replicates our earlier findings of interindividual differences in the correlation of emotion and performance [9][10] and confirms H1b. Unsurprisingly, low performance was associated with high difficulty level, low gaming experience, and high age. As hypothesized in H1a, low performance was also associated with high pupil width, indicating higher arousal during more demanding scenarios. Although conscientiousness and neuroticism showed no significant main effect on performance, participants with a higher neuroticism score tend to perform better on the task.

We found significant improvements of model performance when including arousal and emotional valence. Previous findings regarding the association between low conscientiousness [17] as well as high neuroticism [18] with increased arousal are in line with the results of the present study. Thus, it would be beneficial for affect-adaptive C2 systems to consider both these dimensions of the emotional user state. However, this investigation only analyzed the correlational relationship of emotion and performance. To ensure that emotions causally influence performance, we suggest an experimental design that includes the induction of emotional user states.

We earlier proposed to create Affective Response Categories to cluster users based on what emotional user states are most beneficial for their performance. This would allow affect-adaptive systems to adapt interactions in an appropriate manner based on category membership. Our results suggest that a categorization based on personality traits may be possible, given that we observed interaction effects of (1) neuroticism with arousal and performance, and (2) neuroticism and conscientiousness with arousal and performance. In conditions of low arousal, participants that score higher on the neuroticism scale show lower performance compared to participants that score lower on the neuroticism scale. Therefore, we assumed that subjects with a tendency to neuroticism put in less effort in less demanding situations. We confirmed this hypothesis by analyzing the interaction effect of difficulty level, neuroticism, and pupil width on performance. The results indicate that affect-adaptive systems should monitor participants with higher scores on neuroticism closely, as they tend to lower performance in low arousal conditions.

In order to further investigate this subgroup of participants, we analyzed the interaction of pupil width, neuroticism, and conscientiousness on performance. Subjects with high neuroticism scores and high conscientiousness scores showed higher arousal during low performance than those with low conscientiousness scores. This three-way interaction was significant with a negative estimate of – 3.35. Therefore, we suspect that more conscientious subjects in the subgroup of high neuroticism tried harder to counter the low performance state than those who are less conscientious.

We proposed that interindividual differences observed in our previous investigations emerged at the stage of appraisal and that personality traits have a key role in this process [14][15]. Based on the reported results, appraisal theory offers an explanation for differences in the correlation of arousal and performance. Participants that scored higher on neuroticism and higher in conscientiousness performed worse when arousal was high. Possibly, more conscientious participants executed tasks more carefully and required more time than less conscientious subjects. Especially in high workload scenarios that demand fast task execution in order to avoid score deductions, less conscientious subjects might have had an advantage. To test this theory, a closer look at accuracy and response time would be necessary to analyze the speed-accuracy trade-off [19].

VI. CONCLUSIONS

Our results indicate that people who differ in their personality characteristics also differ in their correlation of emotional arousal and performance. Participants scoring high on neuroticism and low on conscientiousness exhibit a higher arousal level than participants scoring low on neuroticism and high on conscientiousness. Hence, we conclude that the proposed categorization by personality traits shows promising potential for further research.

A starting point for how to consider personality in interactive systems is offered by Sarsam and Al-Samarraie [26], who demonstrated the benefits of integrating a user's personality trait into the design of the user interface. Users scoring high on neuroticism prefer calm colors as well as more structured and divided texts. Furthermore, the use of a personality-tailored interface also increased visual attention during a learning task.

An affect-adaptive system that considers Affective Response Categories to adapt interactions according to the user's individual emotional needs could assist in achieving consistently high performance in a human-machine-system. For example, in a high workload scenario, a user belonging to the subgroup of high neuroticism and high conscientiousness might need extra support in executing the tasks at the required speed, as compared to a user with high neuroticism but low conscientiousness. In a low workload scenario, if the current user belongs to the "high neuroticism" subgroup, it may be possible – according to our results – to avoid performance decrements by increasing arousal. An appropriate adaptation strategy might be to decrease the use of automation. With increasing workload, this user's arousal would increase and performance would improve. In contrast, a user in the "low neuroticism" subgroup may not require adaptive intervention in the same situation.

The preliminary parameters of the Affective Response Categories outlined herein demonstrate the feasibility for the creation of distinct categories and offer a starting point. In order to construct more holistic categories, further associations of individual characteristics and the correlation of emotion and performance will be necessary.

ACKNOWLEDGMENT

The authors would like to thank Mitja Galkin for his valuable contributions to the customization of the RATE task environment.

REFERENCES

[1] T. Åkerstedt, R. Mollard, A. Samel, M. Simons, and M. Spender, "The role of EUFTL legislation in reducing cumulative fatigue in civil aviation," ETSC Meeting, 2003.

[2] M. S. Young and N. A. Stanton, "Malleable attentional resources theory: a new explanation for the effects of mental underload on performance," Hum. Factors: J. Hum. Factors Ergon. Soc., pp. 365–375, 2002.

[3] S. Fuchs et al., "Application-oriented realization of adaptive human-machine interaction for safety-critical systems (ARAMIS)," Final project report, grant no. E/E4BX/HA031/CF215, Fraunhofer FKIE, Wachtberg, 2019.

[4] J. Schwarz and S. Fuchs,"Multidimensional real-time assessment of user state and performance to trigger dynamic system adaptation," International Conference on Augmented Cognition, July 2017, pp. 383-398, Springer, Cham.

[5] E. Hudlicka, "To feel or not to feel: The role of affect in human-computer inter-action," International Journal of Human-Computer Studies, vol. 59, no. 1-2, pp. 1-32, 2003, https://doi.org/10.1016/S1071-5819(03)00047-8.

[6] J. R. Gray, "Emotional modulation of cognitive control: Approach–withdrawal states double-dissociate spatial from verbal two-back task performance," Journal of Experimental Psychology, pp. 436–452, 2001.

[7] G. Tenenbaum, "A conceptual framework for studying emotions–cognitions–performance linkage under conditions that vary in perceived pressure," Progress in Brain Research: Mind and Motion: The Bidirectional Link between Thought and Action, Elsevier, pp. 159–178, 2009.

[8] J. A. Russell, "A circumplex model of affect," Journal of Personality and Social Psychology, vol. 39, no. 6, pp. 1161–1178, 1980. https://doi.org/10.1037/h0077714

[9] A. Schmitz-Hübsch and S. Fuchs, "Challenges and Prospects of Emotional State Diagnosis in Command and Control Environments," International Conference on Human-Computer Interaction, July 2020, pp. 64-75, Springer, Cham.

[10] A. Schmitz-Hübsch, S. M. Stasch, and S. Fuchs, "Individual Differences in the Relationship between Emotion and Performance in Command-and-Control Environments," International Conference on Human-Computer Interaction, July 2021, in press.

[11] R. S. Lazarus, "Emotion and adaptation," Oxford University Press on Demand, 1991.

[12] A. Moors, "Appraisal Theory of Emotion," In: Zeigler-Hill V., Shackelford T. (eds) Encyclopedia of Personality and Individual Differences. Springer, Cham., 2017, https://doi.org/10.1007/978-3-319-28099-8_493-1.

[13] I. J., Roseman, "A model of appraisal in the emotion system," Appraisal processes in emotion: Theory, methods, research, pp. 68–91, 2001.

[14] E. Tong et al., "The role of the Big Five in appraisals," Personality and Individual Differences,vol. 41, no. 3, pp. 513-523, 2006.

[15] P. Kuppens and E. M. W. Tong, "An appraisal account of individual differences in emotional experience," Social and Personality Psychology Compass, vol. 4, no. 12, pp. 1138–1150, 2010.

[16] J. A. Penley and J. Tomaka, "Associations among the Big Five, emotional responses, and coping with acute stress," Personality and Individual Differences, vol. 32, no. 7, pp. 1215–1228 , 2002.

[17] A. M. Brouwer, M. G. Van Schaik, J. H. Korteling, J. B. van Erp and A. Toet, "Neuroticism, extraversion, conscientiousness and stress: physiological correlates," IEEE Trans. Affect. Comput. Vol. 6, no.2, pp. 109–117, 2014.

[18] N. S. Roslan et al., "An Investigation of Physiological Correlates of Neuroticism During Speaking Task: A Preliminary Study," In 2018 IEEE-EMBS Conference on Biomedical Engineering and Sciences, IECBES, Dec. 2018, pp. 515-519, IEEE.

[19] R. Becker, S. M. Stasch, A. Schmitz-Hübsch, and S. Fuchs, "Quantitative Scoring System to assess Performance in Experimental Environments," International Conference on Advances in Computer-Human Interactions, July 2021, in press.

[20] Warship Commander 4.4; Computer Software; San Diego, CA: Pacific Science & Engineering Group; 2003.

[21] T. D. Greef and H. Arciszewski, "Triggering adaptive automation in naval command and control," Frontiers in adaptive control, 2009.

[22] P. Borkenau and F. Ostendorf, "NEO-FFI : NEO-Fünf-Faktoren-Inventar nach Costa und McCrae," Manual, 2nd ed., Göttingen: Hogrefe, 2008.

[23] D. Bates, M. Mächler, B. Bolker, and S. Walker, "Fitting Linear Mixed-Effects Models Using lme4," Journal of Statistical Software, vol. 67, no.1, pp. 1–48, 2015. doi: 10.18637/jss.v067.i01

[24] R Core Team, "R: A language and environment for statistical computing," R Foundation for Statistical Computing, Vienna, Austria, 2021, [retrieved: March, 2021 from https://www.R-project.org/].

[25] A. Kuznetsova, P. B. Brockhoff, and R. H. B. Christensen, "lmerTest Package: Tests in Linear Mixed Effects Models," Journal of Statistical Software, vol. 82, no. 13, pp. 1–26, 2017 doi: 10.18637/jss.v082.i13.

[26] S. M. Sarsam, and H. Al-Samarraie, "Towards incorporating personality into the design of an interface: a method for facilitating users' interaction with the display," User Model User-Adap Inter 28, pp. 75–96, 2018. https://doi.org/10.1007/s11257-018-9201-1

Assessing the Willingness of Elder Users in Using Virtual and Augmented Reality Technologies

Zoe Anastasiadou
Visual Media Computing Lab
Department of Multimedia and Graphic Arts
Cyprus University of Technology
Limassol, Cyprus
Email: Zx.anastasiadou@edu.cut.ac.cy

Andreas Lanitis
Visual Media Computing Lab
Department of Multimedia and Graphic Arts
Cyprus University of Technology
Limassol, Cyprus
Email: Andreas.lanitis@cut.ac.cy

***Abstract*— Emerging technologies in the form of Virtual (VR) and Augmented Reality (AR) can play an important role in improving the lives of the elderly and as such efforts in designing elderly-friendly applications are of paramount importance. However, despite the importance of this topic, issues related to the attitudes of elder users towards new technologies are not thoroughly investigated in the literature. With our work, we aim to analyze issues related to the willingness of older people to use emerging technologies, determine the difficulties faced, and define design requirements that will make emerging technologies more accessible to elder users. Our investigation involves a three-stage hierarchical structure where in each step the participants are exposed to more technologically intensive interaction styles. Our study revealed, that elder people are willing to use advanced technologies in the form of Augmented and Virtual Reality provided that the issues of useful functionality, usability, and neat design are met. The results of this study are important for designers and developers of VR/AR applications for the elderly, who need to address the issues indicated by the target group, to allow them to regularly use such applications in their everyday life.**

Keywords-Virtual Reality; Augmented Reality; Elderly; Interface Design;

I. INTRODUCTION

The use of emerging technologies by the elder people is becoming increasingly important, especially in periods of social isolation caused either by external factors (i.e., a pandemic) or by internal factors associated with reduced mobility in the elderly. Through the use of emerging technologies, the elderly could be offered a way to reduce the side-effects caused by social distancing [1]. Also, AR can be used for assistive technology applications [2]. However, despite the importance of this topic, issues related to the attitudes of elder users towards new technologies and their intention to use such technologies are not thoroughly investigated in the literature.

Elder people experience a decline in many characteristics that may prevent them from using effectively emerging technologies like Virtual (VR) and Augmented Reality (AR) that rely on the activation of numerous senses. Indicatively elder people may face a) reduced mobility, due to arthritis, less muscle strength, and Parkinson, [3] b) reduced eyesight due to several age-related eye diseases such as cataract, macular degeneration, presbyopia, etc., [4] c) hearing loss that is usually accompanied with inability to perceive high frequencies or low volume sounds [5] and d) cognitive declines such as dementia [6].

The aim of our work is to determine, the factors that facilitate the use of emerging technologies by elder users, in order to empower the use of such technologies by the elderly through the design of VR / AR applications that suit the needs of elder users. The ultimate aim of this effort is to develop contemporary emerging technology applications that provide high levels of user experience to elderly users. Towards this end, we run a series of evaluations to determine the factors that influence the use of emerging technologies by older users. The design of the experiment is based on a three-stage hierarchical structure where in each step the participants are exposed to more technologically intensive interaction styles. Initially, at Stage 1 of the experiment, the general issues related to the use of the basic technology in conjunction the use of a common smartphone medical dose management application are explored. This experiment is mainly aimed at confirming the findings of other studies [7], i.e., to define the most important features that motivate users to utilize technological solutions provided by standard smartphone applications. During Stage 2 of the evaluation, we investigate the reactions of older people towards the use of more specialized application that goes beyond the standard use of a smartphone through the need to engage in a more technologically demanding interaction using the smartphone camera, like in the case of augmented reality applications. Stage 3 of the experiments involves the exposure of volunteers from the target group to using a Virtual Reality application with a dedicated VR headset. This experiment exposes the volunteers to new ways of interacting with 3D environments, enabling the derivation of conclusions related to the reactions/concerns of the target group towards using emerging technologies in the form of Virtual Reality.

Our study revealed, that elder people are willing to use advanced technologies in the form of AR and VR, provided that the requirements of useful functionality, usability and design are met. The results of this study are important for designers and developers of VR/AR applications for the elderly, who need to address the issues indicated by the target group, to allow them to use regularly such applications. In the remainder of the paper, we present a literature review on the topics of VR and AR applications for the elderly, followed by a description of the experimental evaluation. In Section IV a discussion, plans for future work and concluding comments are presented.

II. LITERATURE REVIEW

Technology has the potential to enhance the lives of older adults by improving their safety, security, and self-confidence in everyday life. However, too often older adults' abilities and limitations are not reflected in the design of current and future technologies. Although older adults experience specific limitations as they age, the word old does not necessarily identify people who are disabled or sick. Many people over the age of 65 are reportedly in good health [8]. There is a generally supported view of the interest of keeping older adults in sync with the latest technological developments. As well as joining with family and friends, technology can support older adults in improving social support [9], increasing access to medical knowledge [10], enabling them to engage as citizens in decision-making processes, and allow them to keep fit using dedicated fitness apps [11]. In many studies, the importance of using new technologies by elderly is considered.

Levy et al., [12] investigate how virtual reality related to serious games can be used to handle the pathological phobia of falling. Specifically, the fear of falling is the continuing fear of falling that cannot be explained by physical examination. In their experiment, 16 participants were randomly selected from either a treatment group or a waiting list, and the duration of the virtual reality therapy with serious games consisted of 12 weekly sessions. The mean age for the treatment group was 72 years and for the control group was 69 years. Participants' ratings of fear of falling were improved after treatment, leading to a significant difference between the two groups. As they mention, serious games-based virtual reality exposure therapy can be used to treat the fear of falling, though further studies are needed to confirm its effectiveness and determine its underlying mechanism.

Optale et al., [13] tested the efficacy of a program of VR Memory Training (VRMT) in improving the cognitive functioning of elderly adults with memory impairment. For the experiment, they assigned 36 elderly residents of a rest care facility with middle age the 80 years old. The experimental group experienced six months of VR Memory Training that involved auditory stimulation and VR activities in path finding while the control group experienced equivalent face-to-face training sessions using music therapy. The results indicate that the participants who received the VR Memory Training presented an improvement of general cognitive functioning and oral memory after the initial training period. The greatest results were observed in long-term memory, in keeping with the cognitive abilities stimulated by the auditory session of the VR Memory Training. The improvements in executive function capabilities, in contrast, were small and did not perform corrections for the reduced depression scores of the experimental group participants.

Lera et al., [14] rely on a human robot interaction architecture called MYRA, to build a system for elderly support and medical dose control that includes augmented reality to improve the interaction with the robot. Through their prototype, it is possible for the users to follow simple medical guidelines related to everyday pill dose, based on help provided once a pillbox is presented to the robot or to a camera. As they mention the elderly has the interaction with the robot and the pillbox and with the use of AR, the task could be complete. To the other side, somebody can control the robot and offer real-time assistance to the elderly, using the camera speakers and phone mounted onboard. The research concluded that the use of AR had indeed positive impacts on the users.

Peleg-Adler et al., 11] empirically investigate the feasibility of AR technology for older adults. In particular, they tested how older adults interact and use AR for a path plan task, considering the deficits and the constraints to their performance as compared to young adults. Both older and younger participants made a route plan task using both a see-through handheld AR application and a regular (non-AR) phone application. The estimated task completion time, error rate, device movements, and subjective impressions were recorded. These measures were used to evaluate the performance, learning, and user experience of participants when using an AR interface. Forty-four participants were selected from two age groups. The first group consisted of 22 community-dwelling, healthy adults over the age of 65, and the second group consisted of 22 younger people of the age of 25–40 mostly students from a large research-intensive university. It is important to mention that both groups reported daily use of a mobile device, with the younger group reporting a higher level of the smartphone experience. According to the results, older adults performed slower than younger adults in both interfaces. This is expected, as it is well known that perceptual and cognitive skills decline over age. This indicates that the effect of AR was similar for both age groups; the group's gains in speed and losses inaccuracy were of the same magnitude when using the AR in comparison to the non-AR application. This shows that although AR was unfamiliar to the older participants, their performance differences (compared to the non-AR) were similar to the younger adults. Thus, it suggests that AR impacts the performance of older adults in a similar way it impacts the younger population.

Gao et al., [15] mention that virtual reality technology is a tool that can provide effective treatment for the elderly by applying non-immersive virtual reality to the hallway or immersing a patient in a realistic environment, such as a city or park with a head-mounted display or inside a CAVE. In this way physical and occupational therapy sessions can be improved, thereby increasing the chance of successful adaptation to the real world. An example of an experiment was when participants found that exercising on a stationary bike with VR that immersed them in nature was much more enjoyable than traditional cycling without VR. Since VR was an interesting activity for older adults, this could lead to better compliance with a rehabilitation program, which in turn can lead to better outcomes for patients' health.

III. EXPERIMENTAL EVALUATION

The aim of the evaluation is to investigate if the elderly are interested and willing to use AR and VR technologies, and what are the factors that will facilitate the regular use of AR and VR technologies by elder users. Our motivation for this research is to give some really useful tools that will benefit the elderly during periods of social isolation. The design of the experiment is based on a three-stage hierarchical structure where in each step the participants are exposed to more technologically intensive interaction styles. Stage 1 of the evaluation, concerns a collection and analysis of user reviews in relation to a health-related application that is popular among elder users. Through the specific application that they use in their daily life, the real needs that arise from the reviews are defined. Stage 2 of the evaluation that was carried out based on the use of a custom-made pharmaceutical management application, the goal was to expose users to a more technological demanding interface that requires the use of the camera as a means of obtaining comprehensive information about different medicines. Stage 3 of the evaluation involves the use a Virtual Reality application using a dedicated VR headset. Since this experiment involves the use of VR equipment for the first time for the majority of the users, the experiment included the necessary steps of introducing this type of technology to the volunteers. A more detailed description of the experiments carried out is described hereunder.

A. Stage 1: User evaluation of a Smartphone application

a) Aim: The aim of this study is to determine the most important design-related factors that motivate the target group to use a basic form of technological application in the form of a smartphone application. For the experiment, the free commercial application Pill Reminder and Medication Tracker by Medisafe [16] have been selected for evaluation. The application helps users to receive their medicines correctly so that they don't miss doses or receive double dosing by accident. To achieve the goal of this study a large number of user reviews are analyzed, in an effort to deduct conclusions related to the most important issues that attract users towards using this particular application.

b) Experimental Set-up: For the analysis of the results, 1000 user reviews were collected using the software Appbot that allows the collection of user reviews for an application and automatically categorizes customer feedback by theme with topics and tags. Among the reviews collected 166 reviews were not used in the analysis because they did not contain any information related to the parameters under investigation. All reviews were divided into the negative reviews (104 reviews rated with 1-2 stars indicating dissatisfied users) and positive reviews (654 reviews rated with 4-5 stars indicating satisfied users). In addition, user reviews were divided into the ones where users declared that they have a medical condition (116 users) and the ones where users do not state that they have a medical condition. Although, we did not have any data on the age of the users, it is reasonable to assume that most users who indicated a medical condition involve older people who are receiving medication due to some medical condition.

c) Results: User review analysis was carried out by initially filtering the reviews based on keyword analysis followed by content-based analysis in order to classify the reviews into the ones referring to functionality, usability, interface design, cost, number of existing users and user reviews (see Fig.1). Overall functionality, usability and interface design are determined as the most important factors for users, whereas issues like cost, number of existing users and user reviews do not seem to be important issues in all user reviews considered.

d) Discussion: The results indicate that to attract users to use an application the most important factors are the actual usefulness of the application (functionality), the usability, and the interface design. Also, there was no noticeable difference in these observations between the groups of people with or without health issues.

B. Stage 2: Evaluation of a pilot application that requires camera-based interaction

a) Aim: The experiment in Stage 1 reconfirmed the need to provide functionality and usability to attract the target population to using an application. In Stage 2, we explore the reactions of elder people towards the use of applications with a more technologically enhanced interaction style. More specifically, the aim of this experiment is to investigate the reaction of the target group in relation to a new technology and whether they are willing to use such technologies. More specifically the application under evaluation offers more advance capabilities than a simple smartphone application since it incorporates the use of the camera and audio-visual feedback.

b) Description: This experiment is based on the Easypharm application (see Fig.2), an application designed by Anastasiadou [17] as a means of providing an easy to use

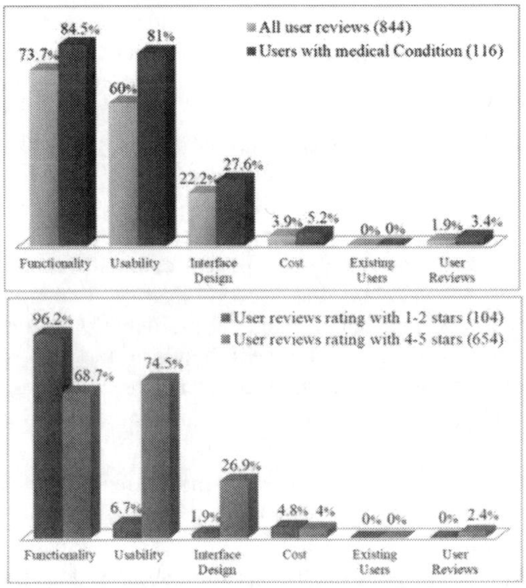

Fig. 1. Top: Results of all user reviews and the users with a medical condition, Bottom: Results of user reviews of dissatisfied users who rated the application with 1 or 2 stars and satisfied users who rated the application with 4 or 5 stars.

and universally acceptable application for managing medicine administration. Among other features, the Easypharm application aims to help the user, who may have reduced vision, by directly identifying, by scanning a QR code, the necessary information that is available on medicine packages.

c) Experimental Set-up: Fifteen adults (6 male, 9 female) aged 50-70 years (mean 57 years) participated in the experiment. The selection of the target group was done based on the typical target group expected to use pharmaceutical applications. Each volunteer who participated in the experiments was an experienced smartphone user who received a pharmaceutical treatment at some stage in his/her life. Both aforementioned factors are important to safeguard that participants could evaluate objectively the pharmaceutical management application. All volunteers were asked to complete a series of actions in relation to specific tasks. Through the process, results were obtained through observation of the actions of the participants while they were completing the preset tasks. At the end of the process, the participants completed a questionnaire that contained 11 questions (see Table I) and attended an interview where they were asked to answer questions related to their experience.

d) Results: According to the results, 33% of users would like to use the application in their daily lives. In relation to the usefulness of the application only 7% of users disagreed with the question stating that the application is designed to meet the needs of users. Based on the results of question 11 it is derived that the most important factors that make users use the application are the functionality, usability, and interface design of the application. In contrast, volunteers did not consider the cost of an application or the user's reviews as an important factor in selecting the application. With the above data we conclude that the target group that was evaluated is willing and would be interested to learn more and use on daily basis more advanced applications. As part of the analysis of the results, the fifteen volunteers were divided into two groups where the first group (with six volunteers) contains the ones who had a severe medical problem and had to use a pharmaceutical management application whereas the second group contains the volunteers with no serious medical problems. A comparison of the responses of volunteers between the two groups indicates no significant differences between the responses from each group were detected.

e) Discussion: Through the monitoring during the evaluation, it was observed that most users were able to complete the script process. Only a small section of users was unable to locate some buttons on the screen. It was obvious that people over the age of 65 are less familiar with new applications and need more time to adapt to new interfaces. When assessing the application, participants tried to adapt directly to the application environment to quickly identify the commands they were asked, although it was not easy for everyone.In conclusion, it was observed that users are willing to use a more technologically intensive application as long as the factors of functionality, usability, and interface design are covered.

Fig. 2. Interface design of Easypharm application.

TABLE I. INDICATIVE QUESTIONS USED DURING THE EVALUATION

	*A**	*N**	*D**
Q1. The overall response to the application was satisfactory.	33%	60%	7%
Q2. It was difficult to read the characters on the screen.	-	13%	87%
Q3. The application information organization was clear.	33%	60%	7%
Q4. The text in the application was readable.	33%	53%	14%
Q5. It was easy to remember the information displayed on the screen.	33%	60%	7%
Q6. Implementing actions in the application was complex.	7%	7%	86%
Q7. The application was designed to compete with the needs of users	33%	60%	7%
Q8. I was able to quickly complete the tasks and scripts using the application.	33%	53%	14%
Q9. The information contained in the application is clear.	33%	60%	7%
Q10. I would like to use the application in my everyday life.	33%	53%	14%
Q11. Which parameters will make you use this type of app: functionality, usability, design, cost, existing users, and reviews.	-	-	-

A=Agree, N= Neutral, D = Disagree

C. *Stage 3: valuation of the use of a virtual reality application by the elderly*

a) Aim: The results of the experiments in Stage 1 and 2 show that if a target population is presented with an application with useful functionality and friendly interface, they are willing to use the application, even if the application demands more dedicated interaction styles. The experiment in Stage 3 aims to investigate whether these observations are still valid for a completely new type of applications, in the form of Virtual Reality. More specifically, the aim of the experiment was to test the reactions of elderly towards the use of a virtual reality application.

b) Experimental Set-up: Ten participants aged between 50 to 70 years participated in the experiment (see Fig.3) which was completed using an Oculus Go running the application "First Aid Training" [18]. For the purposes of the experiment, users were asked to complete a series of operations in order to obtain results related to the reactions of the volunteers towards the use of a virtual reality application.During the process, volunteers completed a pre-experiment questionnaire that contained questions about their attitude towards Virtual Reality. To get acquainted with using a virtual reality interface, all volunteers had the chance to use for a few minutes a game that required them to move in a virtual space and interact with virtual objects. During the actual experiment users used the "First Aid Training" application according to the voice instructions given to them by the experiment administrator, and finally they were asked to answer a post-experiment questionnaire. Initially the instructions were given so that for any reason the user felt unwell to stop the process immediately. Furthermore, in order to prevent possible accidents, the evaluation was done with the users sitting.

c) Results: Participants were 50% women and 50% men with a mean age of 62 years. 50% of the participants were suffering from some disease while only 30% had used virtual reality applications again. The experiment was performed to get an inside of the factors that prevent members of the target group to use advanced technology. It was found that a large percentage of the participants used virtual reality for the first time and yet would like to practice using it to learn about health issues. Users' responses before and after (see Table II) using the virtual reality app indicate that several users have changed their view on whether virtual reality is useful for seniors after they used the VR application. Before running the experiment only 20% considered that VR can be useful for older people but this rate increased to 50% after the exposure to the VR application (see questions B5 and C8 in Table II). A percentage of 30% initially disagreed on whether is it useful to use virtual reality to practice on health issues, while after the use of the VR application, this figure dropped to 10% (see questions B4 and C7 in Table II). Finally, users were asked to answer what kind of applications they would be interested in using virtual reality applications and the most popular answers were around social platforms, relaxing, news, and education. These results show that initially, users out of ignorance were negative towards using such technologies in everyday life, but after they had the chance to be introduced to VR technology it was evident that they are willing to incorporate VR in their everyday activities. It was also noticed that the cost of virtual reality equipment is an issue that concerns them so that they can make daily use of the application, while they seem to be quite satisfied with the interface design as 70% would not like a change in the interaction style.

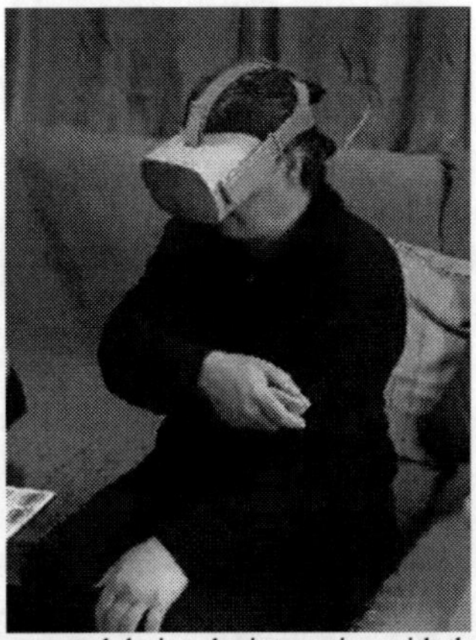

Fig. 3. Picture captured during the interaction with the virtual reality environment and the use of Oculus Go VR Headset.

TABLE II. MAIN QUESTIONS FROM THE QUESTIONNAIRE

Before using virtual reality	***A****	***N****	***D****
B1. I believe that VR applications are intended for entertainment.	90%	-	10%
B2. I believe that using VR can improve my daily life.	30%	10%	60%
B3. I believe that I can integrate the use of VR in my daily routine.	10%	10%	80%
B4. I would like to use the VR to practice on health issues.	60%	10%	30%
B5. I think the VR is useful for older people.	20%	40%	40%
After using virtual reality	***A****	***N****	***D****
C1. It was easy for me to navigate the VR area.	60%	30%	10%
C2. My experience with the VR was enjoyable.	90%	10%	-
C3. I believe that I have learned about the resuscitation position.	60%	30%	10%
C4. The experience in the VR makes me dizzy.	40%	10%	50%
C5. I had a hard time figuring out what to do.	60%	10%	30%
C6. I managed to complete the process.	90%	-	10%
C7. I would like to use the VR to practice on health issues.	70%	20%	10%
C8. I think the VR is useful for older people.	50%	30%	20%
			****A=Agree, N= Neutral, D = Disagree***

d) Conclusion: Based on the results from the experiment, we concluded that before getting exposed to the VR application, the target group believed, due to ignorance, that VR was mainly for fun. After using the application, they thought it was useful for their own needs and they see the possibilities it offers to them. Also, users indicate that they are willing to use such technologies and although it was new for them did not find particular difficulties in using the application with the interface. A new parameter that was included in Experiment 3 and did not exist in the other experiments, was the cost as a high-quality VR experience requires the purchase of equipment to use virtual reality and this could be an obstacle for the elderly, in adopting this technology. Given the possibility of using cardboard-based VR systems, the issue of cost can be partially addressed. Finally, it was observed that functionality is a main factor that attracts users to use VR applications, so particular emphasis should be placed on the development of useful applications. The limitations of our experiments are the small sample of users who participated in the experiments that was mainly attributed to the difficulty of attracting volunteers during the pandemic. Due to the same reason, it was not possible to use the same group of volunteers for all phases of the experiment.

IV. CONCLUSION AND FUTURE WORK

A three-stage experimental evaluation aiming to investigate if the elderly use advanced technologies, if they are interested and willing to use them, and lastly the factors that influence users in terms of using new technology for their daily lives was presented. Also, the aim was to increase the accessibility of emerging technologies and user satisfaction. Based on the results, we conclude that older people are not put off by the prospect of using more technologically advanced technologies as long as the requirements of functionality, usability and design are met.

On top of that, in the case of the need of using dedicated equipment, the issue of the cost is also introduced as an important factor. Furthermore, in the case of new technologies, it is important to provide training, as this will allow elder people to realize the full; potential offered by emerging technologies. Covering these needs of the users, then they can use VR and AR applications on a daily basis with satisfaction. Also in this case, functionality and usability are the key points that the user needs to meet his needs. In addition, with a specific audience, the desire to use such technologies and learn more information on how to integrate them into their daily lives has been observed. Results indicate the main factors to be considered for developing successful VR/AR applications. These results will be utilized for fulfilling our goal of designing VR and AR applications to support the elderly during periods of social isolation.

This research, aims to study more generally the use of technologies in the elderly to see the rationale behind the use of technologies and not as targeted as the above examples. An additional goal is to study how really useful and beneficial it is to use such technologies in the elderly so that they do not have any hesitation to use them in real life. Based on the outcome of our experiments, in the future we plan to develop a virtual reality application where it will create in the user the feeling of joy and nostalgia at the same time, in a way that is deemed to raise interest among older users. Also, in the future we plan to run evaluation experiments with more users in order to reinforce the validity to the results. According to the needs of the users, we will try to create new applications and implicate the target audience at each stage of the design in order to make sure that we meet their requirements and needs. The implication of members from the target group in the design process will guarantee that the requirements of functionality and usability will be met.

REFERENCES

[1] J. Tomaka, S. Thompson, and R. Palacios, "The relation of social isolation, loneliness, and social support to disease outcomes among the elderly." Journal of aging and health, 18(3), pp. 359-384, 2006.

[2] M. P. Cazorla, L. M. Sanju´an, M. V Fiel and J. L. H. Calvet, "Accessibility and Augmented Reality into Heritage Site Interpretation." ACHI: The Sixth International Conference on Advances in Computer-Human Interactions, 2013.

[3] R. Wichert and H. Klausing, "Ambient Assisted Living: 6. AALKongress", Berlin, Germany, January pp. 22.-23., Springer Science Business Media, 2013.

[4] C. Zavlanou and A. Lanitis, "An age simulated virtual environment for improving elderly wellbeing." In XIV Mediterranean Conference on Medical and Biological Engineering and Computing 2016, pp. 891-896. Springer, Cham, 2016.

[5] V. G. Payne and L. D. Isaacs, "Human motor development: A lifespan approach." ,Routledge, 2017.

[6] C. M. Borelli, D. Grennan, and C. C. Muth, "Causes of Memory Loss in Elderly Persons." Jama, 323(5), pp. 486-486, 2020.

[7] S. Carmien and A. G. Manzanares, "Elders using smartphones–a set of research based heuristic guidelines for designers." In International conference on universal access in human-computer interaction pp. 26- 37. Springer, Cham, 2014.

[8] W. A. Rogers, A. J. Stronge and A. D. Fisk,"Technology and aging." Reviews of human factors and ergonomics, 1(1), pp. 130-171, 2005.

[9] R. I. Garcia-Betances, V. Jim´enez-Mixco, M. T. Arredondo and M. F. Cabrera-Umpi´errez, "Using virtual reality for cognitive training of the elderly." American Journal of Alzheimer's Disease Other Dementias®, 30(1), pp. 49-54, 2015.

[10] F. Kamieth et al. "Exploring the potential of virtual reality for the elderly and people with disabilities." INTECH Open Access Publisher, 2010.

[11] R. Peleg-Adler, J. Lanir, and M. Korman, "The effects of aging on the use of handheld augmented reality in a route planning task." Computers in Human Behavior, 81, pp. 52-62, 2018.

[12] F. Levy et al. "Fear of falling: efficacy of virtual reality associated with serious games in elderly people." Neuropsychiatric disease and treatment, 12, p. 877, 2016.

[13] G. Optale et al. "Controlling memory impairment in elderly adults using virtual reality memory training: a randomized controlled pilot study." Neurorehabilitation and neural repair, 24(4), pp. 348-357, 2010

[14] F. J. Lera, V. Rodrıguez, C. Rodrıguez, and V. Matellan, "Augmented reality in robotic assistance for the elderly." In International Technology Robotics Applications, pp. 3-11, Springer, Cham, 2014.

[15] Z. Gao, J. E. Lee, D. J. McDonough, and C. Albers, "Virtual reality exercise as a coping strategy for health and wellness promotion in older adults during the COVID-19 pandemic.", 2020.

[16] Medisafe, 2021, "Medisafe." URL: https://www.medisafeapp.com/ [retrieved: May, 2021].

[17] Z. Anastasiadou, "Development of interactive application for understanding information in medicinal packaging." Cyprus University of Technology, 2016, unpublished.

[18] Dual Good Health Limited, 2019, "DualGood." URL: https://www.dualgoodhealth.com/healthcare [retrieved: May, 2021].

MARIoT: a Framework for Creating Customizable IoT Applications with Mobile Augmented Reality

Meral Kuyucu
Department of Computer Engineering
Istanbul Technical University
email: korkmazmer@itu.edu.tr

Gökhan İnce
Department of Computer Engineering
Istanbul Technical University
email: gokhan.ince@itu.edu.tr

***Abstract*—The programming overhead related to the implementation of intelligent environments is a major obstacle keeping non-technical technology enthusiasts from harnessing the advantages of bringing such technologies into their lives. Commercially available alternatives lack the customization angle that makes these technologies desirable in the first place. In this study, we propose a Low-Code/No-Code (LCNC) Mobile Augmented Reality for Internet of Things (MARIoT) framework that alleviates the requirement of programming expertise otherwise necessary in both the Internet of Things (IoT) and Augmented Reality (AR) fields. With the MARIoT framework, users can create customized AR interfaces to be used for interacting with devices and sensors in a smart home environment. The usability of this framework with participants of different educational and programming backgrounds was tested. Experimental results show that the proposed framework facilitates the intuitive integration of the two technologies.**

***Index Terms*—AR; IoT; Smart Home; LCNC.**

I. INTRODUCTION

Big data, Artificial Intelligence (AI), Augmented Reality (AR), the Internet of Things (IoT), cloud computing, and autonomous robots are among today's cutting-edge technologies. Brought together, these technologies can make smart decisions instead of people in various environments including households, factories, hospitals, transportation, and cities amongst others [1].

AR is the superimposition of digital information onto the real-world view of users to create a richer, compound representation of the surrounding environment [2]. IoT can be loosely described as the concept of connecting everything to the internet [3]. In this sense, the term "everything" encompasses things that can collect data (i.e., sensors), things that can perform actions based on input commands (i.e., home appliances), or things that can do both.

Two technologies can be fused if they are cooperative and complement each other [4]. The fusion of cooperative and complementary technologies often creates an opportunity to harness the advantages of both technologies and mitigate the weaknesses which arise when using the technologies separately. In this study, we motivate the fusion of AR and IoT.

The IoT often exists in the form of ubiquitous devices in our environment [3]. That is, they exist in 3D space. In such a data-driven environment, users must be able to visualize data and communicate with devices seamlessly and intuitively. We believe that in order to achieve this intuition, the interaction surface must also be in 3D.

To better illustrate, consider a scenario in which a user sitting in the living room wishes to observe the setting of the thermostat across the room. With AR-enabled IoT, it will be possible for him to simply point his mobile phone towards the IoT device in question. The context-aware AR interface will then adapt and present the user with a thermostat reading and controller. Using the virtual slider controller, he can adjust the temperature and turn his mobile device towards the light. The context-aware interface will then adapt again and display the light control options.

This seamless context-aware integration of AR and IoT can potentially revolutionize the already progressive concept of smart homes. However, many challenges lie in the way of achievement. Often, people do not have the necessary knowledge and skills to create end-to-end personalized solutions. Moreover, commercial solutions are not customized to fit the needs of different individuals, defeating the purpose of having a customized smart home.

In this study, a Low-Code/No-Code (LCNC) Mobile AR for IoT (MARIoT) framework for customized smart home applications is proposed. We assemble a framework consisting of an IoT network, an AR interface template generator, a dynamic mobile AR application that creates an interface based on the template in real-time, and a messaging protocol between the AR interface and IoT sensors and devices. The main goal of the framework is to provide necessary abstractions so that users can build customized applications by taking advantage of technologies that require coding knowledge without actually having to write code. This framework was tested to answer the following research questions:

1) Will tech-savvy but not necessarily code-savvy users find the suggested framework helpful when creating customized AR-enabled smart environments?
2) Will users find an AR interface for interacting with IoT devices intuitive?

There are three main contributions of this study. First, an end-to-end framework integrating AR and IoT using open source technologies is presented. Second, an LCNC framework that provides users with necessary abstractions so that they can create a personalized smart home application is established.

Lastly, this study assesses the usability of the framework using an application generated with this framework.

The rest of this paper is organized as follows. Section II presents a review of the literature. The design of the proposed framework is given in Section III. Experiments and results are discussed in Section IV. Finally, Section V presents concluding remarks.

II. Literature Review

Numerous studies have focused on applications generated by the fusion of AR and IoT. Studies have targeted medical assistance [5], energy management [6], technical instruction [7], crop monitoring [8], machine fault diagnostics [9], and even military applications [10]. The attitude toward domestic AR was investigated in a study conducted by Knierim et al. [11]. In light of semi-structured interviews at the end of a technology probe, they conclude that participants are interested in using AR within a domestic environment for its ability to enhance perception, provide on-demand information and assistance, and augment devices.

Especially in recent years, many implementation-level studies have been published in this field. These works present direct applications integrating AR and IoT in varying domains. Jang and Bednarz suggest head-mounted AR for visualizing data from various sensors. The output of their work is an application that communicates data from sensors in the network to the AR application [12]. Ankireddy et al. propose a mobile AR application promoting interaction with devices. They also design and implement a low-cost plug-and-play smart glass that can be used to control devices [13]. Fredericks et al. argue that energy consumption is inherently invisible in nature and can be made visible by employing augmented reality to raise awareness and promote energy-conserving behaviors [14]. Another study by Mahroo and colleagues investigates the possibility of communicating with household devices using Microsoft HoloLens [15]. Blanco-Novoa and colleagues set forth an open-source AR-IoT framework facilitating the utilization of AR and IoT in real-time [16]. Wright et al. suggest a cross-platform open-source mixed reality framework capable of communicating with headless IoT devices [17]. Marques et al. propose a context-aware AR application to configure and create uninterrupted management and control of smart home sensors and devices [18]. Mishra et al. describe an AR framework for home automation and telemetry application with IoT. They implement a prototype with which users can control household appliances such as a fan or a light [19]. The common shortcoming of all of the aforementioned studies is that no investigation of usability has been conducted.

Studies that assess the usability of prototype applications also exist in literature. Ullah et al. suggested a prototype that uses AR to control home appliances [20]. Test results suggest that most users would consider using AR interfaces. Jo and Kim introduce a framework for visualizing IoT data with augmented reality and conduct a usability test with 10 participants [21]. Experimental results show that most participants preferred AR-based interaction over Graphical User Interface (GUI) based interaction. Putze et al. design a head-mounted AR Brain-Computer Interface (BCI) which can be controlled by the user's eye movements [22]. Results of their usability tests also show that users are highly in favor of AR interfaces over standard GUI-based modes of interaction. In these studies, users were given a prefabricated interface capable of controlling a fixed set of IoT elements. Users were expected to use the interface and assess usability. We are curious about what happens when the user wishes to create an interface that can control a set of user-determined IoT elements.

Most of the studies found in this field are at the implementation level. Studies that do conduct usability tests do not aim for LCNC solutions. Our study differs from these works because we suggest a framework that can be used by non-programming users who wish to create personalized applications. A smart home was selected as the domain of our study because it appeals to many potential users. Yet, the framework suggested in this study can be generalized to a variety of disciplines.

III. An AR-IoT Enabled Interactive Framework for Smart Home Use

In this section, we present our LCNC framework for creating personalized AR-IoT enabled applications called MARIoT. Figure 1 is an illustration of the system.

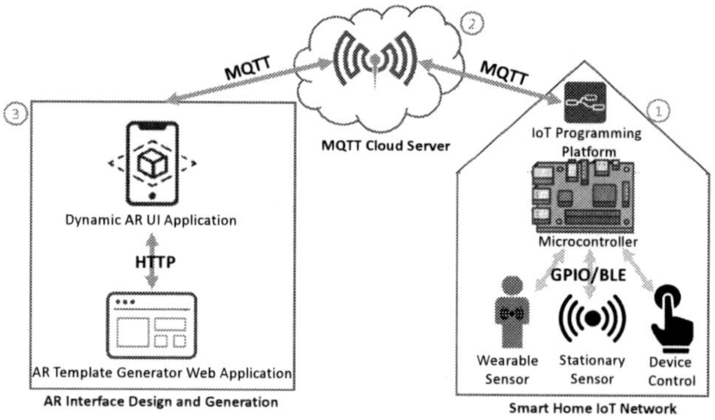

Fig. 1: Overview of the proposed MARIoT framework.

The main components of the system can be divided into three. A smart home IoT network (Figure 1①) consists of different types of sensors and actuators connected to a microcontroller via General Purpose Input Output (GPIO) pins of the controller or Bluetooth Low Energy (BLE). Sensors (i.e., photoresistor) collect data which can be displayed to the user, analyzed, or used in a machine learning application to make smart decisions. For the purposes of this study, we have chosen the name actuator for devices to which commands can be issued by the user via an interface (i.e., a desk lamp). The microcontroller is programmed to send collected data to a cloud server and listen to the server for device input commands. This is done utilizing a visual (flow-based) development tool. A set of configurable generic flows helps the user easily bring up the IoT end of the system. The cloud server (Figure 1②) relays messages between the AR interface and the IoT network. The third and final constituent of the system is the AR interface template generator and mobile AR application (Figure 1③). First, the template generator web application can be utilized to create a template for an AR interface. The output is utilized by the mobile AR application to dynamically and automatically create the user-designed AR interface at runtime. Data from IoT sensors will be visualized with text labels and users will be able to input a number of discrete-valued input commands via several GUI buttons. These components can be utilized to create personalized AR applications for interacting with smart homes.

A. *Design of MARIoT framework*

Figure 2 illustrates a layered architecture of the proposed framework. The IoT elements, cloud server, and AR Engine lie in the lowest layer. These components all require the user to have programming expertise. The second layer consists of the abstractions we added to the base layer so that users can benefit from the base layer technologies without having to write code. Customizable flows enable the user to create IoT scenarios and the template generator assists the user in designing a personalized AR interface to interact with IoT sensors and devices. User-generated applications lie at the top layer of the architecture.

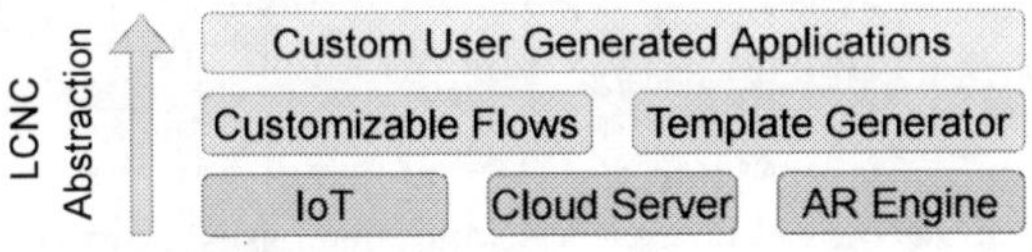

Fig. 2: Layered architecture of the proposed framework.

1) Customizable Task Flow Generator for IoT Devices: This component is responsible for IoT management. Processes in the IoT system are carried out in the form of flows, modular sequential ways of representing more complex tasks.

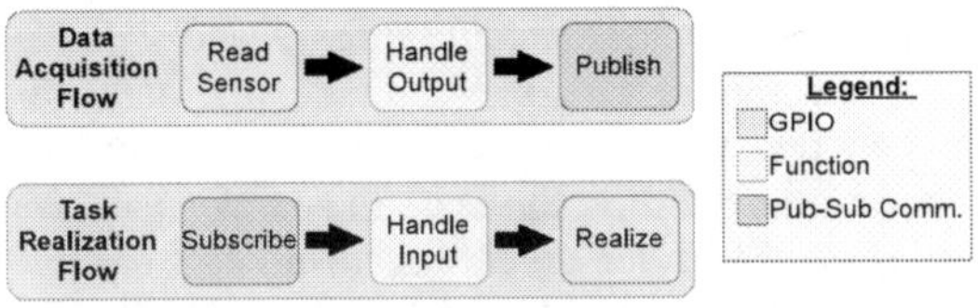

Fig. 3: Set of customizable task flows.

In order to manage IoT processes, we recommend two generic customizable task flows. To configure the IoT system, users can simply import these flows into their workspaces and configure only the device and server-specific aspects. The set of essential flows is illustrated in Figure 3 and detailed as follows:

- **Data Acquisition Flow:** The flow is triggered by a sensor reading which occurs when there is a change in the environment. In the second step, the digital output received from the sensor is converted to a message determined by the user. For example, a photoresistor reading of "1" can be converted to "Light is on". The user-defined message is then combined with a timestamp to indicate the freshness of the data. The third step consists of sending this data to the cloud server.
- **Task Realization Flow:** The IoT device listens to the server for a message from the AR interface. The flow is triggered when a message arrives. In the second step, the message content of the command is parsed. The necessary control signals are applied to the device in the third step. For example, an "OFF" message sent to a desk lamp can be converted to a "0" digital signal to turn off the lamp.

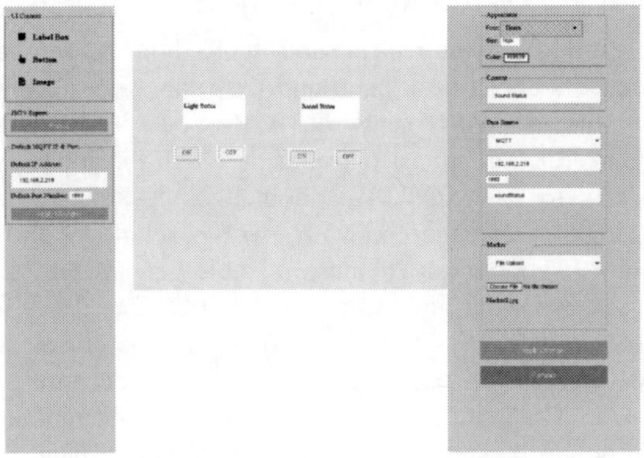

Fig. 4: Template generator web application.

2) Template Generator for Designing Augmented Reality Applications: To facilitate the task of creating an AR user interface for non-programmer users, we introduce a template generator. This web application allows users to drag-and-drop User Interface (UI) elements onto a canvas to design an interface. These elements can be customized in terms of appearance, content, and data source. Additionally, image markers can be added for each UI element to support context awareness.

The template generator application with an example template can be seen in Figure 4. The sidebar on the left contains the UI elements that can be placed onto the canvas. These elements include label boxes, images, and buttons. When an element on the canvas is clicked on, it becomes active and the edit form appears from the right. The user can modify the appearance (i.e., font size and color), content (i.e., text placeholder), data source (i.e., the server it connects to for sending and receiving data), as well as the marker image for the UI element using this form. Completed templates can be exported to be used by the mobile application to dynamically create an AR interface.

3) Pub-Sub Messaging Communication Protocol Between IoT Task Flow and AR Interface: Perhaps the backbone of the suggested framework is the communication of elements in the system. We chose to implement communication using the Message Queuing Telemetry Transport (MQTT) protocol. MQTT is a lightweight, publish-subscribe network protocol that transports messages between devices. Two types of clients exist in a pub-sub network. The first of these is the publishing client, which sends messages under a topic. Secondly, the subscribers listen for messages under specific topics.

In our system, sensors act as publishers, collecting environmental data and publishing it to the network. Actuators subscribe to user commands and are controlled based on incoming commands. AR interface elements that display data (i.e., labels) are subscribers. They subscribe to data coming from the IoT sensors and update the displayed data in real-time. AR interface elements that take inputs from the user (i.e., buttons) publish user commands.

B. Implementation of MARIoT framework

In this study, a photoresistor and microphone were chosen as the sensors and a desk lamp and desk fan were chosen as the actuators of an IoT network. A Raspberry Pi computer was preferred as the microcontroller to which the sensors and actuators were connected. We adopted Node-RED, a flow-based visual development tool with a web-based flow editor for controlling IoT devices. The customizable generic task flows we propose were designed using Node-RED. The flows were composed so that only the GPIO information, output message contents, and server-specific information must be configured by the user. Mosquitto MQTT was chosen for the messaging protocol due to its speed and significantly low overhead when compared to the standard HTTP protocol. The AR template generator is a web application created using HTML and JavaScript (JQuery UI). The AR interface is created by a mobile application employing the Vuforia AR library. This application takes the output of the template generator and creates a corresponding mobile AR interface dynamically at runtime.

IV. Experiments and Results

In this section, we illustrate the experimentation procedure in detail. The experimental results and a discussion of the outcomes follows.

A. Experimental Framework

We conducted usability tests for the proposed framework at Istanbul Technical Univerity's UX Lab. The experiment setup is depicted in Figure 5. Two image markers and the selected set of devices and sensors are placed on the table. Additionally, a computer to be used for IoT configuration and AR interface design is provided.

B. Usability Tests

1) Participant Demographics: Due to the COVID-19 pandemic, access to participants was rather limited. After an initial acquaintance with the facilitator, potential participants were asked to complete a screening survey. Participants were selected based on a combination of AR experience, IoT experience, smart home experience, and daily time spent in front of a computer or mobile device. We preferred participants who used computers and mobile devices for a good part of the day and who were familiar with one or more of the technologies utilized in the study. Participants were familiar with IoT devices such as smart locks, robot vacuums, smart scales, and security cameras. They had some AR experience with games, simulators, and applications that employ camera filters.

After the screening procedure, usability tests were conducted with 9 participants (3 male, 6 female) ranging from 18 to 26 years in age. Selected participants had varying educational backgrounds such as computer engineering, textile engineering, and genetics engineering. All selected participants were either college graduates, or students. They were required to have acquired some level of higher learning due to the concentration necessary to complete the experiment. Of the 9 participants, 4 were undergraduate students and 1 was a graduate student in the department of computer engineering. The rest of the participants were from different disciplines of engineering (i.e., textile and genetics engineering). Although they had varying levels of programming knowledge, none had coding experience with Node-RED, MQTT, or AR prior to the experiment.

2) Test Materials: Throughout the test, the information provided to the participant by the facilitator was read to the participants from a script to maintain consistency throughout experiments. The script can also be considered a guide for the facilitator throughout the experiment. Moreover, a carefully constructed script can remove otherwise unnoticed bias from the words of the facilitator.

3) Pre-Training Materials: We prepared a video presentation that defines AR and IoT and discusses how the two technologies will be used in the scope of this study. The video was designed to provide information to a person who knows nothing about these two technologies. First, the primary definitions of AR and IoT were given. Then, the motivation of using these two technologies together in a smart home domain was built. Afterward, each component of the system was explained to the participants so that the connection between AR UI elements and IoT sensors and devices was clear to the participant. A discussion of Figures 1 and 2 have been presented in the training video. When the participants finished watching the video, they were permitted to ask questions about the system before resuming the experiment. We also prepared two pre-training videos demonstrating the process of importing and customizing the Node-RED task flows.

4) Test Procedure and Metrics: We conducted two pilot studies with expert users. The test materials (script and videos) were revised based on the insight gained from the pilot studies. Due to the lengthy and incremental nature of the system, we decided to fix the time to complete a task. The maximum amount of time to complete the experiment tasks was determined based on the outputs of the pilot studies. Allowing participants to roam prior to completing the test may cause them to lose track and interest in the task at hand. Users were given opportunities to ask questions prior to the test. During the test, users were not provided with assistance. After completing the revisions, usability tests were conducted

(a) Task 1: Turning on the light. (b) Task 2: Observing sensor output. (c) Task 3: Visualizing both markers.

Fig. 5: AR application generated automatically based on template designed by the user.

with selected participants.

Our tests were designed so that users can assess both the usability of the end-to-end framework as well as the usability of an AR interface for interacting with IoT sensors and devices. Throughout the tests, users interact with the framework in three consequent tasks:

- Task 1) Importing and customizing two generic flows:
  - Task 1.1) Data Acquisition Flow
  - Task 1.2) Task Realization Flow
- Task 2) Using the template generator to create a template of a mobile AR interface:
  - Task 2.1) Configuration of server settings
  - Task 2.2) Adding labels to template
  - Task 2.3) Adding buttons to template
- Task 3) Using the dynamically and automatically created mobile AR interface:
  - Task 3.1) Observing sensor output
  - Task 3.2) Controlling a device

First, users were briefly informed about the overall system. Afterward, a training and practice session for Node-RED was provided. In the pre-training session, participants were asked to watch a training video demonstrating the usage of the customizable generic task flows. Then, they were given a chance to practice importing and customizing a Data Acquisition flow and a Task Realization flow in the training session. Because Node-RED is an existing development tool, we felt it necessary to provide training because we are not interested in the users' assessment of Node-RED. Rather, we would like to find out how well the entire system consisting of the three components in Figure 1 works as a whole. We did not train the users with the template generator or the mobile AR interface because we are interested in how intuitive users find them to be. Users interacted with the template generator and AR interface for the first time during the test.

The first task (Task 1) constitutes the configuration of the sensors and actuators. The customizable generic task flows users interacted with are given in Figure 6. In Task 1.1, users were asked to import and configure a Data Acquisition flow for a sensor as shown in Figure 6(a). The "Sensor Data" node should be configured so that the pin to which the sensor is connected is read from. Then, the "Handle Sensor Output" node should be configured with the messages to be displayed depending on digital sensor outputs. Finally, the "Publish" node should be configured with the server details

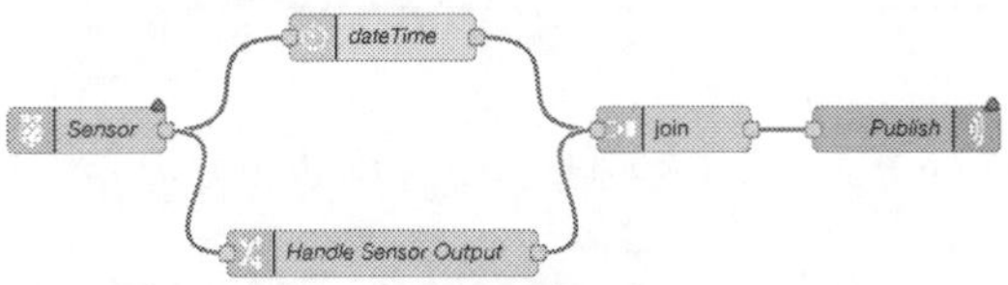

(a) Data Acquisition Flow

(b) Task Realization Flow

Fig. 6: Customizable task flows.

and a topic to publish messages under. In Task 1.2, users were requested to import and configure a Task Realization flow for an actuator. The Task Realization flow is given in Figure 6(b). First, the "Subscribe" node should be configured with server details and a topic to listen for messages. For this flow, the "Handle Message" node does not need modification because currently, the system only supports "ON" and "OFF". Lastly, the "Device" node should be configured so that the pin to which the device is connected is sent a signal.

The objective of Task 2 was to design a template for an AR interface using the template generator. In Task 2.1, users were instructed to configure the server details to which the AR interface elements will be connecting to. This way users do not have to enter sensor details for each dropped UI element. Only the topic should be added. In Task 2.2, users were asked to place two labels onto the canvas. The labels should be configured to subscribe to the topics assigned to the sensors in Task 1.1. In Task 2.3, users were asked to add 4 buttons to the canvas and to configure the buttons as On/Off buttons for two actuators. The buttons should be configured to publish to the topic to which the actuators were subscribed in Task 1.2. A marker image was uploaded for each UI element. An element becomes visible when its assigned marker is in camera view. Once the user finishes designing a template, it can be exported.

The user-designed template from Task 2 is automatically generated by the mobile AR application in Task 3. In this final task, users are asked to hold the mobile device against different markers, make sensor observations, and control devices with buttons.

The metrics used in evaluation can be seen in Table I. We requested users to complete an After Scenario Questionnaire (ASQ) after tasks 1 and 2. Finally, users were invited to

TABLE I: SELECTED EVALUATION METRICS

Usability Dimensions	Evaluation Metrics	Units	Investigation Techniques
Effectiveness	Completion Rate	Percentage (%)	Direct Observation
	Number of Errors	Number	
Efficiency	Task Completion Time	Seconds	Direct Observation
Satisfaction	After Scenario Questionnaire	1-5 Likert Scale	Questionnaire
	System Usability Scale		

evaluate the end-to-end system with a System Usability Scale (SUS).

5) Walkthrough of Test Procedure: Throughout the IoT training and test phases, four flows were configured for the two sensors and two actuators in the experimental setup. Flows for the photoresistor and desk lamp were configured in the IoT training session. Flows for the microphone and desk fan were configured during Task 1.

In Task 2, the template in Figure 4 was designed by the users. The "Light Status" label was configured to subscribe to the same topic that the photoresistor is publishing to. This way, the photoresistor readings will be displayed on the label in real-time. The button pair under the label are publishing On/Off messages to the same topic assigned to the desk lamp. The photoresistor and the buttons for the desk lamp shared a marker. The microphone and the buttons for the desk fan shared a second marker.

In Task 3, participants were asked to launch and use the application they designed. Figure 5 illustrates the mobile AR interface resulting from the template generated in Figure 4. First, the lights are turned off, and the user is requested to hold the mobile device against a marker and observe the sensor status (Figure 5(a)). When the marker related to the desk lamp and light sensor is in camera view, the controls of the desk lamp and the status of the light are displayed. The user is then instructed to turn the desk lamp on and observe the change in the sensor output (Figure 5(b)). After the button press, the "ON" message is published. The subscriber (desk lamp) receives the message and the lamp is turned on (Figure 5(b)). The user is then instructed to hold the mobile device against both markers (Figure 5(c)). The controls for both devices as well as the information from both sensors become visible.

Once participants were finished with all three tasks of the experiment, they were given the opportunity to roam. Some participants chose to change the layout and appearance of the AR interface. Other participants experimented with changing the marker images of different UI elements.

C. Test Results

The results of Tasks 1 and 2 can be seen in Table II. Participants were given 180 seconds to complete Task 1.1. Most users were able to complete the task with little training. In Task 1.1, two participants were unsure about choosing a topic to publish messages under and took time to look back into the documentation provided during the training phase. The time given to complete Task 1.2 was 120 seconds. Only one participant was unable to complete this task within 120 seconds. Four participants were unsure about connecting to the same server (from Task 1.1) as a publisher. The overall satisfaction with Task 1 as given by the ASQ is 4.81/5.00.

TABLE II: TASK 1 AND 2 RESULTS

Evaluation Metrics	Tasks				
	Task 1		Task 2		
	Task 1.1	Task 1.2	Task 2.1	Task 2.2	Task 2.3
Avg. Completion Rate	89%	89%	89%	67%	100%
Avg. Number of Errors	0.23 (± 0.44)	0.45 (± 0.53)	0.12 (± 0.33)	0.56 (± 0.73)	0.34 (± 0.71)
Avg. Task Time (sec.)	119.56 (± 40.46)	75 (± 38.39)	28.44 (± 14.3)	182.89 (± 45.45)	211.67 (± 31.34)

Because Task 2.1 required very few steps to complete, participants were given 45 seconds to complete the task. This task was fairly simple and only one participant misunderstood the task initially. Participants were expected to complete Task 1.2 in 180 seconds. Three participants were unable to finish in time and the average time was slightly higher than the allotted time. The participants who did not finish on time failed to distinguish the topic and the content of a label. Because Task 2.3 required the insertion and customization of four buttons, users were given 420 seconds to complete it. Most participants did not even need half of the allotted time to complete the task. The errors were due to confusion between the topic and the content of a button. Even though users saw the web application for the first time and no training was provided for this task, most users were able to complete the task within the given amount of time. Unsuccessful users were allowed to continue if they wished. Although they were unsuccessful, these users were also eventually able to complete the tasks with extra time. The overall satisfaction with Task 2 was 4.74/5.00.

When asked to hold the mobile device against a marker in Task 3, participants saw that the related UI elements appeared. They were interested in controlling devices–most participants attempted to turn on the devices without being asked to do so. Participants tested turning the light on and off and observing the changes in the state of the photoresistor. The sound created when the fan was turned on triggered the state of the microphone and was noted by the participants. After using the application, most participants commented that they found the concept of topics and pub-sub messaging more intuitive. Participants were also keen to notice that the interface was updated as the mobile device was turned to face different markers. The SUS summarizes the results of Task 3. In general, users indicated that they were satisfied with the system, however, some did think that the system required users to learn. The overall SUS score was 81.9 (A).

D. Discussion

During unstructured conversations with the participants, 6 of the 9 participants indicated that they would like to use these technologies in their homes without directly being asked the question. Participants 4 and 7 mentioned that they felt accomplished and satisfied after completing the test. Most participants were excited to suggest scenarios in which the proposed framework can be used. For example, participant 2 commented that she would like to use this system to monitor and control her kitchen appliances such as her coffee machine. Participant 2 also mentioned that this would not only be useful in the home but also in the workplace. Participant 8 commented on the potentials of integrating wearable technologies into this framework for an even richer, more continuous interaction experience. He suggested integrating textile-based sensors as wearable components of the system. Participant 6 mentioned that different methods of visualizing data such as graphs could be integrated to better present information to the user. Participant 7 mentioned that even though this was completely new material, she was very comfortable and found it intuitive even. She mentioned the concept of pub-sub messaging was similar to a biological process. Participant 9 stated that she was hesitant to participate in the experiment because she did not think she was tech-savvy enough but after testing the system, she found it to be simple to use.

An important angle to consider when evaluating the results of this experiment is the performance comparison of participants with computer engineering training and participants who come from different backgrounds. Table III emphasizes these differences. For each metric, the "CE" column presents the results for participants with computer engineering experience. The "NCE" column depicts the results of participants who do not have computer engineering knowledge. It can be observed from Table III that the CE group was more successful in Task 1.1 and the NCE group outperformed in Task 1.2. While the CE group had a higher completion rate in Task 2.1, the NCE group completed the task in fewer seconds. That is to say, both groups had similar performance throughout the experiment.

TABLE III: PERFORMANCE COMPARISON

	Completion Rate		Completion Time		Num. of Errors	
Tasks	**CE**	**NCE**	**CE**	**NCE**	**CE**	**NCE**
1.1	100%	75%	103.2	114.65	0	2
1.2	80%	100%	76.5	56.75	4	0
2.1	100%	75%	29	18	0	1
2.2	80%	50%	150.25	174	2	3
2.3	100%	100%	193.2	234.75	0	3

While there are no major usability problems with the suggested framework, the wording in the template generator application can be modified to help users distinguish between the content and the topic of a UI element. The targeted audience for this study was a tech-savvy population. This is why tests were conducted with younger individuals. Because there is a significant amount of cognitive load involved with configuring the system end-to-end, elder adults who may not be as computer literate may have difficulties with this system.

In the future, we plan on re-designing the template generator so that it can collect information regarding the flows on Node-RED and make suggestions to the user to reduce this cognitive load. This way, users do not have to remember the topic they entered in the IoT configuration phase. Once the user determines a topic in Node-RED, the same topic can be presented to the user in a drop-down menu refreshed in real-time. Numerous functionalities can be added to the architecture so that users can take complete advantage of the system. The set of supported UI elements available to the user are to be expanded to include various types of graphs, and different methods for inputs (i.e., slider input). Next, support for head-mounted gears will be integrated. Finally, multiple methods of context-awareness will be added to the system so that the user-defined apps can be context-aware in a way that is most convenient to the user.

V. Conclusion

In our study, we introduced an LCNC framework that detaches coding from the process of creating personalized AR-IoT enabled applications. This way, people with little knowledge regarding coding can easily set up and control a custom smart environment. We conducted usability experiments and found that even participants with no programming background can easily create an end-to-end AR-enabled IoT system using our framework. In the light of experimental results, it can be concluded that tech-savvy users were able to use the suggested framework to communicate with IoT sensors and devices using mobile AR. Moreover, participants were excited to suggest ways in which they can use mobile AR in their own homes to interact with their devices.

Acknowledgment

In this work, Meral Kuyucu has been supported by the Turkcell Academia-ITU Research Grant Program.

References

[1] G. Lampropoulos, K. Siakas, and T. Anastasiadis, "Internet of things in the context of industry 4.0: An overview," *International Journal of Entrepreneurial Knowledge*, vol. 7, pp. 4–19, 06 2019.

[2] J. Carmigniani and B. Furht, *Augmented Reality: An Overview*, 07 2011, pp. 3–46.

[3] K. Patel, S. Patel, P. Scholar, and C. Salazar, "Internet of things-iot: Definition, characteristics, architecture, enabling technologies, application & future challenges," 05 2016.

[4] J. Tidd and T. Sammut-Bonnici, *Technology Fusion*, 2015.

[5] F. Ghorbani, M. Kia, M. Delrobaei, and Q. Rahman, "Evaluating the possibility of integrating augmented reality and internet of things technologies to help patients with alzheimer's disease," in *2019 26th National and 4th International Iranian Conference on Biomedical Engineering (ICBME)*, 2019, pp. 139–144.

[6] K. Cho, H. Jang, L. W. Park, S. Kim, and S. Park, "Energy management system based on augmented reality for human-computer interaction in a smart city," in *2019 IEEE International Conference on Consumer Electronics (ICCE)*, 2019, pp. 1–3.

[7] P. Hořejší, K. Novikov, and M. Šimon, "A smart factory in a smart city: Virtual and augmented reality in a smart assembly line," *IEEE Access*, vol. 8, pp. 94 330–94 340, 2020.

[8] P. Phupattanasilp and S.-R. Tong, "Augmented reality in the integrative internet of things (ar-iot): Application for precision farming," *Sustainability*, vol. 11, p. 2658, 05 2019.

[9] V. Rajan, N. Sobhana, and R. Jayakrishnan, "Machine fault diagnostics and condition monitoring using augmented reality and iot," in *2018 Second International Conference on Intelligent Computing and Control Systems (ICICCS)*, 2018, pp. 910–914.

[10] S. Jalui, T. Hait, T. Hathi, and S. Ghosh, "Advanced military helmet aided with wireless live video transmission, sensor integration and augmented reality headset," in *2019 International Conference on Communication and Electronics Systems (ICCES)*, 2019, pp. 123–127.

[11] P. Knierim, P. W. Woundefinedniak, Y. Abdelrahman, and A. Schmidt, "Exploring the potential of augmented reality in domestic environments," in *Proceedings of the 21st International Conference on Human-Computer Interaction with Mobile Devices and Services*, ser. MobileHCI '19. New York, NY, USA: Association for Computing Machinery, 2019, pp. 1–12. [Online]. Available: https://doi.org/10.1145/3338286.3340142

[12] J. Jang and T. Bednarz, "Holosensor for smart home, health, entertainment," in *ACM SIGGRAPH 2018 Appy Hour*, ser. SIGGRAPH '18. New York, NY, USA: Association for Computing Machinery, 2018. [Online]. Available: https://doi.org/10.1145/3213779.3213786

[13] M. A. Ankireddy, A. Rajath, M. Ruthwik Ganesh, and M. Anuradha, "Augmented reality rendered for iot applications," in *2019 IEEE 16th India Council International Conference (INDICON)*, 2019, pp. 1–4.

[14] A. D. Fredericks, Z. Fan, and S. I. Woolley, "Visualising the invisible: Augmented reality and virtual reality as persuasive technologies for energy feedback," in *2019 IEEE SmartWorld, Ubiquitous Intelligence Computing, Advanced Trusted Computing, Scalable Computing Communications, Cloud Big Data Computing, Internet of People and Smart City Innovation (SmartWorld/SCALCOM/UIC/ATC/CBDCom/IOP/SCI)*, 2019, pp. 1209–1212.

[15] A. Mahroo, L. Greci, and M. Sacco, "Holohome: An augmented reality framework to manage the smart home," in *Augmented Reality, Virtual Reality, and Computer Graphics*, L. T. De Paolis and P. Bourdot, Eds. Cham: Springer International Publishing, 2019, pp. 137–145.

[16] O. Blanco-Novoa, P. Fraga-Lamas, M. Vilar-Montesinos, and T. Fernández-Caramés, "Towards the internet of augmented things: An open-source framework to interconnect iot devices and augmented reality systems," in *Multidisciplinary Digital Publishing Institute Proceedings*, vol. 42, no. 1, 11 2019, p. 50.

[17] D. Wright, R. Skaggs-Schellenberg, and S. Tayeb, "Networked mixed reality framework for the internet of things," in *2020 IEEE International IOT, Electronics and Mechatronics Conference (IEMTRONICS)*, 2020, pp. 1–7.

[18] B. Marques, P. Dias, J. Alves, E. Fonseca, and B. S. Santos, "Configuration and use of pervasive augmented reality interfaces in a smart home context: A prototype," in *Human Systems Engineering and Design II*, T. Ahram, W. Karwowski, S. Pickl, and R. Taiar, Eds. Cham: Springer International Publishing, 2020, pp. 96–102.

[19] A. Mishra, S. Karmakar, A. Bose, and A. Dutta, "Design and development of iot-based latency-optimized augmented reality framework in home automation and telemetry for smart lifestyle," *Journal of Reliable Intelligent Environments*, vol. 6, no. 3, pp. 169–187, 2020. [Online]. Available: https://doi.org/10.1007/s40860-020-00106-1

[20] A. M. Ullah, M. R. Islam, S. F. Aktar, and S. K. A. Hossain, "Remote-touch: Augmented reality based marker tracking for smart home control," in *2012 15th International Conference on Computer and Information Technology (ICCIT)*, 2012, pp. 473–477.

[21] D. Jo and G. J. Kim, "Ariot: scalable augmented reality framework for interacting with internet of things appliances everywhere," *IEEE Transactions on Consumer Electronics*, vol. 62, no. 3, pp. 334–340, 2016.

[22] F. Putze, D. Weiß, L.-M. Vortmann, and T. Schultz, "Augmented reality interface for smart home control using ssvep-bci and eye gaze," in *2019 IEEE International Conference on Systems, Man and Cybernetics (SMC)*, 2019, pp. 2812–2817.

Quantitative Scoring System to Assess Performance in Experimental Environments

Ron Becker, Sophie-Marie Stasch, Alina Schmitz-Hübsch, Sven Fuchs
Fraunhofer Institute for Communication, Information Processing and Ergonomics FKIE
53343 Wachtberg, Germany
Email: {ron.becker, sophie-marie.stasch, alina.schmitz-huebsch, sven.fuchs}@fkie.fraunhofer.de

***Abstract* – A quantitative scoring mechanism based on signal detection theory was developed in the context of an experimental command-and-control environment. The scoring approach was designed to include well-established evaluation criteria of performance metrics and to enable insights into various cognitive and behavioral processes of the subjects. Cognitive processes on a perceptual, sensory, and motor level were linked to subtasks similar to the warship commander task. Signal detection theory provides a theoretical rationale for the quantitative scoring mechanism. Due to the generalizability of the scoring approach, a flexible application to a wide range of experimental tasks should be possible. Considerations and lessons learned are discussed.**

Keywords* – *Behavioral processes; Cognitive processes; Human machine interaction; Command-and-control; Quantitative performance metrics, signal detection theory

I. INTRODUCTION

Measuring human performance in complex experimental tasks can be challenging. Generally, two approaches are available to measure user performance in such experiments: Qualitative performance assessment aims at gaining an in-depth understanding of the matter of interest as well as its context. Since the observer's point of view is internal, the results tend to be subjective and difficult to verify. Consequently, conclusions based on qualitative assessments may not be replicable. In contrast, quantitative approaches objectify performance assessment and enable the use of inferential statistics, such as significance testing [1][2]. Quantitative performance assessment aims at measuring human performance through predefined metrics that can be calculated in an automatic manner, resulting in a numeric value, such as a score. Moreover, it allows for flexible adjustment of the scoring mechanism to reflect specific characteristics of an experimental task (e.g., task priorities). This is important, given that adequate scores can reveal underlying cognitive processes involved in task performance. For instance, by combining time and the amount of errors to complete a given task, one can derive insights about the speed-accuracy tradeoff of the participant.

Ducheneaut, Moore and Nickell [3] provide an example of how a quantitative assessment method can reveal deeper insights into complex behavioral processes than a qualitative assessment method could. While exploring the concept of sociability in massive multiplayer online games, the authors gained better understanding of the matter by investigating the number, frequency, and length of visits in social places. However the qualitative results could not reveal how generic and how representative the observed activities were, so they turned to quantitative analysis. Other experimental testbeds benefit from a quantitative performance assessment in the same way, for example the Warship Commander Task (WCT) [4].

Safety-critical vigilance tasks can be found in many domains, such as air traffic control, driving on highways, or in the control room of nuclear power plants. The Warship Commander Task is one example of such a task. With the primary goal of protecting their own ship from hostile tracks appearing on a simulated radar-screen, WCT users must complete multiple subtasks of different priorities within limited time. These hierarchically organized subtasks include identifying all unknown tracks, as well as warning and engaging identified hostile tracks. The engagement of a hostile track can only be performed after its warning. Similarly, the warning of a hostile track can only be performed after its identification (see Figure 1), resulting in a hierarchical task structure.

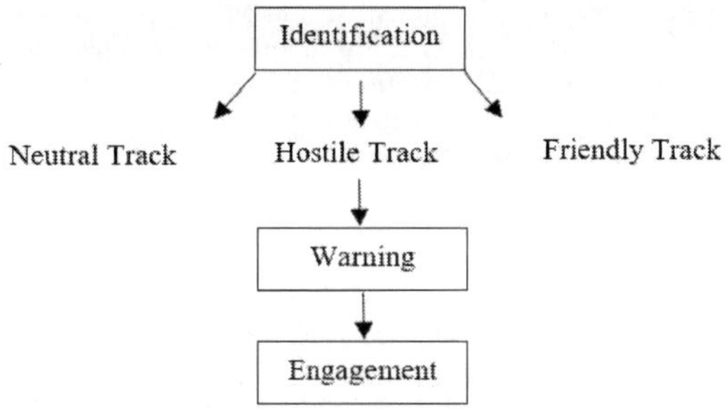

Figure 1. Subtasks of the WCT

Cognitive processes involved in executing a subtask in the WCT are identified based on the human processor model developed by Card, Moran and Newell [5]. The human processor model describes the calculation of reaction times based on the time needed for perceptual, cognitive, and motor processes. Figure 2 illustrates the cognitive processes involved in executing a subtask of the WCT: Visual attention and perception are a necessary prerequisite for detecting an object and discriminating it from the background of the screen. After successful detection of a relevant object, a rule-based decision is necessary to identify the object and determine if further action is necessary. In case of the WCT, such a rule can be found in the warning and engagement subtasks. The operator must decide if a track has to be warned or engaged based on its identity and distance.

The decision-making process is followed by task execution. The physiomotor response of clicking the button representing the required action concludes the subtask. For the identification subtask, the operator clicks on a button named "IFF" ("identify friend foe"). For executing a warning or an engagement, the operator clicks on a button named "warning" or "engagement".

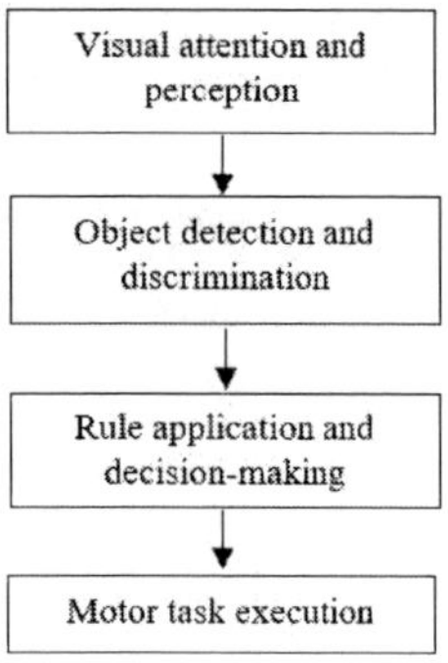

Figure 2. Cognitive processes involved in WCT based on [5]

While performing the main task, different kinds of errors (e.g., late or incorrect execution) can occur at various stages of cognitive processing. For instance, at the stage of perception, the operator may fail to direct visual attention to the relevant areas. Consequently, an approaching track may not be perceived. If the operator attends to the relevant area but does not process the stimulus or cannot discriminate the object from its environment, an error during the stage of object detection and discrimination occurs. At the decision-making stage, the incorrect application of decision rules can lead to decision errors. Finally, errors can also occur during the stage of task execution, e.g., by selecting the wrong response or omitting a response altogether.

The amount and complexity of the cognitive processes involved in tasks like the WCT require a performance mechanism that adequately represents the operator's performance. However, the original performance assessment employed in the WCT neither considers the speed of task completion, nor the type and amount of errors of the operator. For example, in vigilance tasks with temporal components like reaction time, a single overall performance score cannot consider the speed-accuracy tradeoff that describes the process of sacrificing accuracy for speed in task execution [6]. Specifically, accuracy cannot be defined by a single numerical value in complex tasks like the WCT due to the various sources of possible errors and mistakes.

For our purposes of creating affect-adaptive interaction, these are serious limitations. Trading accuracy for faster task completion (speed-accuracy tradeoff) is unfavorable in a command-and-control (C2) task where errors can have fatal consequences. An adaptive system could employ strategies to shift the internal criterion of the operator to complete tasks with more accuracy.

Quantitative analyses of the different error types allow for an in-depth understanding of the decision-making processes of the operator. With a scoring approach that captures the multidimensionality of performance decrements, researchers can exploit the advantages of an objective, quantitative assessment method while learning more about the operators' decisions that lead to the performance decrement.

In section 2, Signal Detection Theory (SDT) is introduced as theoretical background. Section 3 describes the scoring mechanism as it was developed for the chosen task environment followed by a discussion of lessoned learned and a generalized scoring system in section 4. Section 5 sums up the results, provides a conclusion and outlines future work.

II. Signal Detection Theory

Signal Detection Theory (SDT) provides a theoretical rationale on which quantitative measurement techniques in a wide range of application domains can be based on. Originating from signal detection in psychophysics [7], the theory successfully explains phenomena in the study of visual search [8], recognition memory [9], decision making in supervisory control [10], air combat training [11], essay grading [12] or social anxiety [13]. All these domains seem unrelated at first sight. However, the application of signal detection theory lead to a greater understanding by quantifying the underlying cognitive and behavioral processes.

SDT describes the process of detecting a signal [7] that can either be present or absent as well as detected or missed. This results in four possible outcomes, namely Hit, Miss, Correct Rejection or False Alarm (see Table I).

TABLE I. Decision-Making in SDT

		Signal	
		Present	***Absent***
Response	***Present***	Hit	False Alarm
	Absent	Miss	Correct Rejection

Based on that categorization, the operator's criterion and ability to discriminate the signal (+ noise) from a noise-only condition can be determined. The operator's tendency to exhibit a response independent from the presence of the nature of the signal is referred to as the criterion. An operator with a liberal criterion has higher False Alarm and Hit rates, whereas an operator with a conservative criterion has higher Correct Rejection and Miss rates. Discriminability is defined as the number of correct decisions (Correct Rejection and Hit) relative to the number of incorrect decisions (Miss and False Alarm) [14].

III. The Scoring Mechanism

We used signal detection theory as a basis in the development of a detailed scoring mechanism to assess the operator's response bias and performance across multiple performance criteria in a command-and-control environment (see section 3A). The first application of the scoring approach is described in section 3B.

A. Command-And-Control Tasks

The scoring mechanism was implemented in the Rich And Adaptable Test Environment (RATE), a modular and scalable task environment developed by Fraunhofer FKIE that allows for flexible design of experimental tasks. One instantiation of RATE is the described command-and-control task. This setup, coined RATE for C2, was used to investigate the relationship between performance and emotion in a command-and-control task [15]. In accordance with the WCT described in section 1A, the operator's task in RATE for C2 is to identify unknown tracks on a simulated radar screen and categorize them into neutral, hostile, or friendly tracks. Furthermore, hostile tracks that enter certain ranges around the own ship must be warned or engaged, respectively.

The operator's performance was measured by accuracy and speed in task completion. To assess performance at the subtask level, negative and positive scores for each category (accuracy and speed) were assigned to every subtask (identification. warning and engagement). The division into separate positive and negative scores is necessary to cover all categories of the SDT, as described in section 2.

The accuracy scores are based on the correctness of the operator's action. For instance, the engagement of a hostile track gains points on the positive accuracy score, whereas engagement of a neutral or friendly track increases the negative accuracy score. Similarly, positive and negative speed scores were used to capture the temporal performance aspects based on response time. For instance, timely engagement of a hostile track leads to an increase in the positive speed score, whereas a missed or delayed engagement of a hostile track increases the negative speed score. Figure 3 demonstrates how the subtasks of the WCT relate to the assigned performance scores.

The criterion of the operator is determined by the relationship between positive and negative scores of each category (accuracy and speed). An operator with a liberal criterion would tend to engage many tracks – including friendly or neutral ones - leading to an increase in positive as well as negative scores of accuracy. This corresponds to a high Hit and False Alarm rate in SDT. In contrast, a conservative operator would be hesitant in engaging tracks, leading to an increase in negative speed score. This corresponds to a high Miss Rate in SDT.

Insights into the cognitive processes associated with the subtasks of RATE for C2 arise from the analysis of individual scoring components. Problems with visual attention and perception, as well as object discrimination become evident in a high negative speed score for the subtasks of identification, warning, and engagement.

A high negative accuracy score results from problems occurring during the stage of decision-making and rule application. For instance, if the operator assigns a false identification to the corresponding track the negative accuracy score increases. This again results from incorrect interpretation of the IFF code.

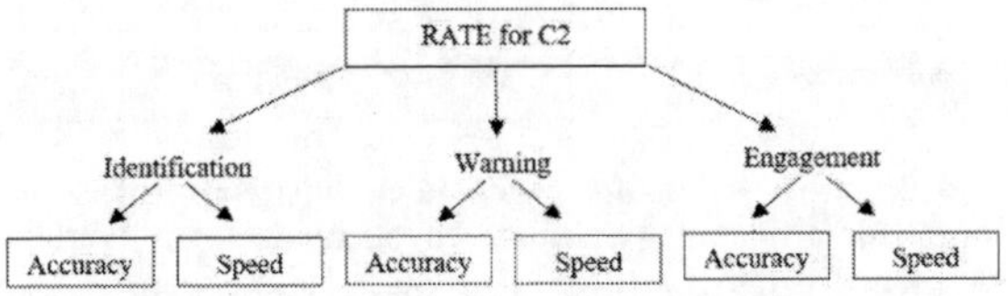

Figure 3. Subtasks of RATE for C2 and performance scores

Furthermore, a high negative speed score in combination with a high positive accuracy score indicates problems within the motor task execution.

To calculate total subtask and task performance, we deducted the negative from the positive score because high positive and low negative scores display high performance. However, achievable scores may vary greatly across conditions or scenarios. For example, in our task environment, difficulty levels were determined by the total number of tracks and the relative proportion of hostile tracks. In order to be able to compare absolute performance scores across conditions and scenarios it is necessary to normalize the absolute score. Our approach was to divide the absolute delta between positive and negative scores by the maximum achievable score within each category (see Table II), resulting in a comparable performance.

TABLE II. The Scoring Mechanism for accuracy and SPEED Adapted To A C2-Task

Individual Scoring Components	**Conditions**
Accuracy	
Positive Score	Correct Decisions: Correct Identification, Correct Warning of Hostile Tracks, Correct Engagement of Hostile Tracks
Negative Score	Incorrect Decisions: False Identification, False Warning (friendly/neutral Track), False Engagement (friendly/neutral Track)
Total Score	Positive Score - Negative Score
Max Score	∑ Achievable Positive Scores
Performance	Total Score / Max Score
Speed	
Positive Score	Correct Decisions: Identification in <=30 seconds, Warning of Hostile Tracks in <=20 seconds, Engagement of Hostile Tracks in <=10 seconds
Negative Score	Incorrect Decisions: Identification in >30 seconds, Warning of Hostile Tracks in >20 seconds, Engagement of Hostile Tracks in >10 seconds

Individual Scoring Components	Conditions
Total Score	Positive Score - Negative Score
Max Score	∑ Achievable Positive Scores
Performance	Total Score / Max Score

All described scores were generated separately for each subtask (identification, warning, engagement). An overall total score is the sum of all subtask total scores. An operator's overall performance for the experiment is calculated along the lines of subtask performance (by dividing the experiment's total score by the maximum achievable points across all subtasks).

B. *Application of the Scoring Approach*

The scoring mechanism was used in a study with Fifty-one ($N = 51$) subjects aged 18 to 57 years ($M = 32.75$, $SD = 9.8$) to examine the relationship between performance and emotion in the command-and-control task [15] described above. Task load was modulated across scenarios by varying the total number of tracks and the relative proportion of enemy tracks. This approach was based on the cognitive task load model validated with a command-and-control task by de Greef and Arciszewski [16]. Cognitive task analysis and the review of similar tasks covered in literature helped us to identify and to rank all relevant subtasks, their priorities and dependencies, as well as all possible behaviors associated with each subtask. Figure 4 illustrates that our implementation of the described scoring mechanism was sensitive to task load, as the overall performance decreased with higher task load.

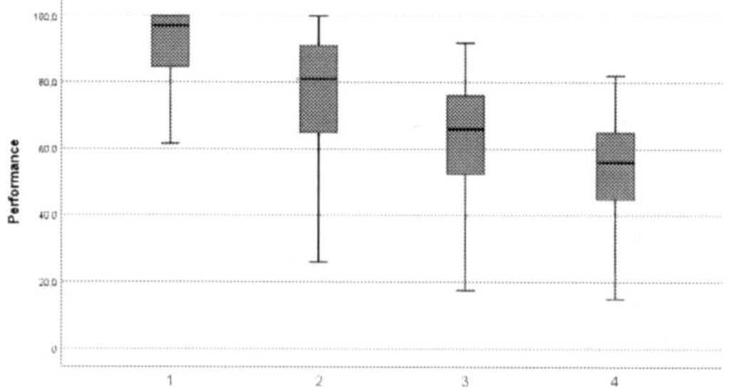

Figure 4. The performance score was sensitive to the number of tracks within a scenario (1=6 tracks, 2= 12 tracks, 3= 18 tracks, 4= 24 tracks)

IV. DISCUSSION

The developed scoring system offers several benefits for measuring human performance in complex task environments. Using "accuracy" and "speed" as performance criteria, we were able to gain insights into the cognitive processes associated with specific subtasks. The scoring approach itself does not isolate the specific information processing resource involved but it provides separate scores for each subtask and all performance criteria that can be mapped to cognitive processing steps. As mentioned above, problems with visual attention and perception as well as object discrimination were reflected in a high negative speed score whereas problems occurring during the stage of decision-making and rule application lead to a high negative accuracy score. Thus, careful choice of categories and/or tasks allows researchers to map subscores to cognitive processes and determine possible causes of observed behaviors.

However, a profound understanding of the experimental task and the cognitive processes involved is required to exploit these benefits. For example, being able to break down subtask performance and consider the hierarchical order of subtasks avoids misleading performance scores, but finding adequate ways for dealing with task omissions and conditional subtasks proved challenging.

The following lessons learned are meant to raise awareness for issues we encountered and provide possible ways to address them.

A. *Lessons learned*

1) Task structure: In order to define the actions leading to increases in positive and negative scores, respectively, decision trees have emerged to be a valuable tool to test the logical order of every possible subtask sequence and its associated scores.

2) Subtask priority: The priority of a subtask in the context of the overall task can be reflected in the amount of points earned on the corresponding positive/negative score. This allows the scoring mechanism to be adapted to other tasks environments, even beyond the command-and-control domain. Keeping in mind the research question and hypotheses of the study also helped to assess the relevance of subtasks and the relationship between them.

3) Conditional subtasks: Caution is advised when scoring conditional subtasks. Conditional subtasks are subtasks that occur in dependence of the outcome of a previous subtask. For example, in the described command-and-control task, only hostile tracks have to be engaged. If the operator incorrectly identifies a friendly track as hostile and then engages it (correctly, from the operator's point of view), no points should be awarded, otherwise he could earn more points than the maximum possible. Therefore, correct actions in conditional subtasks must not be rewarded if the action was only correct because of a preceding error. Whether incorrect actions lead to points on the negative score should be determined in the specific task context.

4) Task omissions: When determining point allocation, omission of necessary actions should neither lead to points on the positive nor on the negative score in order to separate omission errors from correct or incorrect explicit behavior. In case of the accuracy score, points on the positive score represent Hits in SDT and points on the negative score represent False Alarms in SDT as described above. Giving points for omissions would falsify this representation of SDT categories. This, however, does not apply if the omitted action represents incorrect behavior. For example, if the performance criterion is speed, operators should be given points on the negative score when the omission represents a missed identification.

5) Normalization: Normalization of the absolute performance score enabled comparisons of operator performance across conditions or scenarios, and even across different experiments. With a normalized performance score, it is possible to capture and analyze changes in performance over time (e.g., to compare implemented usability improvements or new interaction mechanisms). The impact of changes or improvements can then be analyzed at the task and even at subtask level. Test-retest reliability is ensured because the calculation of the score is independent from any dynamic components except the actions of the operator himself.

B. *Use With Other Tasks*

The developed scoring approach is not limited to use in command-and-control environments. It could also be generalized and adapted to other tasks that consist of multiple subtasks, including hierarchical task structures. Validation is still pending but the generalized concept is described below.

As a first step, applicable performance criteria must be determined for the task at hand. For our task detailed above, we chose accuracy and speed but there may be other options. In our case, the operator has the option of performing a subtask correctly or incorrectly depending on the considered category. For instance, in the case of speed, correct means "within a time limit" and incorrect means "outside the time limit" but the scoring approach is not limited to these categories. The scheme provided in Table II can be adapted and enhanced to calculate performance metrics for each criterion and each subtask in other task environment.

To assess multiple performance criteria, the above procedure can be repeated for each criterion separately. Performance across all subtasks can be calculated by dividing the sum of all subtask total scores by the sum of all subtask max scores (see Table III). It is also possible to quantify overall performance across all subtasks and categories.

TABLE III. GENERALIZED SCORING MECHANISM FOR TWO CATEGORIES AND TWO SUBSTASKS

Scoring-Components	Conditions
Category A (i.e., accuracy)	
Subtask 1	
Positive Score$_{A1}$	Correct Decisions
Negative Score$_{A1}$	Incorrect Decisions
Total Score$_{A1}$	Positive Score$_{A1}$ - Negative Score$_{A1}$
Max Score$_{A1}$	$\sum$ All possible achievable Positive Scores$_{A1}$
Performance$_{A1}$	Total Score$_{A1}$ / Max Score$_{A1}$
Subtask 2	
Positive Score$_{A2}$	Correct Decisions
Negative Score$_{A2}$	Incorrect Decisions
Total Score$_{A2}$	Positive Score$_{A2}$ - Negative Score$_{A2}$
Max Score$_{A2}$	$\sum$ All possible achievable Positive Scores$_{A2}$
Performance$_{A2}$	Total Score$_{A2}$ / Max Score$_{A2}$
Overall subtasks in category A	
Total Score$_{A}$	Total Score$_{A1}$ + Total Score$_{A2}$
Max Score$_{A}$	Max Score$_{A1}$ + Max Score$_{A2}$
Performance$_{A}$	Total Score$_{A}$ / Max Score$_{A}$
Category B (i.e., speed)	
Subtask 1	
Positive Score$_{B1}$	Decisions made within 15 seconds.
Negative Score$_{B1}$	Decisions made in more than 15 seconds.
Total Score$_{B1}$	Positive Score$_{B1}$ - Negative Score$_{B1}$
Max Score$_{B1}$	$\sum$ All possible achievable Positive Scores$_{B1}$
Performance$_{B1}$	Total Score$_{B1}$ / Max Score$_{B1}$
Subtask 2	
Positive Score$_{B2}$	Decisions made within 15 seconds.
Negative Score$_{B2}$	Decisions made in more than 15 seconds.
Total Score$_{B2}$	Positive Score$_{B1}$ - Negative Score$_{B1}$
Max Score$_{B2}$	$\sum$ All possible achievable Positive Scores$_{B2}$
Performance$_{B2}$	Total Score$_{B2}$ / Max Score$_{B2}$
Overall subtasks in category B	
Total Score$_{B}$	Total Score$_{B1}$ + Total Score$_{B2}$
Max Score$_{B}$	Max Score$_{B1}$ + Max Score$_{B2}$
Performance$_{B}$	Total Score$_{B}$ / Max Score$_{B}$
Overall categories	
Total Score	Total Score$_{A}$ + Total Score$_{B}$
Max Score	Max Score$_{A}$ + Max Score$_{B}$
Performance	Total Score / Max Score

V. CONCLUSION

Measuring human performance in complex task environments is a challenge, especially when multiple subtasks of varying priority are present or when subtasks depend on one another, resulting in a hierarchical task structure. With the reported scoring mechanism, we addressed some of these challenges and illustrated an approach to quantitatively assess human performance in complex experimental tasks. We have begun and illustrated first steps to generalize the scoring mechanism developed for our task environment, using SDT as a theoretical foundation, so that it can be adapted to different task environments and applicable performance criteria.

One limitation of the reported approach is that the scoring mechanism is currently limited to subtasks with dichotomous responses (correct or incorrect). Whether (and how) more gradual responses could be mapped into the score will be investigated in the future.

ACKNOWLEDGMENT

The authors would like to thank Stephanie Hochgeschurz for valuable thoughts on the scoring mechanism and Mitja Galkin for his crucial contributions to the customization of the RATE task environment and the implementation of the scoring mechanism.

REFERENCES

[1] P. A. Ochieng, "An analysis of the strengths and limitation of qualitative and quantitative research paradigms",. Problems of Education in the 21st Century, vol. 13, pp. 13-18, 2009.

[2] A. Queirós, D. Faria, and F. Almeida, "Strengths and limitations of qualitative and quantitative research methods", European Journal of Education Studies, vol. 3, no. 9, pp 369-387, 2017.

[3] N. Ducheneaut, R. J. Moore, and E. Nickell, "Virtual "third places": A case study of sociability in massively multiplayer games" Computer Supported Cooperative Work (CSCW), vol. 16, no. 1, pp. 129-166, 2007.

[4] Warship Commander 4.4; Computer Software; San Diego, CA: Pacific Science & Engineering Group; 2003.

[5] S. K. Card, T. P. Moran, and A. Newell, "The Model Human Processor: An Engineering Model of Human Performance" Handbook of Perception and Human Performance. vol. 2, Cognitive Processes and Performance, pp. 1-35, 1986.

[6] A. Osman et al., "Mechanisms of speed–accuracy tradeoff: evidence from covert motor processes", Biological psychology, vol. 51, no. 2-3,pp. 173-199, 2000.

[7] D. M. Green and J. A. Swets, "Signal detection theory and psychophysics", Wiley, 1966.

[8] P. Verghese, "Visual search and attention: A signal detection theory approach" Neuron,vol. 31, no. 4, pp. 523-535, 2001.

[9] J. T. Wixted, "Dual-process theory and signal-detection theory of recognition memory" Psychological review, vol. 114, no. 1, p. 152, 2007.

[10] A. Bisseret, "Application of signal detection theory to decision making in supervisory control The effect of the operator's experience", Ergonomics, vol. 24, no. 2, pp. 81-94, 1981.

[11] J. L. Eubanks and P. R. Killeen "An application of signal detection theory to air combat training"; Human factors, vol. 25, no. 4, pp. 449-456, 1983.

[12] L. T. DeCarlo, "A model of rater behavior in essay grading based on signal detection theory" Journal of Educational Measurement, vol. 42, no. 1, pp. 53-76, 2005.

[13] L Yoon, J. W. Yang, S. C. Chong, and K. J. Oh, "Perceptual sensitivity and response bias in social anxiety: an application of signal detection theory" Cognitive therapy and research, vol. 38, no. 5, pp. 551-558, 2014.

[14] N. A. Macmillan, "Signal detection theory", Stevens' handbook of experimental psychology, Wiley, 2002.

[15] A. Schmitz-Hübsch, S. M. Stasch, R. Becker, and S. Fuchs, "Personality Traits in the Relationship of Emotion and Performance in Command-and-Control Environments", International Conference on Advances in Computer-Human Interactions. vol. 14, in press.

[16] T. D. Greef and H. Arciszewski, "Triggering adaptive automation in naval command and control", Frontiers in adaptive control, IntechOpen, 2009.

Acquiring and Processing Data Using Simplified EEG-based Brain-Computer Interface for the Purpose of Detecting Emotions

Rafal Chalupnik, Katarzyna Bialas, Ireneusz Jozwiak, Michal Kedziora
Faculty of Computer Science and Management
Wroclaw University of Science and Technology
Wroclaw, Poland
rafal.chalupnik@pwr.edu.pl

***Abstract*—The aim of the paper was to analyze how to acquire and process EEG data with a simplified, commercially applicable EEG interface and to check whether it is possible to recognize human emotions with it. The EEG data gathering station was built and the data was gathered from the subjects. Then, the data was processed to apply it to the classifier training. The AutoML software was used to find the best ML model, and it was also built manually to prove the output accuracy was reliable and there was no overfitting. The AutoML experiment has shown that the best classifier was the boosted decision tree algorithm, and building it manually resulted in an accuracy of recognizing four distinct emotions equal to 99.80%.**

***Index Terms*—EEG; emotion recognition; machine learning; data acquiring**

I. Introduction

There are various studies regarding detecting emotions using electroencephalography (EEG). However, these studies use full-scale EEG devices, which can be difficult to use for commercial purposes [1] [2]. As the market is being filled with more and more devices that are smaller and more convenient [3] than the traditional EEG interface [4], such as NeuroSky MindWave Mobile 2 [5] [6], it is worth trying to acquire the data necessary for building the classifier with such devices and checking the achievable accuracy.

In this paper, we have planned the data acquisition and processing. The data acquisition process was defined and executed to gather the data for further processing, which included filtering by attention level above the preset threshold and signal smoothing by applying Simple Moving Average technique, which replaces the signal value at any given point in time with the average of the neighbors. Such experiment was completed successfully with the achieved accuracy of the built classifier of 99.80%.

The remainder of this paper is structured as follows: first, the available multiclass classification trainers are presented. Then, the stimulus set is prepared and the data acquisition process is described. After that, we described the methods used for signal processing, and finally, the experiment was performed, along with the results and conclusions drawn from them.

II. Related works

Detecting emotions using EEG was part of several research papers; however, they used the full-scale EEG interface instead of the simplified one. In the research done in [7], it was decided to use the emotion model used in [8], which assumes a division into two groups: positive and negative. The group of subjects consisted of three women and three men around the age of 22. They have viewed 12 video clips of length around four minutes. The authors decided to use audiovisual stimuli, as they stimulate more than one sense of the subject. Recording of brain activity in such a scenario gives 310 characteristics in each sample (62 electrodes * 5 channels). Samples were obtained this way and they were preanalyzed. Results with a dominance value lower than 3 were rejected because it implies an insufficient stimulant effect on the subject.

In the research by Chi et al. [9], emotion recognition was done while listening to music. They decided to use a 2D emotion model used in [10] consisting of two factors: arousal and valence of the emotion [11]. The EEG interface had 32 electrodes, distributed evenly through all head surfaces. The authors have tested three approaches to this problem. The first was one multiclass Support Vector Machine (SVM) classifier directly returning the predicted emotion. The second was the SVM classifier per each emotion and selecting the one with the highest score. The third was the tree of SVM classifiers recognizing valence on the first level, then arousal on the second one. The results of the experiments lead to the conclusion that the best approach to be used is to build the classifier for each emotion separately and then aggregate their outputs. The authors achieved an accuracy of 92.57%. In this paper, we conducted a similar experiment, but with the usage of the simplified, more convenient, and commercially available EEG interface to see whether it could achieve similar results.

III. Multi-class classification trainers

In the following section, the multiclass classification trainers are explained.

A. Averaged Perceptron Trainer

The single perceptron predicts the value by estimating the separating hyperplane. Let us say that there is a sample represented by a feature value vector, as shown in Equation 1.

$$F = [f_0, f_1, ..., f_{D-1}] \tag{1}$$

The perceptron simply determines which side of the hyperplane is the feature vector located. It is described by the sign of the weighted sum of the feature vectors, as shown in Equation 2, where $w*$ values are the weights of the perceptron, and the $b*$ are the biases.

$$y = \sum_{0}^{D-1} (w_i * f_i) + b_i \tag{2}$$

$$y - weighted\,sum$$

The learning process starts with initial weights (the best approach is to set them randomly). For each training sample, the weighted sum is calculated. If the sign of the predicted value is the opposite of the real one, the weights are updated by adding or subtracting the current sample features, multiplied by the learning rate and by the gradient of the loss function (Equation 3).

$$w_{t+1} = w_t \pm F * \alpha * l \tag{3}$$

$$w_{t+1} - new\,weights$$

$$w_t - old\,weights$$

$$F - feature\,vector$$

$$\alpha - learning\,rate$$

$$l - loss\,function\,value$$

The Averaged Perceptron model is based on a set of perceptrons. Each sample is processed with every perceptron, and the final prediction is based on the sign of the average output from all perceptrons.

B. Fast Forest Binary Trainer

Decision trees are models that are based on simple tests executed in sequence. The prediction is made by finding a similar input in the training dataset and returning their output label. Each node of the binary tree is representing a simple test to perform on the input data, and the output decision is reached by traversing the tree and finding the leaf node representing the output.

There are several advantages of decision trees. They are efficient in terms of computation and memory usage, both during the training phase and using the trained classifier. Moreover, they can represent the boundaries that cannot be resolved by linear decision (e.g., perceptron).

This particular trainer is a random forest implementation - it builds an ensemble of decision trees and then aggregates the output to find a Gaussian distribution that is the closest one to the combined distribution of aggregated trees. Such an approach provides better coverage and accuracy than single decision trees.

C. Fast Tree Binary Trainer

This trainer uses the efficient implementation of Multiple Additive Regression Trees (MART) gradient-boosting algorithm. It is building every decision tree using a step-by-step approach and using a predefined loss function to measure the error and correct for each step.

MART algorithm uses an ensemble of regression trees, which is a decision tree that contains scalar values in each leaf. The decision can be presented as a binary tree-like flow, where every node decides which of the two children should be used based on one of the features from the input.

The tree ensemble is constructed by computing a regression tree for each step that is an approximation of the loss function gradient and then adding it to the previous tree to minimize the loss function value of the new tree.

D. LBFGS Logistic Regression Binary Trainer

This trainer is using the optimization technique based on the Limited memory Broyden-Fletcher-Goldfarb-Shanno method (L-BFGS). It is a quasi-Newtonian method that is used to replace the Hessian matrix, which is computation-expensive, with an approximation.

Linear logistic regression is a variant of the linear model. It assumes the mapping of the feature vector into a scalar via the scoring function:

$$y(x) = w^T x + b = \sum_{j=1}^{n} w_j x_j + b \tag{4}$$

Since the approximation uses a limited number of states in history to designate the direction of the next step, it is convenient to solve problems having high-dimensional features. The user can set the number of stored historical steps and thus balance between a better approximation and lower cost per step.

E. LBFGS Maximum Entropy Multiclass Trainer

This model is a generalization of linear logistic regression. It can, however, be used in multiclass classification problems, while the regression can only solve binary ones.

This trainer assigns to each class a coefficient vector:

$$w_c \in R^n \tag{5}$$

and bias:

$$b_c \in R \tag{6}$$

Next, each class's score is calculated:

$$y_c = w_c^T x + b_c \tag{7}$$

The probability of the sample belonging to a given class can be defined in the following way:

$$P(c|x) = \frac{e^{y_c}}{\sum^{m} e^{y_c}} \tag{8}$$

F. Light GBM Multiclass Trainer

This Gradient Boosting Machine (GBM) trainer is an implementation of a gradient boosting framework that uses tree-based learning algorithms [12]. The major advantages of this trainer are that it achieves higher efficiency in shorter training time. Furthermore, it is using less memory and provides higher accuracy than similar algorithms.

G. Linear SVM Trainer

Linear SVM is another trainer that relies on finding a hyperplane in the feature space to perform binary classification. As in previous examples, the side of a hyperplane is defined by sign of the equation:

$$y = \sum_{1}^{N} (w_i * x_i) + b_i \tag{9}$$

However, the SVM model builds a representation of training samples as points in the space and the objective is to create a wide gap between points representing particular classes as possible.

H. One Versus All Trainer

One Versus All strategy assumes having a binary classification algorithm for each class. Such a classifier predicts the output class by evaluating all binary classifiers and selecting the result which has the highest score.

In ML.NET [13], such trainer can be used to concatenate binary classifiers to perform multiclass classification. This way, the developer can create a complex model, e.g., using 4 Fast Tree algorithms to achieve 4-class classification.

I. SDCA Maximum Entropy Multiclass Trainer

The Stochastic Dual Coordinate Ascent (SDCA) trainer is dedicated to multiclass classification usage. Assuming that there are C classes and N features in a particular sample, this algorithm assigns to every class a coefficient vector $w_c \in R^n$ and bias $b_c \in R$. For the feature vector, the value y_c is calculated for each class.

$$y_c = w_c^T x + b_c \tag{10}$$

Then, the probability of the feature vector belonging to a particular class is calculated in the following way:

$$P(c|x) = \frac{e^{y_c}}{\sum_{1}^{C} e^{y_{c_i}}} \tag{11}$$

J. Symbolic SGD Logistic Regression Binary Trainer

This trainer, also in its core is using the hyperplane to divide the samples represented as points in space. However, it has one fundamental difference.

While most of the algorithms that are using Stochastic Gradient Descent (SGD) are sequential, which means they are using the result of the previous step to process the current one, this algorithm is training the local models on separate threads and then, the probabilistic model combiner is trained to aggregate the models and provide the same output that the sequential algorithms would produce.

IV. Data Acquisition and Processing

As it is a common approach in related works, it has been decided to use audiovisual stimuli to invoke the particular emotion of a subject while stimulating more than one sense. This approach allows us to stimulate different parts of the brain. The best approach seems to be using music videos [14], as:

- they are fulfilling the audiovisual stimulus criterium,
- music is known to invoke human emotions effectively,
- videos are often well synchronized with music.

As the experiment is conducted based on the two-dimensional emotion model [15] [16], there is a need to find four music videos that would be related to each of the emotions: anger, depression, relaxation and happiness.

To build the classifier, the EEG data needed to be acquired and processed. NeuroSky MindWave Mobile 2 EEG interface is returning the raw data in its own metrics [17], and such data is already split into EEG spectres, This section is describing the two parts of the gathering data problem: how the data gathering station was built, and how the process looked like.

A. Data gathering station

Fig. 1. Data gathering station

To collect the EEG interface data necessary to conduct this experiment, the data gathering station was assembled, as visible in Figure 1. It consists of four most important factors: video stimuli, displayed on the monitor placed directly before the subject; audio stimuli, played through the headphones to reduce the noise around the station and improve the quality of the gathered data; NeuroSky MindWave Mobile 2 EEG interface [18], which is recording the EEG data; data gathering software, running on a separate computer facing away from the subject to not distract the user (for the station presentation, the photo is taken where it is visible for the subject).

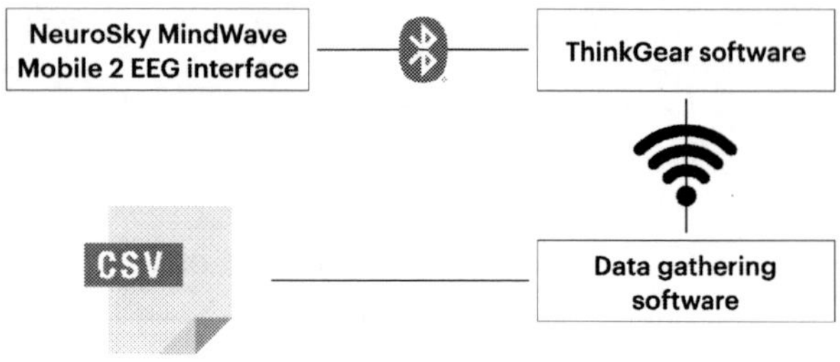

Fig. 2. Data gathering connection diagram

To collect the recorded EEG data and write it to the CSV file, the software needs to be used as presented in Figure 2. NeuroSky ThinkGear software is responsible for handling the Bluetooth connection to the EEG interface and provides this data over the Internet connection (during this experiment, the connection was used only in the localhost scope). Then, the dedicated data gathering software was written that connects to the ThinkGear API, downloading the EEG data and saving it to the CSV file.

B. Data gathering process

The study group consisted of 6 people, both women and men, of age from 15 to 45 years. Each subject had the EEG MindWave interface put on, along with headphones to reduce the outside stimuli that could negatively affect the experiment results.

For each of the stimuli, the subject watched the video for about five minutes, then was allowed to rest for about one minute to clear the mind, so the next recording is not affected by the previous one.

The subject is not told about the emotion that is currently recorded. In a related work, Nie et al [7] were using self-assessment manikin (SAM) to make the subject describe the emotion he was feeling, which later was classified as positive or negative. Such manikin consists of valence and arousal measures, which in our experiment are part of the two-dimensional emotion model. The third measure is the dominance measure, which was used to indicate whether the emotion was felt precisely and deeply or too slightly.

The idea of using SAM was deliberately discarded [19], as three measures are already included, and the third one will be achieved in another way, which will be described later in this work. Moreover, such an approach makes it possible to check in this experiment whether the emotions felt by different people have something in common, even if we are giving it different names. The proposed two-dimensional model has the advantage of not giving name to each of the emotions, we can describe them as valence/arousal positivity/negativity.

Figures from 3 to 10 represent the example visualization of the gathered data for each emotion or each spectrum in the domain of time. The Y axis represents the ASIC_EEG_POWER custom unit, which can be represented as $\frac{V^2}{Hz}$. [17].

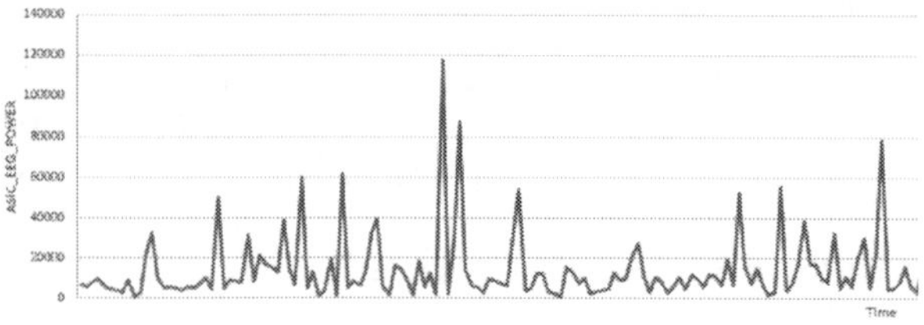

Fig. 3. Visualization of the Alpha High EEG spectrum for anger

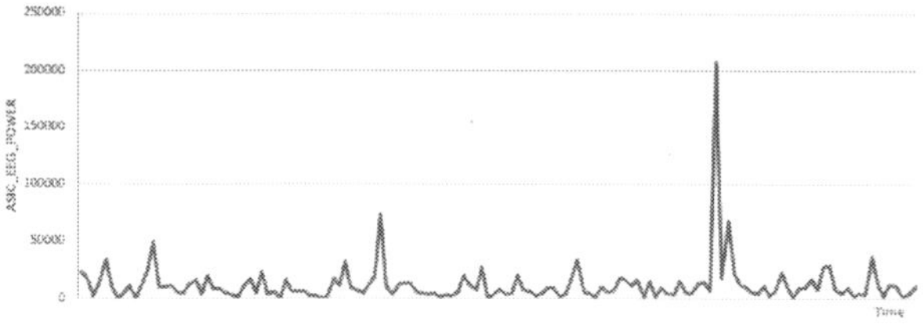

Fig. 4. Visualization of the Alpha Low EEG spectrum for anger

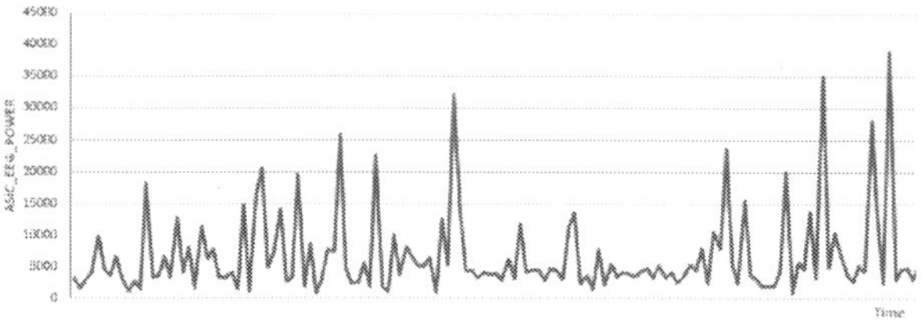

Fig. 5. Visualization of the Beta High EEG spectrum for anger

C. Processing data - filtering

In a related work, Nie et al [7] were using SAM manikins to describe i.a. strength of the felt emotion. As such manikins can be nonintuitive to the subjects, and such a measure does not have to match the reality, it was decided to filter the data using eSense measures provided by the MindWave EEG interface.

The eSense data consists of three measures: Attention, Meditation and Blink. To filter out the not-applicable data,

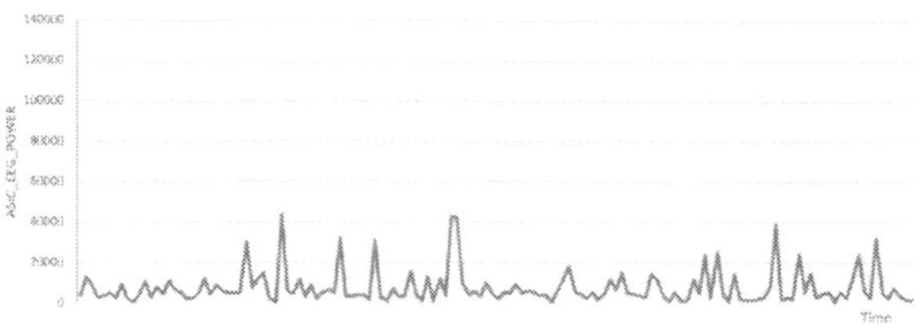

Fig. 6. Visualization of the Beta Low EEG spectrum for anger

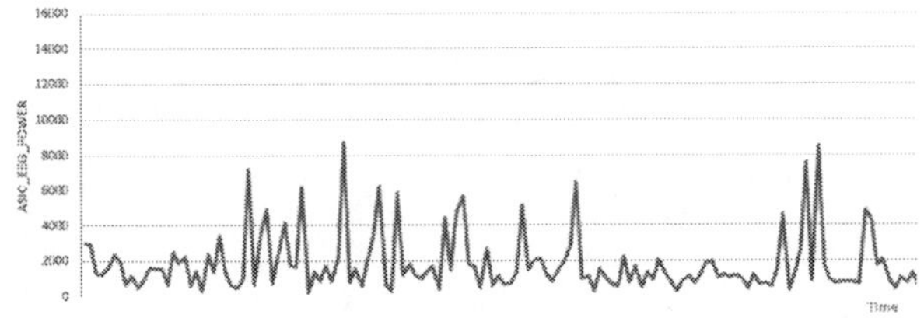

Fig. 7. Visualization of the Gamma High EEG spectrum for anger

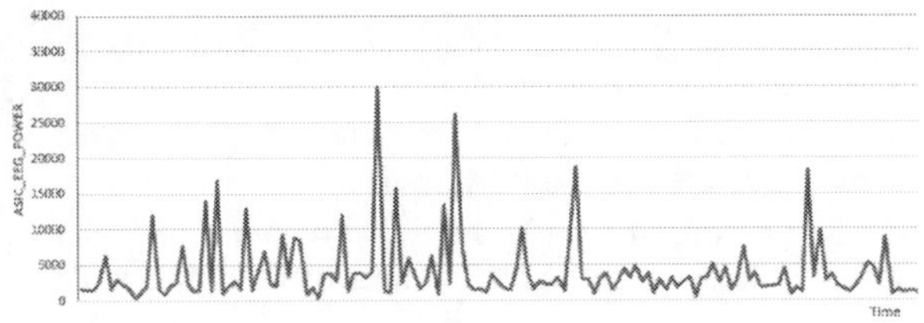

Fig. 8. Visualization of the Gamma Low EEG spectrum for anger

all samples with the attention level below 50 (on a scale from 0 to 100) were discarded. Such a filter can discard all data when the subject was not "concentrated" enough, e.g., there was a noise in the environment that got to the subject through the headphones or there was a fly in the room that distracted the subject.

Using SAM manikins to check the dominance of the emotion has two major disadvantages:

- subject can answer that the emotion was very dominant, but there were times that he was distracted,
- subject can answer that the emotion was not dominant because of distraction, e.g., 3 seconds - then the whole recording was wasted.

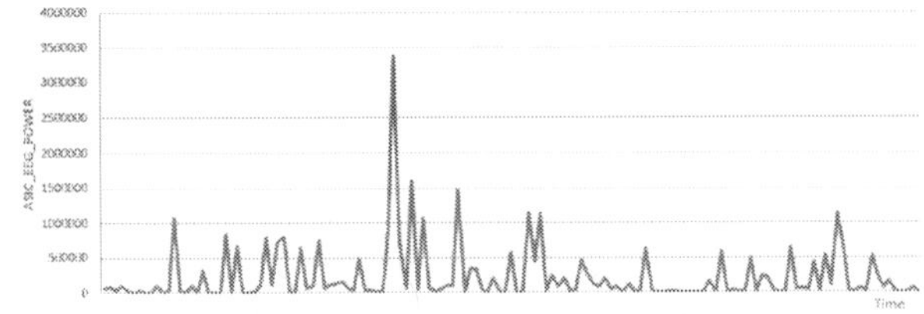

Fig. 9. Visualization of the Delta EEG spectrum for anger

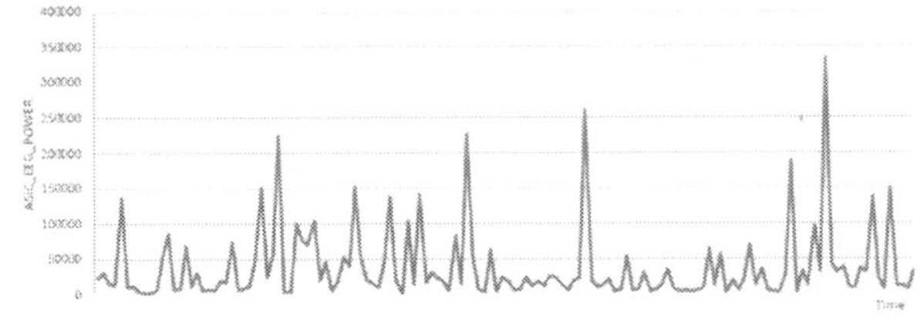

Fig. 10. Visualization of the Theta EEG spectrum for anger

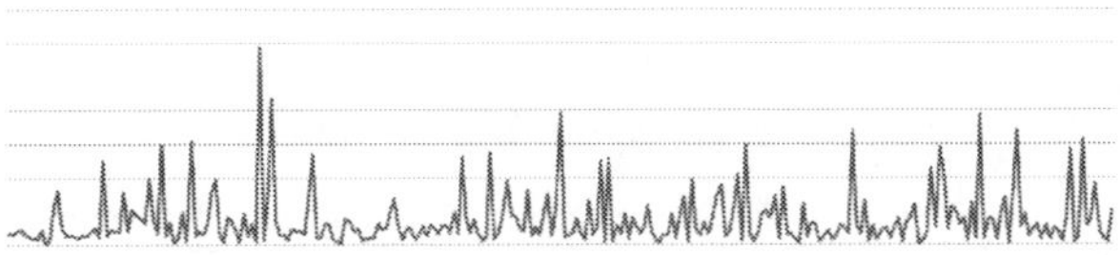

Fig. 11. Original signal

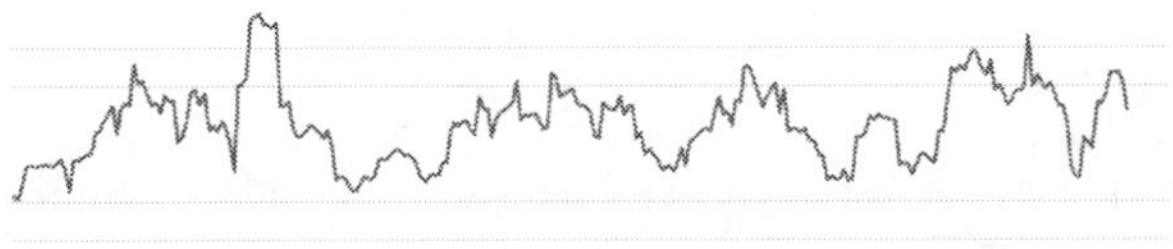

Fig. 12. Smoothed signal

Filtering the recorded samples through their attention score allows removing these two disadvantages, as such a measure is independent of the subject consciousness, and therefore cannot be falsified too easily.

D. Processing data - signal smoothing

The data received from the MindWave EEG interface consisted of eight measures:

- low alpha,
- high alpha,
- low beta,
- high beta,
- low gamma,
- high gamma,
- delta,
- theta.

The problem that appeared is that the signal received from the interface is quite noisy, and trying to train the classifier using a singular sample could result in low efficiency. To avoid that, the received output was smoothed, as presented in Figures 11 and 12.

There are numerous ways to smooth the signal [20] [21]. For this experiment, the Simple Moving Average algorithm [22] has been chosen, which uses the sliding window to calculate the average value of the signal.

For example, let us assume the window width $w = 4$ and step $s = 2$ for the signal values:

$$\lambda = [4, 9, 6, 5, 2, 1, 3, 10, 8, 7] \quad (12)$$

then the new signal will consist of four average values:

$$\lambda\prime = [\frac{\sum_1^4 \lambda_n}{4}, \frac{\sum_3^6 \lambda_n}{4}, \frac{\sum_5^8 \lambda_n}{4}, \frac{\sum_7^{10} \lambda_n}{4}] \quad (13)$$

which after calculation, will be

$$\lambda\prime = [6, 3.5, 4, 7] \quad (14)$$

TABLE I
AUTOML: TOP 5 TESTED CLASSIFIERS

	Trainer	MicroAccuracy	MacroAccuracy	Duration
1	FastTreeOva	0.9233	0.9264	19.4
2	LightGbmMulti	0.9000	0.9001	14.3
3	LightGbmMulti	0.8185	0.8199	17.5
4	FastForestOva	0.8027	0.8051	53.1
5	FastTreeOva	0.8006	0.8035	24.3

TABLE II
SUMMARY CONFUSION MATRIX FOR TESTED BEST CLASSIFIER

	Anger	Depression	Happiness	Relaxation	Recall
Anger	1326	1	2	0	0.97743
Depression	1	1280	2	0	0.97662
Happiness	0	0	1267	1	0.99211
Relaxation	2	2	0	1024	0.96109
Precision	0.97743	0.97662	0.96853	0.99024	

E. Gathered data from time perspective

While it is natural to consider the gathered data as changing in time, as it is recording brain waves, this experiment was conducted using singular samples from the recordings to check whether the time is needed. The ThinkGear Web API [23] used to collect the samples was returning the data 1 sample per second, and that is the granularity used in this experiment. To reduce the noise available in the data, a smoothing filter was used as described earlier, however, the resulting samples were used one-by-one in building the classifier, without keeping the information about the relationship between them. This way, the experiment can check whether it is more important to check the brain waves fluctuations over time, or to observe the plain values of EEG spectres to correctly recognize and classify emotions.

V. EXPLORING THE CLASSIFIERS

The following section describes the classifier exploration with ML.NET.

A. Exploring classifiers using AutoML

After the data processing, the AutoML framework was used to determine the best ML.NET model for the dataset. AutoML is a feature of ML.NET foundation developed by Microsoft. It is a key advantage is that it allows quickly browsing the available classifiers and their achievable accuracy without writing the code. Given 5 minutes of time, AutoML designated the best classifier and the summary of the tested classifiers (top 5 shown in Table I).

B. Building the best classifier with ML.NET

During the experiment, the best classifier found by AutoML was FastTreeOva. To ensure that the achieved accuracy is reliable (e.g, there was no overfitting, the test data were not the same as the training ones, etc.), the FastTreeOva classifier has been built manually, using ML.NET components.

Firstly, the training and test data were prepared and the cross-validation technique was applied.

1) Load the samples from CSV file.
2) Randomize the samples order.
3) Split data into 10 batches.
4) For each batch:
    a) Form the test data from the selected batch.
    b) Form the training data from the rest.
    c) Run the training and gather output.
5) Gather average values from the output of each batch.

The FastTreeOva model constructed with ML.NET components was used in the cross-validation. The results were presented in the confusion matrix, presented in Table II. The real emotions are represented by rows, and the predicted emotions are represented as columns.

The accuracy (a) of the classifier can be presented as a ratio of correctly classified samples (s) to all the samples(Ω):

$$a = \frac{s}{\Omega} = \frac{4897}{4908} \approx 99.8\% \quad (15)$$

The FastTreeOva model has been proven to achieve an accuracy of 99.8%. It is worth noticing that the accuracy was achieved without filtering the data by attention level, which might indicate the difficulty of hiding the felt emotions.

VI. CONCLUSION AND FUTURE WORK

Data that was gathered during the experiment was processed by applying two techniques: eliminating samples with the attention level below the preset threshold and signal smoothing using Simple Moving Average algorithm.

Taking into account the purpose of the study, which is to check whether it is possible to recognize emotions using the simplified EEG interface and to see how many emotions it is achievable to distinguish, the purpose was fulfilled.

The conducted experiment has shown that it is possible to predict 4 distinct emotions using NeuroSky MindWave Mobile 2 device with an accuracy of 99.80%. It seems that filtering the gathered data by attention level did not impact the final results, as opposed to the applied signal smoothing technique, which helped to achieve such an accuracy.

It would be promising to research the improvement ratio for each EEG spectrum and compare it with the accuracy of the classifier built solely on this spectrum, showing that there certainly is a noticeable difference in spectrum influence between the two groups: alpha, beta, gamma and delta, theta. The difference between the calculated values could be observed, which could indicate that some EEG spectres have higher influence on emotion recognition. Furthermore, the built FastTreeOva model research could define the range of each EEG spectrum that is correlated with the particular emotion.

REFERENCES

[1] S. Saganowski, A. Dutkowiak, A. Dziadek, M. Dzieżyc, J. Komoszyńska, W. Michalska, A. Polak, M. Ujma, and P. Kazienko, "Emotion recognition using wearables: A systematic literature review-work-in-progress," in *2020 IEEE International Conference on Pervasive Computing and Communications Workshops (PerCom Workshops)*. IEEE, 2020, pp. 1–6.

[2] Y. Yin, X. Zheng, B. Hu, Y. Zhang, and X. Cui, "Eeg emotion recognition using fusion model of graph convolutional neural networks and lstm," *Applied Soft Computing*, vol. 100, p. 106954, 2021.

[3] S. Saganowski, A. Dutkowiak, A. Dziadek, M. Dzieżyc, J. Komoszyńska, W. Michalska, A. Polak, M. Ujma, and P. Kazienko, "Emotion recognition using wearables: A systematic literature review - work-in-progress," in *2020 IEEE International Conference on Pervasive Computing and Communications Workshops (PerCom Workshops)*, 2020, pp. 1–6.

[4] E. Niedermeyer, *Electroencephalography : basic principles, clinical applications, and related fields*. Philadelphia: Lippincott Williams & Wilkins, 2005.

[5] K. Bialas and M. Kedziora, "Analiza mozliwosci sterowania aplikacja mobilna za pomoca interfejsu mozg-komputer," in *XII Ogolnokrajowa Konferencja Naukowa MLODZI NAUKOWCY W POLSCE – BADANIA I ROZWOJ (paper accepted)*, 2020.

[6] "NeuroSky official website," http://neurosky.com, accessed: 2020-06-08.

[7] D. Nie, X. Wang, L.-C. Shi, and B.-L. Lu, "Eeg-based emotion recognition during watching movies," 06 2011, pp. 667 – 670.

[8] P. Ekman and D. Cordaro, "What is meant by calling emotions basic," *Emotion Review*, vol. 3, no. 4, pp. 364–370, 2011.

[9] Y.-P. Lin, C.-H. Wang, T.-L. Wu, S.-K. Jeng, and J. Chen, "Eeg-based emotion recognition in music listening: A comparison of schemes for multiclass support vector machine," 04 2009, pp. 489–492.

[10] M. N. Shiota, "Ekman's theory of basic emotions," *The SAGE Encyclopedia of Theory in Psychology*, 2016.

[11] C. Osgood, G. Suci, and P. Tenenbaum, *The Measurement of meaning*. University of Illinois Press, 1957.

[12] "LightGBM documentation website," https://lightgbm.readthedocs.io/en/latest/index.html, accessed: 2020-06-14.

[13] "ML.NET official webpage," https://dotnet.microsoft.com/apps/machinelearning-ai/ml-dotnet, accessed: 2020-05-21.

[14] D. Plass-Oude Bos, "Eeg-based emotion recognition," *The Influence of Visual and Auditory Stimuli*, 01 2006.

[15] D. L. Schacter, *Psychology*. New York, NY : Worth Publishers, 2011.

[16] P. Ekman, "What scientists who study emotion agree about," *Perspectives on Psychological Science*, vol. 11, no. 1, pp. 31–34, 2016.

[17] "NeuroSky EEG Band Power values meaning," http://support.neurosky.com/kb/development-2/eeg-band-power-values-units-amplitudes-and-meaning, accessed: 2020-06-14.

[18] "NeuroSky MindWave Mobile 2 official product page," https://store.neurosky.com/pages/mindwave, accessed: 2020-06-08.

[19] M. Dzieżyc, J. Komoszyńska, S. Saganowski, M. Boruch, J. Dziwiński, K. Jabłońska, D. Kunc, and P. Kazienko, "How to catch them all? enhanced data collection for emotion recognition in the field," in *2021 IEEE International Conference on Pervasive Computing and Communications Workshops and other Affiliated Events (PerCom Workshops)*, 2021, pp. 348–351.

[20] H. He, Y. Tan, J. Ying, and W. Zhang, "Strengthen eeg-based emotion recognition using firefly integrated optimization algorithm," *Applied Soft Computing*, vol. 94, p. 106426, 2020.

[21] C. Wei, L.-l. Chen, Z.-z. Song, X.-g. Lou, and D.-d. Li, "Eeg-based emotion recognition using simple recurrent units network and ensemble learning," *Biomedical Signal Processing and Control*, vol. 58, p. 101756, 2020.

[22] C. Clapham, J. Nicholson, and J. Nicholson, *The Concise Oxford Dictionary of Mathematics*, ser. Oxford Paperback Reference. OUP Oxford, 2014. [Online]. Available: https://books.google.pl/books?id=c69GBAAAQBAJ

[23] "NeuroSky ThinkGear chip technical specifications," http://neurosky.com/biosensors/eeg-sensor/, accessed: 2020-06-08.

Scalability of the Size of Patterns Drawn Using Tactile Hand Guidance

Dhanya Nair
Fowler School of Engineering
Chapman University
Orange, USA
email: dnair@chapman.edu

Abstract— **Haptic feedback for handwriting training has been extensively studied, but with primary focus on kinematic feedback. We provide vibrotactile feedback through a wrist worn sleeve to guide the user to recreate unknown patterns and study the impact of vibrational duration (1, 2, 3 seconds) on pattern scaling. User traces a line at 90° angles, while attempting to maintain a constant speed, in the direction of the motor activated till a different motor activation is perceived. Shape and size are two features of good letter formation. Study performed on three subjects showed the ability to utilize four vibrotactile motors to guide the hand towards correct shape formation with high accuracy (> 95%). The overall size of the letter was observed to scale linearly with the vibrational duration. Implications for utilizing the vibrational feedback for handwriting correction are discussed.**

Keywords-wearable haptics; tactile sleeve; handwriting; letter size and shape; tactile hand guidance.

I. INTRODUCTION

Handwriting is an important lifelong skill that can be challenging to acquire for children with learning disabilities and post-stroke patients with agraphia. Tracing, copying, and completing paper worksheets, with the help of corrective auditory feedback, remains the common mode of teaching this skill. Providing haptic feedback in addition to the audio-visual format has shown to improve visuo-motor skills (a prerequisite to handwriting training) [1]][2], character retention [3] and the overall handwriting quality [4]. Several haptic guidance methods have been developed for handwriting training [1][3][5]-[11], with their suitability depending on the complexity of the task. For example, partial haptic guidance may be better suited for medium complexity letters/handwriting tasks, while disturbance haptic guidance for high complexity letters and full haptic guidance for the low complexity letters [8]; and combining the different haptic guidance methods over the training period has been more effective than utilizing either of them alone [9]. These systems while benefiting the sighted can also provide the visually impaired an accessible means of learning to write/sign their name [12][13].

Owing to its ready availability to the research community, Phantom Omni has been the primary platform for developing these systems [1][3][5]-[11][13]. Although Phantom Omni based handwriting training has shown to be effective, it is still not a common training tool in classrooms. Their bulk and tethered nature, requiring allocated workstations in addition to their cost, might be a hinderance in their widescale adaptability. Utilizing similar force feedback principles of hand guidance, other ergonomically focused stylus systems like RealPen [14] and KATIB [15] are currently being developed. While technologically promising, they are not cost-effective options yet.

Meanwhile, there is growing research in utilizing tactile feedback for hand movement guidance [16]-[24]. These systems employ inexpensive vibrators/motors to develop affordable wearable solutions that could be easily accessible to the educators, as well as the research community. We are investigating the efficacy of vibrotactile wearable system for handwriting training. To this effect, we provide a brief overview of the vibrotactile hand guidance methods that have been investigated.

In a large trial study, Matscheko et al. [16] achieved higher information transfer rate by placing tactors around the wrist vs. placing them in a grid on the dorsal side, while also demonstrating a lower impact of distraction load. They concluded that wrist worn tactile systems should place tactors around the wrist instead of in a grid form. They attributed the reduced accuracy (in the latter case) to space restriction of placing the grid beneath "the watch face" area while meeting the two-point discrimination requirement of about 38mm. Most systems have followed this guideline for motor placement with the motor type, number, or actuation method being the differentiators.

Sergi et al. [17] used four Direct Current (DC) motors to provide tactile feedback on the four quadrants (dorsal, volar, radial, ulnar sides) of the wrist for angular directional guidance of the entire forearm in performing 2-Degree Of Freedom (DOF) tasks and showed an increased accuracy by including the tactile feedback in comparison to visual alone. Causo et al. [18] utilized 6 vibrating disk motors worn on a stationary arm for posture correction of the other arm in a 3D space with each axis being assigned to two motors. The user is supposed to move their wrist (and then elbow, and later forearm) towards the direction of increasing vibration till a maximum vibration is felt indicating the correct final position. Salazar et al. [19] arranged six vibrational motors at equal distances around the wrist circumference for wrist guidance in 2D space using phantom sensation illusion (produced by simultaneously actuating two adjacent motors resulting in a perceived stimulus at their midpoint). Hong et al. [20][21] developed different wristbands for angular path finding/tracing in 2D surface, one with four vibrating disk motors placed along four quadrants of the wrist (like Sergi et al.) and the second with an additional four motors placed in between these, totaling to eight motors around the wrist. They found the 4-motor wristband to be faster, more accurate and preferred over the 8-motor design. They also performed comparative study between activating single motor vs. providing illusions by activating two adjacent motors and found that participants could non-visually trace paths more quickly and accurately using the single motor activation design.

VibroSleeve [22] proposed placement of 16 vibrating disk motors on a sleeve worn around the forearm (a row of four motors on each forearm quadrant: dorsal, ventral, medial and lateral) for arm guidance in 3D Cartesian space. In a test where they examined the user's ability to correctly identify the stimulation side (top/bottom/left/right), they simultaneously activated all the four motors on that side for 500ms before requesting participant response resulting in 100% accuracy. They aimed to study the perceived direction of motion using movement illusion generated by the sequential stimulation of motors, from the proximal to distal end of the forearm for forward motion (or vice versa for backward motion). They also utilized Amplitude Modulation (AM) where the intensity of the previous motor was reduced before the activation of the next motor in the sequence. While they found highest directional accuracy (85-90%) and subjective ease of interpretation in the AM pattern representation method, this was also the only activation sequence where they had provided a break (100ms) between the activation of successive motors. Hence, it is inconclusive whether the increased direction recognition was due to the AM pattern or the difference between continuous activation vs. with breaks, or even due to the introduction of movement illusion.

StrokeSleeve [23][24] design utilized two sleeves (worn on the wrist and biceps respectively), each embedded with four eccentric mass motors for hand guidance and movement training. The arm motion was tracked, and upon detecting a deviation from the desired trajectory, visual and vibratory feedback was provided. They found that vibratory feedback significantly reduced the angular error in motion during the training, especially for simpler tasks. Although they did not observe a significant angular error reduction during their retention trials, they attributed this to the short training period and the meaninglessness of the motions performed reducing the intrinsic motivation to memorize the trajectories.

In vibrotactile hand guidance research area, there are limited studies in utilizing tactile wearable systems for handwriting training. A few exceptions are Morikawa et al. [25][26] and Narita et al. [27][28] that utilize wrist worn pressure presentation device for calligraphy training. They use two levers mounted on the wrist to provide stimulations (gentle taps) to correct the user's hand position along the horizontal direction, for self-training. They do not provide any vertical direction feedback.

Towards the goal of developing wearable vibrotactile handwriting training system, this study investigates the ability to utilize a sleeve for guiding the user towards the correct form (shape) and size/scale of different characters. Therefore, vibrations are provided at different spatial locations on a forearm (representing the direction of desired motion), and participants are asked to draw unseen patterns on graph paper (with grids) as the only visual guide.

Appropriate form and size are key features of good letter formation [29]. Focusing on the proper sizing of the letters (prior to the form) has shown to improve letter form and handwriting legibility [30]. Hence, this work aims to study the applicability of utilizing a vibrotactile sleeve embedded with four motors for presenting the correct form of select letters from English, Arabic and Malayalam (a south Indian language) that are hidden from the user. We investigate the ability of using vibrotactile cues for controlling the size of each of these letters.

This paper demonstrates the preliminary results of utilizing tactile feedback for controlling the form and size of letters drawn by the user. In Section II, an overview of the vibrotactile sleeve is provided, section III lists the scope of this study, section IV describes the experimental setup for data collection, section V explains the results, and section VI concludes with a summary and future work.

II. BACKGROUND

The sleeve and the system architecture being utilized in this study has been presented in prior works [31][32] with a learn-to-write software that tracks pen movement (based on a webcam input) as the user tries to trace a pattern displayed on the screen. If the pen deviates from the pattern being traced, motors embedded within the sleeve provide vibrational feedback guiding the user's hand in the correct direction. Different arrangements of the motors on the sleeve were considered and the accuracy of perceived location and user response time were investigated to identify the best location for motor placement [32]. A summary of the sleeve design is provided below for completeness.

A. Motor placement

Since four motor wristbands were found to be accurate and intuitive for hand guidance in 2D space [21], our hardware utilizes four mini vibrating disk motors. Only a single motor is activated at a time, thus enabling faster response by reducing the cognitive load/confusion introduced by providing illusions [19]. The activated motor represents one of the four directions (up, down, left, or right) of desired motion.

Four different arrangements of motor placement on the sleeve were considered. Initially, the motors were placed around the four quadrants of the wrist (ring configuration) as recommended by literature [16]. Since the two-point discrimination on the forearm is between 25mm [33] and 38mm [34], we also performed initial testing by placing the four motors in other configurations with spacing of 50mm or more.

In top-arm configuration, two motors were placed on the dorsal side of the forearm, one near the wrist/distal region and the other 10cm apart on the proximal region, with none on the ventral side and in bottom-arm configuration both were placed on the ventral side with similar spacing as previous, with none on the dorsal side. In spaced-ring configuration, one motor was placed near the wrist on the dorsal side of the forearm and another one was placed on the ventral side near the proximal side of the forearm (10cm from the wrist motor). The other two motors were each placed on the radial and ulnar side midway between these (i.e., 50mm from the wrist).

Preliminary testing performed on three subjects on the ability to identify the activated motor showed an average accuracy of 94% using the wrist-ring arrangement and 98% using the spaced-ring arrangement. Spacing the motors on the same side (dorsal or ventral alone) also gave higher average accuracy (96%) but there appeared to be a directional bias wherein the down motor was often misidentified as the right motor. It was also observed that the spaced-ring arrangement had the fastest user response speed (average 1.02s, ranging from 0.45s to 1.6s) among the four configurations [32].

Hence, the spaced-ring arrangement was chosen for our sleeve design with a motor embedded on each side of the forearm: up motor on the dorsal side near the wrist, down motor on the ventral side near the proximal region 10mm away from wrist, left motor on the lateral side 5mm away from wrist, and right motor on medial side 5mm away from wrist.

B. *Motor Control*

Four mini vibrating disk motors by Adafruit (ADA 1201) were embedded into a fabric sleeve. The motors are controlled using ESP32 microcontroller and two dual DC motor drivers (TB6612FNG). Pulse Width Modulated (PWM) signal from the ESP32 is used to control the intensity of vibrations. In this study, the vibrational intensity is kept constant using a square waveform (50% duty cycle) at 250Hz frequency. The ESP32 is powered using a 3.7V 500mAh Lithium-ion battery.

III. SCOPE

This study evaluates the feasibility of utilizing the tactile sleeve for handwriting intervention, with the eventual goal of providing a corrective feedback to their hand in case they deviate from the alphabet/pattern they are trying to trace/draw. Hence, it investigates the following:

a) will the user be able to respond to a vibration and correct their hand movement in the desired direction, while they are attempting to draw a pattern?

b) can the user's hand move a consistent distance for identical vibrational cues (same vibrational intensity for the same time)?

The response of a user in drawing a pattern projected on their arm via the tactile sleeve, was tested to understand the accuracy, scalability, and variability in the drawn pattern as a function of tactile duration.

The study uses a wrist worn sleeve embedded with four mini vibrating disk motors, with a single motor being activated in the desired direction of movement (up, down, left, or right), thus providing 90° directional cues only. The vibrotactile sleeve was used to guide participants through blind patterns of low, medium, and high complexity, grouped based on the number of directional changes required to complete the pattern.

It was hypothesized that the participants will be able to identify the vibrational direction provided by the sleeve and trace these blind patterns with high accuracy. Also, another hypothesis was that the size of the patterns drawn will scale with the duration of vibration. Finally, it was hypothesized that shorter vibrational durations (< 3 seconds) will show higher variability in the pattern size, due to a significant portion of the duration (approx. 1 second) being used for comprehending the direction to be moved in.

IV. EXPERIMENTAL SETUP

Due to COVID-19 restrictions on large scale human subject testing, this pilot study performed initial data collection on three healthy adult volunteers, with no prior experience of using wearable haptics. All the participants were right-handed and wore the sleeve on the dominant forearm (Figure 1).

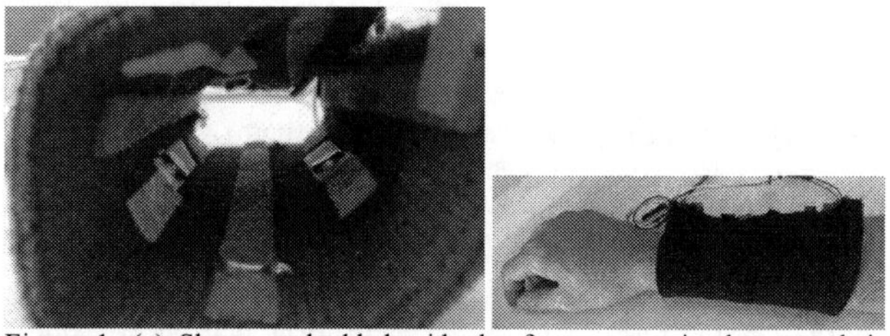

Figure 1. (a) Sleeve embedded with the four motors in the spaced-ring arrangement. (b) Sleeve worn by one of the participants.

Data was collected to test the accuracy of the (a) perceived location, (b) pattern formation (shape), and (c) pattern sizing (scaling) based on the vibrational duration provided. Prior to the data collection, each subject was given 5 minutes to self-train by activating a desired motor on the sleeve using directional keys on a keyboard. The testing was performed as described below.

A. *Training*

The participants were asked to use a pen and draw straight lines in the direction of the activated motor on a graph paper (with 0.5cm x 0.5cm grids). They were provided a pattern, corresponding to English letter *f* for training.

The letter *f* was converted into square font such that it required the following pen movements to draw: 2cm towards right, 4cm up, 3cm right, 3 cm left, 2cm down, 1cm left and 2 cm right as shown (Figure 2). Each 1cm distance expected to be traced was encoded into 1s of continuous motor vibration in that direction, when presented using the sleeve. Continuous movement in one direction is considered one segment. Hence, the letter f consisted of 7 segments. The change from one segment to next is also continuous, i.e., as soon as the first 2s of vibration on the right motor are completed, the up motor starts vibrating and the participant has no prior information that the vibration location is about to change.

Initially, the participants were provided a graph paper and asked to draw the pattern based on straight movements in the direction of vibration perceived. Then, they were provided the graph paper with the letter f already drawn to the expected size/scale. They practiced tracing on this letter multiple (3-4) times while receiving the vibrations corresponding to the pattern through the sleeve.

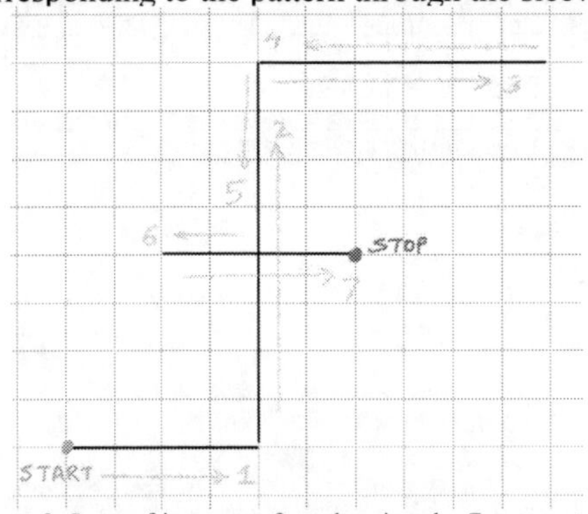

Figure 2. Letter f in square font showing the 7 segments to be drawn in the order numbered. Each grid is 0.5cm and each 1cm distance is encoded using a 1s vibrational duration/movement in that direction.

B. Blind Pattern Drawing

Five patterns, corresponding to English cursive letter (a), Arabic letters (s, f) and Malayalam letters (a, sh), converted into square font were randomly projected to the participant's arm through the activation of corresponding motor. Based on the number of directional changes (segments) required to complete the pattern, the patterns were grouped as low, medium, or high complexity.

English letter *a* was broken into 9 segments (medium complexity) of equal lengths in the following direction: right, up, right, left, down, right, up, down, right (Figure 3. a). The Arabic letter *s* had 9 segments (medium complexity) and letter *f* had only 6 segments (low complexity). High complexity Malayalam letters *sh* had 12 segments and *a* had 16 segments.

The shortest length (1cm) was encoded into 1s of continuous motor vibration in that direction. The low and medium complexity letters were presented at three scales: at 1s, 2s, and 3s. i.e., the same pattern was presented with 2x and 3x the duration of vibration per 1cm distance, to evaluate how the same pattern would be scaled by the participants based on modulating the vibrational duration. To avoid fatigue, the high complexity letters were only presented once to the participant at 1s scale.

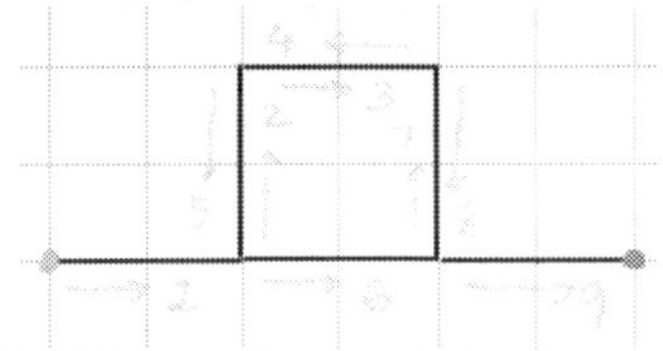

(a) English letter *a* in square font, with 9 segments

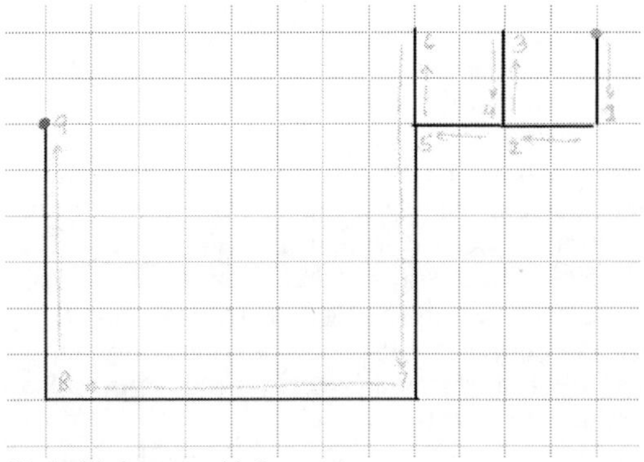

(b) Arabic letter *s*, with 9 segments

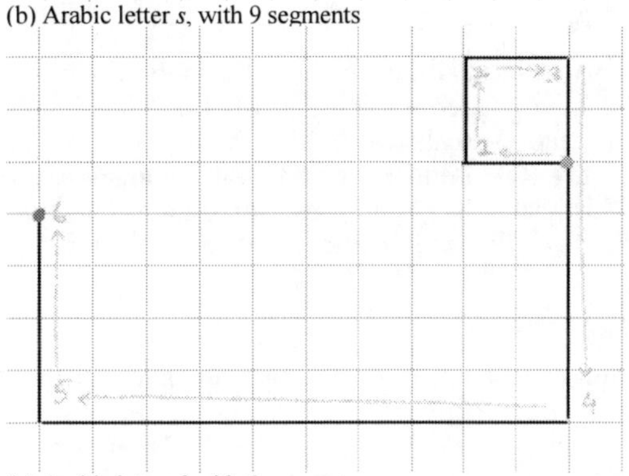

(c) Arabic letter *f*, with 6 segments

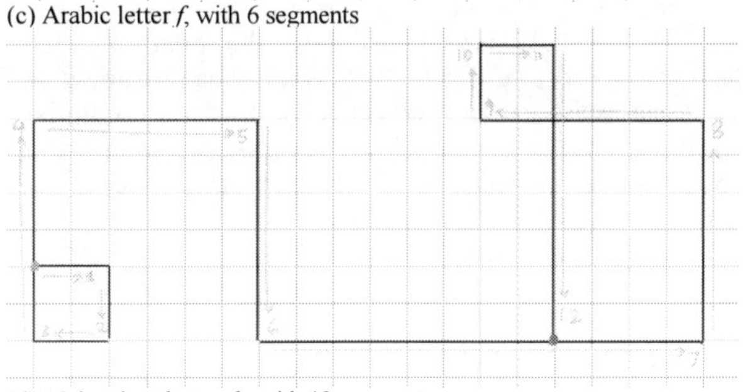

(d) Malayalam letter *sh*, with 12 segments

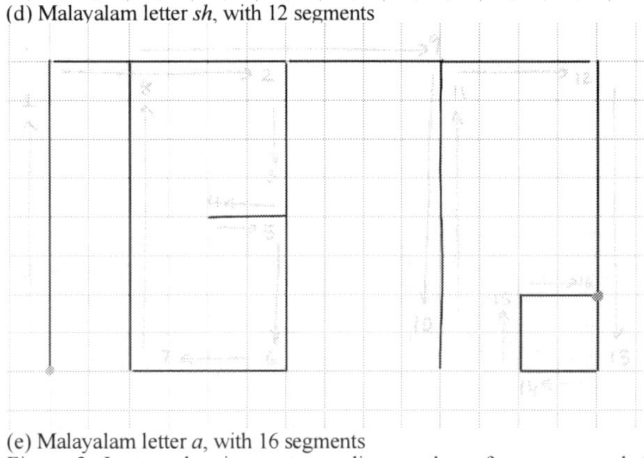

(e) Malayalam letter *a*, with 16 segments

Figure 3. Letters showing corresponding number of segments and their order.

The letter/pattern and the duration were randomly picked. The participants were not informed on what pattern they were being provided, although a countdown was provided to prepare them for the start of the pattern. None of the participants knew to read Arabic or Malayalam alphabets and no feedback was provided (during or after any trial) on whether the pattern was correctly drawn or not. Blind patterns were provided so that the subject's ability to identify the vibrational location and respond to changes in the vibrational direction while performing the task of tracing a pattern could be isolated from their ability to trace known/seen patterns. They were asked to try and maintain their speed of drawing but were not provided any cues during (or after) the trials to modify their speed. They were provided 2-3 minute break between each pattern.

V. PRELIMINARY RESULTS

The data was collected from three participants. Each of them drew 11 blind patterns (3 scales of 3 low/medium complex letters and 1 scale of 2 high complex letters) corresponding to 100 segments/directional changes per participant. This data was analyzed for the accuracy, scalability, and variability of drawn patterns as a function of the vibrational duration.

A. Pattern Shape

The participants were able to replicate the shape of the unknown pattern with a high accuracy. Pattern accuracy was measured as the movement in the correct direction for a given segment with respect to the direction presented by the activated motor. The participants drew the blind patterns with an average accuracy of 95.67% (individual accuracy of 96%, 95% and 96% per subject). This corroborates the initial measurements made on perceived location accuracy and demonstrates that subjects can distinguish and move in the direction of the vibration even while drawing patterns.

The error was either due to the subject drawing a segment in the wrong direction or missing a segment/directional change completely and continuing in the same direction. Missed segments: Two subjects missed one segment while the third subject missed two segments. Each of the missed segments were the shortest 1cm segments, though not from the same pattern and not for the same time duration.

B. Pattern Size and Scalability

To determine whether the participants could maintain a steady size for the segments with same vibrational duration, and how the sizing of segments with longer duration scaled – length of each of the 100 segments were measured. The segment length/size (in cm) vs. continuous tactile duration, cumulative for all the subjects, is shown in Figure 4.

As seen from the Figure 4, the size of the segments drawn by the subjects increases linearly with the increase in tactile duration. That is, the size of the patterns can be scaled linearly as a function of the tactile duration. Hence, once trained on a pattern, the user can be expected to move their arm relatively steadily for the same intensity of vibration.

It should be noted that the participants in this study were not aware of how long any of the segments were (or how long the vibration would be felt in that direction) and when a new segment (or change in direction) would occur. Thus, they could not have predicted the segment length to be drawn.

TABLE I. STATISTICS OF SIZES DRAWN FOR THE DIFFERENT DURATIONS

Duration (s)	1	2	3	4	6	8	9	12
Avg. size (cm)	0.982	1.281	2.595	3.818	6.163	8.536	9.800	14.068
Variance (cm ^ 2)	0.013	0.062	0.242	0.524	1.198	2.522	3.410	10.251
Std. dev. (cm)	0.114	0.248	0.492	0.724	1.094	1.588	1.847	3.202
Median (cm)	1	1.25	2.5	3.75	6.1	8.4	9.875	13
CV	0.116	0.194	0.189	0.190	0.178	0.186	0.188	0.228

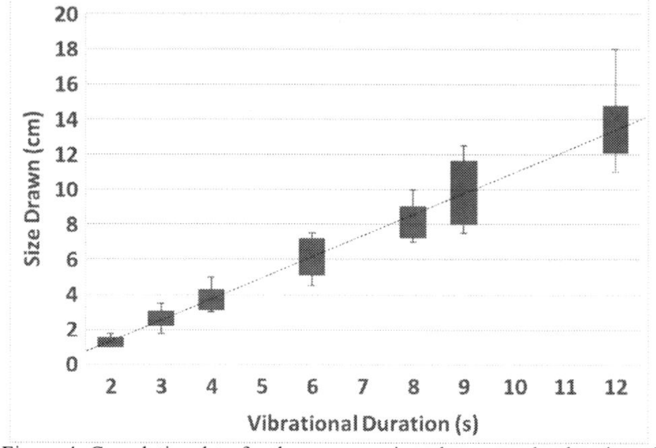

Figure 4. Cumulative data for the segment sizes drawn vs. the duration of continuous vibrational stimulation.

C. Variability in Pattern Size

Since the initial user response time had an average of 1s, it was hypothesized that it might be difficult to maintain a steady size for the shorter segments, due to the cognitive load of decoding the direction. However, in contrast to the assumption, as observed in Figure 4 and Table 1, the standard deviation in the drawn size for smaller segments is very low and increases as the segment length increases. Thus, as the tactile duration is increased, the error in size increases. Although the pattern scales almost linearly with tactile duration, the high variability for larger lengths indicates that when the vibrations provided continuously for a longer duration, it becomes more difficult to maintain the steady speed.

Breaking down the larger lengths into multiple shorter durations might provide a more controlled size. Considering the broken segments are independent of each other, the variance sum law (1) provides that the individual variances can be added together to determine the total variance for that segment. For example, the 12cm distance covered using 12s continuous vibrations results in a variance of $10.25cm^2$. Breaking the 12s continuous vibrations into six shorter 2s continuous vibrations ($\sigma^2_{2cm} = 0.062cm^2$) with breaks in between would result in total variance of six times σ^2_{2cm} (2). Hence, reducing the overall variance to $0.36cm^2$ in the 12cm length.

$$\sigma^2_{x+y} = \sigma^2_x + \sigma^2_y \quad (1)$$

$$\sigma^2_{N.x} = N.\sigma^2_x \quad (2)$$

where σ^2_x is the variance of segment with length x, $\sigma^2_{N.x}$ the variance of segment with length N times x, and N is the number of segments the total length is broken into.

The low variability for shorter lengths (< 5 cm) indicates the feasibility of utilizing continuous tactile durations for correcting handwriting movements that are expected to be within the short lengths.

VI. CONCLUSION AND FUTURE WORK

There is limited research on utilizing tactile feedback for handwriting training. This study shows the feasibility of utilizing a tactile sleeve to control the shape and size of blind patterns presented to the hand. A wrist worn sleeve embedded with four vibrating motors was utilized to guide the hand of three subjects. The subjects were asked to draw patterns, unknown to them, using the tactile feedback from the sleeve alone and were able to reproduce the patterns with high accuracy.

The impact of continuous vibrations on the sizing of the drawn segments was evaluated. It was observed that the segment lengths can be scaled linearly using vibrational durations. It is proposed that shorter segments, of less than 5cm, be provided using continuous vibrations. However, if longer segments need to be drawn, they can be broken into multiple small segments represented using continuous vibrations of less than 5s with a short break (eg. 100ms) between the segments. In handwriting training, the size of lines/segments drawn is usually less than 5cm and hence continuous vibrations of different time duration might be sufficient to provide the necessary scaling of the letter/pattern.

Currently, work is in progress to test this sleeve on a larger number of participants. The ability of subjects to draw more complex patterns using phantom sensations is also being explored. Future work includes testing this system on individuals with visuo-motor skills issues and/or handwriting learning disabilities. Furthermore, the impact of modulating the vibrational intensity on the handwriting patterns is yet to be studied.

REFERENCES

[1] F. Bara, and E. Gentaz, “Haptics in teaching handwriting: The role of perceptual and visuo-motor skills,” *Human movement science*, Elsevier, Aug. 2011, vol. 30. pp. 745-759.

[2] S. Chang, and N. Yu, “Visual and haptic perception training to improve handwriting skills in children with dysgraphia,” *The American Journal of Occupational Therapy*, Jan. 2017, vol. 17(2). doi: 10.5014/ajot.2017.021311.

[3] S. Fisackerly and M. H. Zadeh., "Haptic-enabled virtual handwriting: Multimodal handwriting instructions for young students," *IEEE International Symposium on Haptic Audio-Visual Environments & Games*, 2010, pp. 1-6, doi: 10.1109/HAVE.2010.5623963.

[4] R. Karlsdottir “Development of cursive handwriting,” *Percept Mot Skills*, Apr. 1996, vol. 82, no. 2, pp. 659-73, doi:10.2466/pms.1996.82.2.659.

[5] J. Mullins, C. Mawson, and S. Nahavandi, "Haptic handwriting aid for training and rehabilitation," In *Proc. IEEE International Conference on Systems, Man and Cybernetics*, 2005, vol. 3, pp. 2690-2694.

[6] C. L. Teo, E. Burdet, and H. P. Lim, "A robotic teacher of chinese handwriting," In *Proc. Symposium on Haptic Interfaces for Virtual Environment and Teleoperator Systems (HAPTICS)*, 2002, pp. 335-341, doi: 10.1109/HAPTIC.2002.998977.

[7] Y. Kim, M. Collins, W. Bulmer, S. Sharma, and J. Mayrose, "Haptics Assisted Training (HAT) system for children's handwriting," In *Proc. IEEE World Haptics Conference (WHC)*, Korea, 2013, pp. 559-564, doi: 10.1109/WHC.2013.6548469.

[8] W. Park, G. Korres, T. Moonesinghe, and M. Eid, "Investigating haptic guidance methods for teaching children handwriting skills," *IEEE Transactions on Haptics*, 2019, vol. 12, no. 4, pp. 461-469, doi: 10.1109/TOH.2019.2922284.

[9] Teranishi, G. Korres, W. Park, and M. Eid, "Combining full and partial haptic guidance improves handwriting skills development," *IEEE Transactions on Haptics*, 2018, vol. 11, no. 4, pp. 509-517, doi: 10.1109/TOH.2018.2851511.

[10] Y. Kim, Z. Duric, N. L. Gerber, A. R. Palsbo and S. E. Palsbo, “Poster: Teaching letter writing using a programmable haptic device interface for children with handwriting difficulties," In *Proc. IEEE Symposium on 3D User Interfaces*, March 2009, pp. 145-146, doi: 10.1109/3DUI.2009.4811228.

[11] M. Eid, M. Mansour, Mohamed, A. El Saddik, and R. Iglesias, “A haptic multimedia handwriting learning system,” In *Proc. International Workshop on Educational Multimedia and Multimedia Education*, Germany, Sep. 2007, pp. 103-108, doi: 10.1145/1290144.1290161.

[12] B. Plimmer, P. Reid, R. Blagojevic, A. Crossan, and S. Brewster, “Signing on the tactile line: A multimodal system for teaching handwriting to blind children,” *ACM Trans. Computer Human Interaction*, July 2011, vol. 18, no. 3, pp. 1-29, doi: 10.1145/1993060.1993067.

[13] A. S. Bayousuf, H. S. Al-Khalifa, and AbdulMalik S. Al-Salman, “Towards the development of haptic-based interface for teaching visually impaired arabic handwriting,” In *Proc. 15th International ACM SIGACCESS Conference on Computers and Accessibility*, Oct. 2013, pp. 1-2, doi: 10.1145/2513383.2513400.

[14] Y. Cho, A. Bianchi, N. Marquardt, and N. Bianchi-Berthouze, “RealPen: Providing realism in handwriting tasks on touch surfaces using auditory-tactile feedback,” In *Proc. 29th Annual Symposium on User Interface Software and Technology*, Oct. 2016, pp. 195–205, doi: 10.1145/2984511.2984550.

[15] G. Korres, and M. Eid, “ KATIB: Haptic-visual guidance for handwriting,” In *Proc. 12th International Conference EuroHaptics*, 2020, pp. 279-287, doi: 10.1007/978-3-030-58147-3_31.

[16] M. Matscheko, A. Ferscha, A. Riener, and M. Lehner, “Tactor placement in wrist worn wearables.” In *Proc. International Symposium on Wearable Computers (ISWC)*, Oct. 2010.

[17] F. Sergi, D. Accoto, D. Campolo, and E. Guglielmelli, "Forearm orientation guidance with a vibrotactile feedback bracelet: On the directionality of tactile motor communication," In *Proc. 2nd IEEE RAS & EMBS International Conference on Biomedical Robotics and Biomechatronics*, 2008, pp. 433-438, doi: 10.1109/BIOROB.2008.4762827.

[18] A. Causo, L. D. Tran, S. Huat Yeo, and I-Ming Chen, “Vibrotactile motors on stationary arm as directional feedback

to correct arm posture" In *Proc. IEEE/ASME International Conference on Advanced Intelligent Mechatronics*, 2012, pp. 202-207, doi: 10.1109/AIM.2012.6265990.

[19] J. Salazar, K. Okabe, and Y. Hirata, "Path-following guidance using phantom sensation based vibrotactile cues around the wrist," *IEEE Robotics and Automation Letters*, July 2018, vol. 3, no. 3, pp. 2485-2492, doi: 10.1109/LRA.2018.2810939.

[20] J. Hong, L. Stearns, J. Froelich, D. Ross, and L. Findlater, "Evaluating angular Accuracy of Wrist-based Haptic Directional Guidance for Hand Movement," In *Proc. 42nd Graphics Interface Conference*, 2016, pp. 195-200.

[21] J. Hong, A. Pradhan, J. E. Froehlich, and L.. Findlater, "Evaluating wrist-based haptic feedback for non-visual target finding and path tracing on a 2D surface." In *Proc. 19th International ACM SIGACCESS Conference on Computers and Accessibility (ASSETS),* Oct. 2017, pp. 210-219, doi: 10.1145/3132525.3132538.

[22] D. Prabhu, M. M. Hasan, L. Wise, C. MacMahon and C. McCarthy, "VibroSleeve: A wearable vibro-tactile feedback device for arm guidance," In *Proc. 42nd Annual International Conference of the IEEE Engineering in Medicine & Biology Society (EMBC)*, 2020, pp. 4909-4912, doi: 10.1109/EMBC44109.2020.9176028.

[23] K. Bark et al., "Lessons in using vibrotactile feedback to guide fast arm motions," In *Proc. IEEE World Haptics Conference*, June 2011, pp. 355-360, doi: 10.1109/WHC.2011.5945512.

[24] K. Bark et al., "Effects of vibrotactile feedback on human learning of arm motions," *IEEE Trans. on Neural Systems and Rehabilitation Engineering*, Jan. 2015, vol. 23, no. 1, pp. 51-63, doi: 10.1109/TNSRE.2014.2327229.

[25] A. Morikawa, N. Tsuda, Y. Nomura, and N. Kato, "Self-training system of calligraphy brushwork," In *Proc. Companion of the 2017 ACM/IEEE International Conference on Human-Robot Interaction.*, Mar. 2017, pp. 215-216, doi: 10.1145/3029798.3038422.

[26] A. Morikawa, N. Tsuda, Y. Nomura, and K. Norihiko, "Double pressure presentation for calligraphy self-training", In *Proc. Companion of the 2018 ACM/IEEE International Conference on Human-Robot Interaction*, Mar. 2018, pp. 199–200, doi: 10.1145/3173386.3177010.

[27] M. Narita, and T. Matsumaru, "Calligraphy-stroke learning support system using projection", In *Proc. 24th IEEE International Workshop on Robot and Human Interactive Communication (RO-MAN)*, Nov. 2015, pp 640-645, doi: 10.1109/ROMAN.2015.7333576.

[28] T. Matsumaru, and M. Narita, "Calligraphy-stroke learning support system using projector and motion sensor", *Journal of Advanced Computational Intelligence and Intelligent Informatics (JACAII)*, 2017, vol. 21, no. 4, pp. 697-708, doi: doi: 10.20965/jaciii.2017.p069.

[29] C. Meyers, T. F. McLaughlin, M. Derby, K. P. Weber, and M. Robison, "The effects of "Handwriting without Tears®" on the handwriting skills of appropriate size, form, and tool for a four year-old boy with a developmental delay," *Journal of Special Education Apprenticeship*, Dec. 2015, vol. 4, no. 2.

[30] B. Pfeiffer, G. Rai, T. Murray, and E. Brusilovskiy, "Effectiveness of the size matters handwriting program," *OTJR : occupation, participation and health*, 2015, vol. 35, no. 2, pp. 110-119, doi: 10.1177/1539449215573004.

[31] D. Nair, S. Duback, R. Geoffrion, and J. B. Jackson, "Visuo-tactile handwriting training system using wearable sleeve," presented at *IEEE Haptics Symposium*, March 2020.

[32] D. Nair, G. Stankaitis, S. Duback, R. Geoffrion, and J. B. Jackson, "Handwriting correction system using wearable sleeve with optimal tactor configuration," In *Proc. of IEEE International Conference on Ubiquitous Robots,* July 2021, in press.

[33] R. W. Cholewiak, and A. A. Collins, "Vibrotactile localization on the arm: Effects of place, space, and age," *Perception & psychophysics*, Oct. 2003, vol. 65, no. 7, pp. 1058–1077, doi: 10.3758/BF03194834.

[34] S. Weinstein, "Intensive and extensive aspects of tactile sensitivity as a function of body part, sex, and laterality," *The skin senses, Springfield,* 1968, pp. 195–218.

[35] T. McDaniel, D. Villanueva, S. Krishna, and S. Panchanathan, "MOVeMENT: A framework for systematically mapping vibrotactile stimulations to fundamental body movements." In *Proc. IEEE International Symposium on Haptic Audio Visual Environments and Games*, 2010, pp. 1-6, doi: 10.1109/HAVE.2010.5623965.